101
Questions & Answers
Series

Law of Contract

Second edition

Editor: Dr Vickneswaren Krishnan
LLB (Hons), LLM, MA, Barrister at Law,
ACI, Arb, AIPFM, AFSALS, ACII, PhD

Old Bailey Press

OLD BAILEY PRESS
at Holborn College, Woolwich Road,
Charlton, London, SE7 8LN

First published 1998
Second edition 2004
Reprinted 2005

ISBN 1 85836 517 1

British Library Cataloguing-in-Publication Data

A catalogue record for this book is available from the British Library.

Printed and bound in Great Britain.

Contents

Foreword

This book is part of a series designed specifically for those students studying at undergraduate level. Coverage is not restricted to any one syllabus but embraces the main examination topics found in a typical examination paper.

This book is concerned with contract law in the context of examinations. Each chapter contains an Introduction setting out the scope of the topic, important recent cases and articles, and other helpful advice as to likely examination questions on that topic.

Additionally, in each chapter there are Interrograms and Examination Questions. The Interrograms are designed as short questions testing knowledge of the fundamentals of the topic being covered. The Examination Questions are a selection of actual questions taken mainly from papers set by a university, and have been selected because they represent the most typical examples of how knowledge of the syllabus is tested. It is intended that students should work through the Interrograms and Examination Questions before checking their knowledge (and presentation style) against the suggested answers contained in each chapter. The answers state the law as at 1 October 2003.

Acknowledgement

Examination questions are the copyright of the University of London (where specified).

The questions are taken or adapted mainly from past University of London LLB Degree for external students examination papers. Our thanks are extended to the University of London for their kind permission to use and publish the questions.

Caveat

Table of Cases

1

Offer and Acceptance

Introduction

Offer and acceptance are the traditional foundations of the law of contract. It is not therefore surprising to see a question on this topic appearing on virtually every examination paper - and very often the question is compulsory. A good student will be expected to demonstrate a clear understanding of the principles relevant to this area.

While there may have been some movement in the courts away from a traditional analysis of a contract in terms of offer and acceptance, it is clear these are exceptional cases. The student (while naturally showing awareness of these cases) is thus expected to perform the traditional analysis on problem questions. This usually requires a detailed consideration of the rules as to acceptance and withdrawal of an offer. From time to time, however, a question will be set on unilateral rather than bilateral contracts and here the student will be required to demonstrate knowledge of the very different set of rules, especially relating to acceptance and withdrawal of the offer.

The consolation for the student is that questions on this topic follow a very similar basic pattern and someone who has learned how to apply the rules should have no difficulty in obtaining a good mark. Some recent cases include the following: *Manatee Towing Co* v *Oceanbulk Maritime SA, The Bay Ridge* (1999), *Barry* v *Davies (t/a Heathcote, Ball & Co)* (2000) and *Inland Revenue Commissioners* v *Fry* (2001).

Questions

INTERROGAMS

1. Explain why it is so important to distinguish between an offer and an invitation to treat and how the courts proceed to do so.
2. What is meant by a unilateral contract?
3. Olivia, in England, sends a fax message to Anna in Germany, accepting her contractual offer. Where is the contract made? Would there be a contract if the fax had been sent to the wrong number?

QUESTION ONE

On Monday, A posted a letter to B offering to buy B's vortex car for £12,000. The postman dropped the letter in the street where it was found by B's neighbour, C. He did not give the letter to B until Friday. In the meantime, on Tuesday, B wrote to A offering to sell the car to him for £11,000 and this letter arrived at A's house on Wednesday. A faxed to B stating, 'Good news! I agree to the deal.' However, because there was a paper failure in B's machine the message was never printed out. On Friday, B posted a letter to A agreeing to sell the car for £12,000. B's letter was not received by A for two weeks.

Advise the parties. What difference, if any, would it make to your advice if the fax had been printed but B did not go into the room where the fax machine was situated for three days?

University of London LLB Examination
(for external students) Elements of the Law of Contract June 2001 Q1

QUESTION TWO

On Monday, A telephoned B and left a message on B's answering machine offering to sell B his sports car for £10,000. B's wife telephoned A, saying that B was away for two weeks. A said he would wait for B's return before doing anything else. B's wife said, 'Good! I promise to inform B as soon as he returns.' On Wednesday, by letter A offered to sell his car to C. On Thursday C posted a reply stating, 'I'll buy it at that price. Is it green?' C's letter was delayed in the post till Saturday. Meanwhile on Friday, B returned earlier than expected, and e-mailed A agreeing to buy the car for £10,000. A replied by e-mail, 'Yes! It is yours.' B did not receive this e-mail till Sunday.

Advise the parties of their contractual position.

University of London LLB Examination
(for external students) Elements of the Law of Contract June 2000 Q1

QUESTION THREE

On Monday, L sent a letter to M offering M £3,500 for M's old van. M telephoned L leaving a message on L's answer phone saying that he was happy to sell it at the suggested price. When L returned home he accidentally deleted all messages before listening to them. On Wednesday, L wrote to M offering £4,000 for the van. On Thursday, M e-mailed an acceptance of the £4,000 offer and the message was downloaded by L's wife but she forgot to tell L about the offer. On Saturday, L met M in the street and M said that as he had heard nothing from L he had sold the van elsewhere.

Advise L who has had to pay £6,000 for a similar van.

University of London LLB Examination
(for external students) Elements of the Law of Contract June 1999 Q6

QUESTION FOUR

On Monday, A telephoned B in response to an advertisement in the Berkhamsted Leader, a local newspaper. B's telephone was answered by B's mother-in-law, C, with whom B was on bad terms. A, having explained who he was, said, 'I agree to buy the advertised caravan at the advertised price. I'll confirm by fax.' C replied, 'OK! I'll pass that message on to B when he comes home from work.' In fact, what C said to B was, 'Some idiot rang up about the caravan and is willing to buy it.' On Thursday B found the fax and replied immediately by e-mail stating, 'I agree the caravan is yours at the agreed price.' Unfortunately, although A received part of the message, it was incomplete because of a defect in A's modem. On Wednesday of that week the value of the caravan had dropped by half because of the introduction of a new model. A refused to take the caravan.

Advise B.

University of London LLB Examination
(for external students) Elements of the Law of Contract June 1998 Q2

QUESTION FIVE

On Tuesday, 6 May, A wrote to B saying, 'Please sell me your vintage MGB for £5,000.' On Wednesday B replied by leaving a message on A's answerphone, 'Sure, provided you pay cash.' B then changed his mind and he posted a letter to A which read, 'I have reconsidered the position. I am no longer able to sell you my MGB.' This letter arrived on Thursday before A played back the messages on his answerphone.

Advise the parties. What difference, if any, would it make to your advice if:

i) B's letter had never arrived, or, alternatively,
ii) because of a fault on A's answerphone B's message had not been recorded, or, alternatively,
iii) on Monday, 5 May, B had asked A if he wanted to buy his MGB?

University of London LLB Examination
(for external students) Elements of the Law of Contract June 1997 Q1

QUESTION SIX

Floyd supplies household goods. He sent a fax to Delia which read: 'Can offer latest "Cookwell" 3 litre pressure cookers @ £70 each.' Delia faxed in reply: 'Will have two dozen. Need delivery by next Thursday.'

Floyd then wrote: 'Thank you for your fax, which is receiving our attention.'

Advise Delia as to the legal position on each of the following *alternative* assumptions:

i) Floyd packed the cookers and loaded them on to a van for delivery to Delia, but before the van set out Delia telephoned to say that she no longer needed the cookers.
ii) Floyd failed to deliver any cookers to Delia.

University of London LLB Examination
(for external students) Elements of the Law of Contract June 1996 Q1

QUESTION SEVEN

On Monday, A wrote to B offering to buy B's picture painted by Augustus John for £25,000. On Tuesday, B replied by leaving a message on A's answerphone stating, 'I assume that you mean the painting of four sisters and I accept.' The painting was worth £20,000. In addition to the painting called 'Four Sisters' B owned another painting by Augustus John called 'Forbidden Fruit' (worth £30,000). It was 'Forbidden Fruit' to which A was referring in his letter. On Wednesday, A was told that B owned two paintings by Augustus John, played back his answerphone and sent a message by electronic mail, via internet, to B's number saying, 'I accept both at £50,000. Unless I hear from you within two days I will assume that they are mine. You need not bother to reply.' B replied by letter to A stating, 'I may be prepared to sell both.' However, this letter was lost in the post.

Advise the parties. What difference, if any, would it make to your advice if (a) because of a computer fault B had not received A's electronic mail message, or (b) because of a transmission failure the electronic mail message was incomplete and all that B received was, 'I accept'?

University of London LLB Examination
(for external students) Elements of the Law of Contract June 1995 Q1

Answers

ANSWERS TO INTERROGRAMS

1. An offer may be accepted, turning it into a contract. An invitation to treat may not. Invitations to treat are merely steps in the negotiation of a contract. They may be an invitation to make an offer but they are not the offer itself. So far as the courts are concerned, it is a question of what was intended. Presumptions of intention are, however, made in certain circumstances. A display of goods in a shop, in a window or on shelves, is an invitation to treat: *Pharmaceutical Society of Great Britain* v *Boots Cash Chemists (Southern) Ltd* (1952); *Fisher* v *Bell* (1961). A newspaper advertisement of goods for sale is also usually presumed to be an invitation to treat (*Partridge* v *Crittenden* (1968)), although not if the contract advertised is unilateral: *Carlill* v *Carbolic Smoke Ball Co Ltd* (1893). Similarly, catalogues, price lists, brochures and other advertising material are usually presumed to be invitations to treat unless there is a clear contrary intention: *Grainger & Son* v *Gough* (1896).

   The question of whether there was an invitation to treat or an offer is important not only in deciding whether there was a contract between the parties but also when the contract was concluded. This has proved to be an important issue in a number of cases where a defendant has sought to rely on an exclusion clause printed on a ticket. If the ticket is a contractual document, the exclusion clauses are incorporated, but if it is a mere receipt they are not. The question is therefore whether the defendant by holding himself out as ready to trade is making an offer or an invitation to treat: *Chapleton* v *Barry UDC* (1940); *Thornton* v *Shoe Lane Parking Ltd* (1971).

2. A unilateral contract is an offer to the world at large which is accepted by someone who performs the conditions of the offer. The offeror is then bound to make good his promise. An example is *Carlill* v *Carbolic Smoke Ball Co Ltd* (1893) where the defendants offered in a newspaper advertisement to make a payment to anyone who wore the smoke ball as instructed and nevertheless contracted influenza. The plaintiff performed this condition and was held entitled to the payment. A common example is the offer of a reward for performing some act such as finding a lost pet or giving information leading to a conviction: *Gibbons* v *Proctor* (1891).

   Unilateral contracts differ from bilateral contracts in some ways. First, as noted above, acceptance is by embarking on performance of the condition. The acceptor does not need to communicate acceptance to the offeror. The offeror is bound, even though he does not know that the acceptor has embarked on performance. Acceptance is, however, not complete until performance is complete. Thus, if a number of people embark on performance, the first to complete will have accepted the offer. Second, the offer can only be withdrawn by giving the withdrawal at least as much publicity as the original offer. Third, there is an implied condition that the offer cannot be revoked once performance has commenced: *Errington* v *Errington and Woods* (1952); *Daulia Ltd* v *Four Millbank Nominees Ltd* (1978).

3. The general rule is that acceptance must be communicated to the offeror: *Brogden* v *Metropolitan Railway Co* (1877). That is to say that it must be brought to his attention (*Entores Ltd* v *Miles Far East Corporation* (1955)). The only exception to this is the 'postal rule' which states that acceptance sent by post is effective when posted: *Adams* v *Lindsell* (1818). A telex is a form of instantaneous communication and therefore the normal rules apply to it (*Brinkibon Ltd* v *Stahag Stahl* (1982)), as is the telephone. By analogy (although there appears to be no reported decision on this question), a fax is also an instantaneous means of communicating acceptance. Acceptance is effective when and where received. The acceptance was received in Germany and the contract was therefore made in Germany.

   Had the fax not been received by Anna, there would have been no contract unless acceptance was communicated by some other means.

SUGGESTED ANSWER TO QUESTION ONE

General Comment

This question on offer and acceptance invites discussion of the problems associated with instantaneous communication and the postal rule.

Key Points

- A's offer and when it was communicated
- B's offer and when it was communicated
- A's fax message, whether it could be deemed to have been communicated
- The position arising from B's failure to go to the room where the fax machine was situated
- B's letter to A, was it communicated?
- The application of the postal rule

Suggested Answer

A has clearly made an offer to B to buy the car at the price of £12,000, and this offer is only communicated to B when the letter is handed to him on the Friday.

B's offer to sell to sell the car for £11,000 is communicated on the Wednesday. A's fax message in reply does appear to be an acceptance of that offer. The question is whether that acceptance has been communicated.

There is no direct authority on the communication of fax messages. In *Brinkibon* v

Stahag Stahl (1983) the House of Lords held that a telex message is communicated only when it is received, and it appears from *Entores Ltd* v *Miles Far East Corporation* (1955) that in instantaneous communications, such as the telephone, the acceptance is only communicated when it is actually heard. A's faxed acceptance, therefore, must have been received in order to have been validly communicated. The problem is the paper failure in B's machine.

B has not seen A's message of acceptance. We are not informed as to whether or not A is aware of this. If he is, then he knows that there has been no communication, and no contract has been concluded: this is the implication of Denning LJ's analysis of telex messages in *Entores* (above). If he is unaware of the failure, then can the acceptance be deemed to have been received by B?

If the paper failure can be attributed to fault on the part of B then, again following the reasoning of Denning LJ in the case just cited, B would be bound because, as his Lordship said, 'he would be estopped from saying that he did not receive the message.': this statement by Denning LJ was in the context of telephone conversations, but it is submitted that they apply also to fax messages. If B is not at fault, we must again refer to the remarks of Denning LJ, where he said 'But if there should be a case where the offeror without any fault on his part does not receive the message of acceptance – yet the sender of it reasonably believes that it has got home when it has not – then I think that there is no contract.'

It is convenient at this point to deal with the hypothesis that the fax had been printed but B did not go the room where the machine was situated for three days. In *The Brimnes* (1975) the Court of Appeal held that a telex message could be deemed to have been received when it should have been read in the normal course of business. Note that this case concerned the termination of a contract, not its formation, but if its principle is applicable then B would be deemed to have received A's faxed acceptance when he should have read it, and a contract would have been concluded for the sale of the car at £11,000.

On the assumption that no contract has been concluded at that price I must consider the effect of B's letter to A.

On the Friday B posted a letter to A accepting the offer (which he had received that day) to buy the car for £12,000. This letter was not received for two weeks. This involves consideration of the postal rule.

In *Adams* v *Lindsell* (1818) it was held that where the acceptance is sent by letter it is deemed to have been communicated when the letter was posted. The question is whether the postal rule applies in the present circumstances.

In *Henthorn* v *Fraser* (1892) Lord Herschell said:

> '... where the circumstances are such that it must have been within the contemplation of the parties that, according to ordinary usages of mankind, the post might be used as a means of communicating the acceptance of an offer, the acceptance is complete as soon as it is posted.'

The use of the post was clearly within the contemplation of the parties: A's offer was by post, and B elected to use the post to communicate his acceptance.

How is the postal rule vitiated by the delay in the receipt of the letter? In *Household*

Fire and Carriage Accident Insurance Co Ltd v *Grant* (1879) Thesiger LJ held that the application of the postal rule meant that contract was made as soon as the letter was posted. It could not, therefore, be 'unmade' by a vagary in the post.

It appears, therefore, that a contract was concluded by the exchange of letters for the sale of the car at £12,000.

A would obviously prefer to be able to enforce the sale at £11,000, but would only be able to do so if he could establish fault on B's part, either because of the paper failure in the fax machine or because of B's failure to go to room where it was situated.

SUGGESTED ANSWER TO QUESTION TWO

General Comment

This is a reasonably straightforward question on offer and acceptance.

Key Points

- A's offer to B: when and if it was communicated - the effect of the promise to keep it open
- A's offer to C: C's reply - an acceptance or a counter-offer? - if an acceptance, the application of the postal rule
- the exchange of e-mails between A and B

Suggested Answer

A's offer to B was left on B's answering machine. Clearly the offer was not communicated at that stage. Whilst there is no clear authority on the communication of messages on telephone answering machines, it appears from *Entores Ltd* v *Miles Far East Corporation* (1955) that an acceptance on the telephone is only communicated when it is actually heard, and it is submitted that this should also apply to an offer. Moreover, there is nothing to suggest that B's wife had authority to act on his behalf.

A undertook, in effect, to keep the offer open until B's return. It is trite law that an offer can be revoked at any time before acceptance: *Routledge* v *Grant* (1828). In the absence of consideration, A's promise to keep the offer open could not be enforced.

We are informed that, on the Wednesday, A made a further offer to sell the car to C. What has to be considered is whether C's reply constituted an acceptance of that offer and, if it did, when that acceptance was communicated.

C's reply is not, on the face of it, an unconditional acceptance of the offer, in view of the query as to the colour of the car. If this query constitutes the introduction of a new term, then C's letter is a counter-offer, which of course destroys the original offer: *Hyde* v *Wrench* (1840). However, it can be argued that C's reply is a conditional acceptance, the condition being satisfied if the car is in fact green. Moreover, it could well be that the query 'Is it green?' is no more than a request for information, which in no way invalidates A's offer: *Stevenson* v *McLean* (1880). On either of the above constructions there has been an acceptance by C of A's offer.

The next question is whether this acceptance has been communicated: this involves consideration of the postal rule. It was established in *Adams* v *Lindsell* (1818) that when the postal rule applies, communication is deemed to have been effected when the letter of acceptance is posted. In *Henthorn* v *Fraser* (1892) Lord Herschell stated that the postal rule would apply, in the absence of contrary indications, where the offer has been made by post, which is the situation here. The fact that the letter of acceptance is delayed in the post does not negate the application of the postal rule: *Household Fire and Carriage Accident Insurance Co Ltd* v *Grant* (1879).

It seems, therefore, that as there was a valid acceptance and that this was effectively communicated, a contract between A and C was concluded on the Thursday.

It remains to consider the position as between A and B.

A has, in fact, purported to revoke his offer to B by his subsequent negotiations with C. But whilst, as stated above, an offer can be revoked at any time before acceptance the revocation must be actually communicated before the acceptance has, or been deemed to have, been communicated: *Byrne & Co* v *Van Tienhoven & Co* (1880). On the Friday A's offer to B has presumably been communicated, and B, being unaware of any revocation, purports to accept it. He does so by e-mail. Whilst it could have been suggested that A, having made the offer by telephone, expected an acceptance by the same medium, this is contradicted by A having replied by e-mail. In any event it is submitted that, as A has not prescribed any particular form of acceptance, an e-mail is equally efficacious: *Tinn* v *Hoffman & Co* (1873); *Manchester Diocesan Council for Education* v *Commercial & General Investments Ltd* (1970).

I have made the assumption that A's offer was still open when B sent his e-mail. If, for some reason, this were not so, then B's e-mail would have constituted the offer, which A then accepted by the same method. It is unnecessary to consider whether an acceptance by e-mail is deemed to be communicated when it is sent, or only when it is received, as B actually receives the e-mail on the Sunday, at which time he is totally unaware of the contract with C.

The somewhat untidy conclusion is, therefore, that A has concluded contracts with both of the other parties. As C's contract was concluded on the Thursday he has the prior right, and might conceivably have a claim for specific performance. B would be limited to a claim for damages for breach of contract.

SUGGESTED ANSWER TO QUESTION THREE

General Comment

This seems to be a straightforward question on offer and acceptance but, as will appear from the suggested answer, it is difficult to find a satisfactory solution to the problem.

Key Points

- M's telephone call: was it an acceptance of L's offer? – has it been communicated?
- The effect of L's second offer
- Was M's acceptance of the second offer communicated?
- M's 'revocation' of his acceptance

Suggested Answer

L's letter clearly constitutes an offer. It is specific as to the goods and as to the price.

M's telephone message purports to be an acceptance of the offer. With regard to instantaneous communications it appears that the acceptance is only deemed to be communicated when it is actually received or heard. Thus an acceptance by telex is communicated when the message is received, not when it is transmitted: ***Brinkibon Ltd*** v ***Stahag Stahl*** (1983). A court might be persuaded that a telex message would be deemed to have been received when it should have been read in the course of ordinary business hours: ***The Brimnes*** (1975). But this case is not a direct authority on this point.

In his judgment in ***Entores Ltd*** v ***Miles Far East Corporation*** (1955) Denning LJ discussed communication by telephone. His Lordship said that if the listener on the telephone does not catch the words of acceptance but does not trouble to ask for them to be repeated, so that the offeree reasonably believes that the message has been received, then the offeror is clearly bound, because he will be estopped from saying that he did not receive the message of acceptance. He went on to say:

> 'But if there should be a case where the offeror without any fault on his part does not receive the message of acceptance - yet the sender of it believes that it has got home when it has not - then I think there is no contract.'

The same principle must apply to a message on an answer phone.

L might be said to be at fault in deleting all the messages before listening to them, and therefore be estopped from saying that he did not receive M's message. But this conjecture is inappropriate; it is not L who would wish to deny receiving the message. Whether M could deny having sent it is a speculation that is irrelevant to pursue. I must conclude that no contract has been formed at this juncture.

L subsequently made a second offer at a higher price, clearly assuming that his first offer has not been accepted. I find some difficulty in determining the effect of this second offer on the first one. It might be impliedly a revocation of the first offer. It is trite law that an offer can be revoked at any time before acceptance: ***Routledge*** v ***Grant*** (1828). But the revocation must be communicated before the acceptance was communicated, or was deemed to be communicated: ***Byrne & Co*** v ***Leon Van Tienhoven & Co*** (1880). But it has been submitted that the first acceptance was not effectively communicated. It will not avail L, at some subsequent time, to allege that there was an acceptance which he did not hear, if this resulted from fault on his part. I would decide, in so far as it is necessary to do so, that the first offer had been revoked.

M e-mailed an acceptance of the second offer. He is perhaps not beyond reproach in doing so, having accepted the first, lower, offer, but this is not legally culpable. This message was downloaded by L's wife (the examiner assumes computer literacy in the candidates), but L was not informed of the message.

The message, having been downloaded had, presumably, been received. But the question is whether L's wife acted as his agent in downloading it. We are not informed whether she was so authorised. Even if she were not, it may be possible for L to ratify her action, which would relate back to the time of the acceptance: ***Bolton Partners*** v

Lambert (1889). This is hypothetical and, in any event, the law of agency is not within the confines of this syllabus.

By telling L that he had sold the can elsewhere, M had purportedly revoked his acceptance. I do not consider that he could legitimately do so, for one of, or perhaps both, of the following reasons:

1. if the agency rule does apply, and L's wife was duly authorised, or ratification is operative;
2. when and if L heard of the e-mailed message of acceptance, M would be estopped from denying that he had sent it.

I would therefore conclude, although not without some doubt, that a contract for the sale of the van for £4,000 was concluded on the basis of the second offer and the acceptance of that offer.

L has, accordingly, an action for breach of contract. He has mitigated his loss by purchasing a similar van elsewhere, and the measure of his damages is the difference between the contract price of £4,000 and the subsequent purchase price of £6,000.

SUGGESTED ANSWER TO QUESTION FOUR

General Comment

This is a question on offer and acceptance, one which frequently appears in London external examination papers. It involves the usual features of communication of the offer and of the acceptance.

Key Points

- Nature of the advertisement
- A's telephone call, whether it was an offer, and if so, whether it was communicated
- The fax message, nature and communication of
- The e-mail and its communication

Suggested Answer

The advertisement in the local newspaper was clearly an invitation to treat: *Partridge* v *Crittenden* (1968).

It is not clear whether A's telephone call was itself an offer, or merely an indication that the offer would follow by fax. However, it does seem that B's mother-in-law would have had the authority to receive it (suggested by the information as to the 'bad terms'), and in any event C's message to B was too vague – it failed to identify the offeror or mention the price – and therefore no offer had effectively been made at this stage.

The fax message appears definitely to have been an offer: it is presumed that it was in the same terms as the telephone call, although this is not expressly stated. The offer was communicated when B found the fax. It can be assumed that a fax, like a telex message, is communicated when it is actually received: *Brinkibon Ltd* v *Stahag Stahl* (1983).

What has now to be considered is whether A's offer has been accepted.

B replied by e-mail, and it is clearly an acceptance of the offer. There is nothing to suggest that an e-mail was not a valid form of acceptance. (But see below.) However, the difficulty is to determine whether the acceptance was effectively communicated. In the case of instantaneous communications by telephone or telex, the message is only deemed to be communicated when it is actually received: *Brinkibon* (above); *Entores Ltd* v *Miles Far East Corporation* (1955). The same rule must apply to messages by fax.

It appears that the message of acceptance was only partially received, because of a defect in A's modem. In *Entores* Denning LJ said:

> '... if there should be a case where the offeror without any fault on his part does not receive the message of acceptance – yet the sender of it reasonably believes that it has got home when it has not – then I think there is no contract.'

There are, unfortunately, gaps in the information furnished to us. We are not told the extent to which there was only partial receipt of B's message. Could the part that was received be considered to be a coherent acceptance of the offer? Could the defect in A's modem be attributed to fault on his part? In the absence of this information one has to entertain certain hypotheses, remembering that it is A, the offeror, who wishes to deny the contract, and B, the offeree, who would presumably want to enforce it.

If the part of the message that A received is sufficient to constitute a coherent acceptance, it is difficult to advise him that he could successfully deny the validity of the contract, although he could, of course, argue that, because of the defect in his modem, he realised that the message was incomplete, and could not, therefore, be reasonably understood as an unambiguous acceptance. In this event, or if the part of the message that was received was not coherent, one must consider who should bear the consequence of the defect.

In the extract of the judgment of Denning LJ in *Entores*, quoted above, his Lordship refers to the offeror not receiving the message – 'without any fault on his part'. Earlier his Lordship had referred to situations where the listener on the telephone does not hear the words of acceptance, but does not trouble to ask for them to be repeated, or where the ink on a teleprinter runs dry, but the recipient does not ask for the message to be repeated. In these circumstances, said His Lordship, the offeror would be clearly bound, because he would be estopped from saying that he did not receive the message of acceptance. It was his own fault that he did not receive it.

It is submitted, with respect, that Denning LJ's reasoning is correct and that it applies, moreover, to the situation in this problem. B would presumably have been unaware of the defect in A's modem, and assumed that his message of acceptance had got through. A was, or should have been, aware of the defect. He is therefore estopped from denying that the acceptance was communicated.

I must deal with one further contention that A might advance. I have stated earlier that there was nothing to suggest that an e-mail was not a valid form of acceptance. A might argue that as he transmitted his offer by fax, he anticipated an acceptance by fax. I suggest that this argument would be without substance. There is authority that where an offer was sent by telegram, the offeror was entitled to expect an acceptance in the same form: *Quenerduaine* v *Cole* (1883). But e-mail is just as swift as a fax. Even if it could be argued that, by sending a fax message, A had impliedly prescribed an acceptance by that means, this would not avail A. There is clear authority that where an offeror, even expressly, prescribes a particular form of acceptance, unless he makes it clear that only that form will do, any other form, equally swift and effective, will also constitute a valid acceptance: *Tinn* v *Hoffman & Co* (1873); *Manchester Diocesan Council for Education* v *Commercial & General Investments Ltd* (1970).

I would advise B, therefore, that he is entitled to enforce the contract.

SUGGESTED ANSWER TO QUESTION FIVE

General Comment

This question raises issues relating to the principles of offer and acceptance with the emphasis on communication of same. The postal rule and methods of instantaneous communications also require consideration.

Key Points

- A's letter to B: an offer, or an invitation to treat?
- B's reply by message on the answerphone: an acceptance or a counter-offer?
- If B's reply an acceptance, whether and when communicated
- The effect of B's subsequent letter
- On assumption (i): B's letter never arriving
- On assumption (ii): B's message not having been recorded
- On assumption (iii): B's query to A on Monday 5 May, offer or invitation to treat?

Suggested Answer

A's letter to B of Tuesday 6 May is an offer, and not merely an invitation to treat. In my submission it is clearly 'an expression of willingness to contract on specified terms, made with the intention that it shall become binding as soon as it is accepted by the person to whom it is addressed' (*Treitel: The Law of Contract,* 9th edn, p8). If it were merely an invitation to treat there would be little further to discuss.

I now have to consider whether B's message, left on the answerphone, is an acceptance or a counter-offer. If it were the latter, the effect would be to destroy the original offer: *Hyde* v *Wrench* (1840). In that event there would be, again, little further to discuss. Whilst an acceptance must be unqualified, this does not mean that there must be precise correspondence with the words of the offer. It appears that the requirement to pay cash merely makes express what the law would imply. I conclude that B's message is an acceptance of A's offer. *Manatee Towing Co* v *Oceanbulk Maritime SA, The Bay Ridge* (1999) recently reiterated the fact that acceptance materialises when parties have concluded negotiations or are no longer in such a process. So long as the presumption of acceptance is not rebutted, the court will conclude that there has been acceptance: *Inland Revenue Commissioners* v *Fry* (2001).

The next question is when B's message is communicated. There are three possibilities: first, when the message was left on the machine; second, when the message was actually heard; and third, when it should have been heard in the normal course of events.

There is no clear authority with regard to telephone answering machines. In his analysis of telephone communications in *Entores Ltd* v *Miles Far East Corporation* (1955), Denning LJ said: 'But if there should be a case where the offeror without any fault on his part does not receive the message of acceptance - yet the sender of it reasonably believes it has got home when it has not - then I think there is no contract.' Whilst it is not a perfect analogy, I submit that a message on a telephone answering machine is only communicated when it is actually heard. I have considered the possibility that the message might be deemed to be communicated when it should have been heard. In *The Brimnes* (1975) the Court of Appeal held that a message by telex must have been regarded as having been received in the normal course of business hours. But this case concerned the termination of a contract, not its formation, and moreover was in the context of business dealings, and I do not consider that it can be applied in the present situation.

It appears, therefore, that as B's letter - rejecting A's offer - arrived on the Thursday before the message of acceptance had been heard, no contract had been concluded between the parties.

I must now consider the alternative assumptions.

B's letter had never arrived

The 'postal rule', by which an acceptance is deemed to be communicated when the letter is posted, does not apply to a revocation: actual communication is required. B's letter, therefore, is ineffective. A's offer has consequently been accepted when he hears the message on his answering machine, and the contract was concluded at that point.

B's message not being recorded due to a fault with the answerphone

In the quotation by Denning LJ, given above, his Lordship referred to the offeror not having received the message 'without any fault on his part'. It could be argued that the failure of A's answerphone could be attributed to fault on his part, in which case the message of acceptance would be deemed to have been communicated. The difficulty would be in deciding when this communication would be deemed to have occurred. As argued above, the suggestion that the message was communicated when it was left on the machine is contrary to principle, and the ratio of *The Brimnes* has no application to the present situation. Moreover, it is difficult to hold that A is bound by a message of which he is completely unaware. The conclusion must be that, A's offer not having been accepted, no contract has been concluded.

B had asked A if he wanted to buy his MGB on Monday 5 May

The answer to this depends on whether B's query is an offer or an invitation to treat. If it were an offer, then A's letter to B could be considered an acceptance of that offer. However, as no price seems to have been mentioned in B's query, it seems more likely that it was no more than an invitation to treat, and this does not affect the finding that no contract was concluded.

SUGGESTED SOLUTION TO QUESTION SIX

General Comment

Another question that requires consideration of both an offer and an invitation to treat. Issues of communication are also raised to determine the existence of a contractual relationship. Remedies for breach of contract must also be discussed.

Key Points

- Floyd's fax to Delia: whether an offer, or an invitation to treat
- Delia's fax in reply: whether an acceptance of the offer, or itself the offer
- the nature of Floyd's further communication
- on assumption (i): the effect of Delia's telephone call
- on assumption (ii): the possibility of a contract having been concluded and, if it has, the liability of Floyd for breach of contract

Suggested Answer

The initial point for discussion is whether the fax from Floyd constitutes an offer in the sense defined by Treitel (*Treitel: The Law of Contract*, 9th edn, p8) as 'an expression of willingness to contract on specified terms, made with the intention that it shall become binding as soon as it accepted by the person to whom it is addressed'. The wording of the fax is somewhat ambiguous; it could be construed merely as an invitation to treat. It is not always easy to distinguish an offer from an invitation to treat, the distinction depends on the intention of the parties, objectively considered. The use of the word 'offer' is not necessarily conclusive: *Spencer* v *Harding* (1870); *Clifton* v *Palumbo* (1944). The expression 'can offer' might suggest that the communication is merely an invitation to treat. However, it seems somewhat pedantic to give this interpretation to it and, in view of Delia's reply, nothing turns on the distinction. But consideration must be afforded to both possibilities.

Attention must now be directed to the nature of Delia's faxed reply. On the assumption that she was responding to an invitation to treat, then her fax constitutes the offer. On the alternative assumption that she was responding to an offer, the question is whether her message constitutes an acceptance of that offer. An acceptance has been defined as 'a final and unqualified assent to the terms of the offer' (*Treitel*, op cit, p16). This was recently confirmed in *Manatee Towing Co* v *Oceanbulk Maritime SA, The Bay Ridge* (1999). A communication is not an unqualified acceptance if it introduces a new term: *Butler Machine Tool Co Ltd* v *Ex-cell-o Corporation (England) Ltd* (1979). It is submitted that the requirement 'Need delivery by next Thursday' does introduce a new term and that, consequently, Delia's message is not an acceptance. If it is not an acceptance it is a counter-offer, which destroys the original offer: *Hyde* v *Wrench* (1840) appears, therefore, that whether the initial communication from Floyd is an invitation to treat or an offer, the only extant offer is the fax sent by Delia.

The further communication from Floyd – presumably a letter – is unfortunately also somewhat ambiguous. It could conceivably be interpreted as merely acknowledging

Delia's fax and indicating that her offer was being considered. In that event no contract was ever concluded. (The packing and loading of the cookers could not constitute an acceptance as there was no communication of this to Delia.) On this interpretation no rights or liabilities were incurred. I shall proceed on the basis, therefore, that Floyd's communication was intended to be an acceptance of Delia's offer.

It remains to consider Delia's position on each of the alternative assumptions presented.

i) On the first assumption it appears that Delia purported to revoke her offer before the van set out. It is trite law that an offer can be revoked at any time before acceptance (*Routledge* v *Grant* (1828)), and that a revocation is ineffective if it is communicated after the acceptance has been (or deemed to have been) communicated: *Byrne & Co* v *Van Tienhoven & Co* (1880). It is presumed that when Floyd 'wrote', as distinct from sending a fax, this communication was by letter. The question is whether this letter of acceptance was communicated before Delia telephoned revoking her offer. We are not told whether Delia received the letter. If she did, then the acceptance was clearly communicated, her purported revocation is ineffective, and she is contractually bound. If she had not received the letter at that time, I have to consider whether acceptance would be deemed to be communicated by the application of the postal rule. Where this rule applies the letter of acceptance is deemed to be communicated when the letter is posted: *Adams* v *Lindsell* (1818). It matters not that the letter may never have been received: *Household Fire and Carriage Accident Insurance Co Ltd* v *Grant* (1879). The postal rule will apply where 'it must have been within the contemplation of the parties that, according to the ordinary usages of mankind, the post might be used as a means of communicating the acceptance of an offer': per Lord Herschell in *Henthorn* v *Fraser* (1892).

   The postal rule is, however, an artificial one, and the parties may, expressly or impliedly, exclude its operation: *Holwell Securities Ltd* v *Hughes* (1974). There are indications here that the use of the post was not contemplated by the parties. The previous communications had been by fax, and it can be assumed that the use of this medium, or at least an equally swift method of communication, would be continued. There is authority to the effect that, if an offer is sent by telegram, the posting of a letter does not constitute an effective communication of the acceptance: *Quenerduaine* v *Cole* (1883).

   My view is, therefore, that Delia could not reasonably be expected to have anticipated a postal acceptance of her offer. I am fortified in this view that her requiring 'delivery by next Thursday' indicates that she expects a speedy response.

   I conclude, on the first assumption, that if Delia had received Floyd's letter she would be contractually bound, but not otherwise. If she were bound, then Floyd would have an action against her for breach of contract. His remedy would lie in damages, an order for specific performance would not be appropriate.

ii) If Floyd failed to deliver any cookers to Delia, I submit that he would be liable for breach of contract. Even if the postal rule did not apply, as previously discussed, it would not lie in his mouth to assert this, as he elected to use the post as the method of communicating his acceptance. In this event Delia would certainly have a claim for damages against him. Again specific performance would not appear to be an appropriate remedy, unless, possibly, the cookers, or similar ones, were not available elsewhere.

SUGGESTED ANSWER TO QUESTION SEVEN

General Comment

Essentially this question requires analysis of whether on the facts there is an offer, or counter offer, or a mere request for information. Issues of communication are also raised and methods of instantaneous communications and their implications need to be discussed.

Key Points

- B's message on A's answerphone: whether it constitutes an acceptance (the question of mistake must be referred to here), a counter offer, or a request for information
- the nature of A's message by electronic mail: whether it constitutes an acceptance or a fresh offer – if a fresh offer, the effect of the attempt to construe silence as acceptance
- B's reply by letter: whether it is an acceptance and, if so, the relevance of the postal rule
- The consequences of B not receiving A's electronic mail message, or B only receiving the incomplete message

Suggested Answer

It is assumed that the letter sent by A on the Monday constitutes a clear offer. There is an element of doubt on this point as there are two paintings by Augustus John, and it may be difficult to determine, objectively, to which painting the offer can be held to relate.

The reply by B, the message on A's answerphone, is termed an acceptance by B. It cannot, however, be effective as such. The offer was made for the painting 'Forbidden Fruit' and the acceptance relates to the painting 'Four Sisters'. The parties are clearly not ad idem as to the subject matter and the contract would be void for mistake: *Raffles* v *Wichelhaus* (1864); *Scriven Bros & Co* v *Hindley & Co* (1913).

It is, in any event, by no means clear that B's message could be construed as an acceptance. Treitel (*The Law of Contract*, 9th edn, p16) defines an acceptance as 'a final and unqualified expression of assent to the terms of an offer'. It would not appear that the message falls within this definition. In *Manatee Towing Co* v *Oceanbulk Maritime SA, The Bay Ridge* (1999) the Queen's Bench Division held that so long as the parties are still negotiating, no agreement has been reached. For there to be acceptance, unqualified assent must be evident. The message could be construed either as a counter-offer, or as a request for information. If it is a counter-offer the effect of it would be to destroy the original offer: *Hyde* v *Wrench* (1840). It may be, however, that the message could be regarded merely as a request for information, which would not amount to a rejection of the offer: *Stevenson Jacques & Co* v *McLean* (1880). The question of whether a communication is a counter-offer or a request for information depends on the intention of the parties, objectively ascertained. It is submitted that, as the message introduces a different subject matter, it must be regarded as a counter-offer, which A is free to accept or reject. Accordingly no contract has been concluded at this point.

On the Wednesday A's message by electronic mail is clearly not an acceptance of B's offer, but a fresh offer to buy both paintings. His use of the words 'I accept' do not contradict the interpretation of the message as an offer; a statement may be an offer although it is expressed to be an 'acceptance': *Bigg* v *Boyd Gibbins Ltd* (1971). The remainder of the message clearly indicates that it was intended as an offer.

In this message A is attempting to impose silence as constituting acceptance. The general rule is that an offeror cannot do so: *Felthouse* v *Bindley* (1862). Whilst the offeree would not be bound by silence, it is possible that the the offeror could be held to have waived communication and to be bound by the offeree's silence - see the discussion by Treitel (*The Law of Contract* (9th edn), p32). This possibility is discussed below.

What has now to be discussed is whether A's fresh offer has been accepted. Two points must be considered: whether B's letter constitutes an acceptance; and, if it does, whether the acceptance can be deemed to have been communicated.

B's reply - 'I may be prepared to sell both' - cannot, it is submitted, be regarded as 'a final and unqualified assent' as required by the quotation from Treitel referred to above. That being so, the question whether it has been communicated is an academic one. The problem does, however, require consideration of it.

When an acceptance is sent by post it may be deemed to have been communicated when the letter is posted. This is the effect of the postal rule established in *Adams* v *Lindsell* (1818). It matters not that the letter is lost in the post: *Household Fire and Carriage Accident Insurance Co Ltd* v *Grant* (1879). The postal rule will apply '[w]here the circumstances are such that it must have been within the contemplation of the parties that, according to the ordinary usages of mankind, the post might be used as a means of communicating the acceptance of an offer' per Lord Herschell in *Henthorn* v *Fraser* (1892). If B's letter had constituted an acceptance, it could be argued that it was deemed to have been communicated by the application of the postal rule. It would not avail A to maintain that, having made the offer by electronic mail, he did not anticipate an acceptance through the post, but an instantaneous one, as he did not require a reply at all. However, it has been suggested that B's letter was not an unequivocal acceptance of A's offer.

My conclusion thus far is that B is not bound by A's offer transmitted by electronic mail, because the rule is that silence cannot be imposed on the offeree: *Felthouse* v *Bindley*. It is, however, possible to argue - as Treitel does (see previous reference) - that this rule was developed for the protection of the offeree, and that there is no reason in principle why the offeror should not be bound; although, as Treitel concedes, this possibility has been judicially doubted: *Fairline Shipping Corporation* v *Adamson* (1975). In the absence, therefore, of clear supporting authority B could not be advised that he could hold A to the offer to buy both paintings.

At this stage I remain of the view that no contract has been concluded.

I am asked to consider two further possibilities: (a) that B had not received A's electronic mail message; and (b) that B received only the incomplete message.

With regard to the first situation it is trite law that an offer must be actually communicated; an acceptance in ignorance of the offer can have no effect. The position would then be that B's counter-offer on A's answerphone to sell the painting 'Four Sisters' had not been accepted by A, and that there had been no further communication between the parties since then. My advice would, in consequence, would be the same, that no contract had been concluded.

The second situation gives rise to more doubt. Here B receives a message which appears to be an acceptance of his counter-offer for the sale of of the painting 'Four Sisters' at £25,000. This clearly was not A's intention, but could it be objectively construed as such? The answer would seem to depend on whether A knew (or had the means of knowing) of the transmission failure. Having chosen to use electronic mail as a method of communication it is arguable that A should bear the risk of imperfect transmission. Moreover his use of the expression 'I accept' would lead a reasonable person to believe that the message was a response – and therefore an acceptance – of the counter-offer. I conclude, although not without doubt, in the absence of clear authority, that on the assumption that A knew, or should have known of the possibility of the transmission failure, a contract would have been concluded on the terms of B's counter-offer.

2

Consideration and Intention to Create Legal Relations

Introduction

The two further elements of a simple contract (one not under seal), consideration and intention to be legally bound, are no less important than offer and acceptance, since without them there is no enforceable contract. Thus, this topic is scarcely less highly-favoured by examiners.

While legal intention is generally straightforward and can be discerned from the nature of the transaction and the relationship between the parties, the concept of consideration often causes difficulty. Consideration merely means that a party who wishes to sue under a contract must have given or promised something of value in return. The main question in this area is what amounts to 'valuable' or 'good' consideration. Examples of consideration which may not be 'good' are acts performed prior to the making of the contract or the performance of an existing legal duty. Students are advised to read the cases and examples carefully in order to discuss this point, and to note the apparent recent change in attitudes of the courts.

The question of promissory estoppel also falls within this area. Promissory estoppel is the equitable principle that when a creditor has agreed to forego part of his debt, he cannot then renege on that agreement, even though there was no consideration for it. Candidates should be fully aware of the circumstances in which this principle may be invoked and the development of rules in relation to it.

Questions

INTERROGRAMS

1. Under what circumstances (if any) is the court prepared to uphold social and domestic agreements?
2. What words in commercial agreements have been deemed evidence that there was no intention to enter into a legally binding contract?
3. 'Consideration must have some economic value but need not be adequate.' Explain.

QUESTION ONE

Les agreed to rent his lorry to Morgan for £500 per week for 104 weeks. Morgan had just started out 'on his own' and was aiming to use the lorry to transport coal to a nearby power station. After paying the agreed sum for 14 weeks Morgan fell ill and Les agreed to accept £200 per week till Morgan recovered. Morgan paid the reduced sum for the following eight weeks when Morgan's wife, Noreen, won £250,000 on her premium savings bond. Although they had agreed to share any winnings Noreen refused to share any of her prize with Morgan. Ten weeks after Noreen's win, Morgan was left £10,000 by his Uncle Oliver. Morgan continued to pay the reduced sum till in the 52nd week Les discovered what had transpired. Two weeks later Morgan made a full recovery. Les claimed the full arrears of £300 per week and requested that the lorry be returned to Les immediately. Morgan refused. At that time Les could have rented the lorry for £600 per week.

Advise Les.

University of London LLB Examination
(for external students) Elements of the Law of Contract June 2001 Q8

QUESTION TWO

'Payment of a sum less than that due does not discharge the original contractual obligation. This is why the courts have gone to extraordinary lengths to provide the person who has paid the lesser sum with some form of protection. But this protection is heavily circumscribed.'

Discuss.

University of London LLB Examination
(for external students) Elements of the Law of Contract June 2000 Q5

QUESTION THREE

H let his London flat to P, a visitor from Australia, for two years from 1 January 1998. It was agreed that P would take good care of the flat and pay a monthly fee of £1,200 a month. On 1 June 1998 P fell ill and on 1 September he lost his job. As a result P was in financial difficulties. H agreed to accept half rent till P's financial state improved. Three months later P won a large sum on the national lottery. Two months afterwards P recovered his health. P had paid half rent for three months when H discovered that P had won the money. H insisted that P repay the outstanding arrears as well as full rent for the future.

Advise H.

University of London LLB Examination
(for external students) Elements of the Law of Contract June 1999 Q3

QUESTION FOUR

'The requirement of consideration is an unnecessary complication in the formation of contracts.'

Discuss.

University of London LLB Examination
(for external students) Elements of the Law of Contract June 1998 Q1

QUESTION FIVE

a) 'A promise to do what a person is already obliged to do cannot constitute consideration.'

Discuss.

b) E let his caravan to F, a university law student, for £120 per month for three years while she was studying. After F had paid the rent for 18 months she gave birth to a son, G, who proved to be sickly and delicate. As a result of looking after G, F failed her examinations and her grant (her sole source of income) was withdrawn. E took pity on F and said, 'You can pay £80 a month till you get yourself sorted.' After F had paid the reduced rent for six months, she received a large payment from social services to cover arrears. F did not tell E about this payment and continued to pay £80 per month for three months till E discovered the full facts. E demanded arrears of payment and full rent for the future.

Advise E.

University of London LLB Examination
(for external students) Elements of the Law of Contract June 1997 Q8

QUESTION SIX

Trevor and Una are neighbours. Last month Una erected a high fence along the side of her garden next to Trevor's garden. When Una took no notice of Trevor's complaints about the fence, Trevor threatened that he would 'go to the court for an injunction to have the fence pulled down'. To avoid trouble, Una promised Trevor that she would reduce the size of the fence if he agreed not to go to court. Trevor agreed.

Later on the same day Una was talking to her other neighbour, Vernon, who is a law lecturer. Vernon told her (correctly) that the existing fence was perfectly lawful. The next morning she promised Vernon that she would pay him £50 for his help, after she had been to the bank.

Una still refuses to change the fence and has failed to pay the £50 to Vernon.

Advise Trevor and Vernon.

University of London LLB Examination
(for external students) Elements of the Law of Contract June 1996 Q6

QUESTION SEVEN

'Consideration is a form as much as seal.' Discuss.

Written by the Editor

QUESTION EIGHT

'The concept of consideration is antiquated and must now be made obsolete. All that is needed to create binding relations is intention.'

Discuss.

Written by the Editor

Answers

ANSWERS TO INTERROGRAMS

1. There is a presumption that the parties to social and domestic agreements do not intend them to be legally binding (*Balfour* v *Balfour* (1919)). However this is a rebuttable presumption, which is to say that it will not apply if strong evidence is shown to the contrary: *Pettitt* v *Pettitt* (1970).

   In *Jones* v *Padavatton* (1969) a mother induced her daughter to leave her job in America and read for the Bar in England by the promise of a monthly allowance, for which was later substituted an agreement that the daughter would live rent-free in a property of hers. The court found an intention to create legal relations in the promise to pay a monthly allowance but not in the agreement for rent-free accommodation which was deemed a family arrangement.

   The courts are, however, sometimes more ready to find intention to create legal relations where the agreement concerns the occupation of real property, even if the arrangement is between family members: *Hardwick* v *Johnson* (1978).

   Separation agreements between spouses have been held to be legally binding (*Merritt* v *Merritt* (1970); *Gould* v *Gould* (1970)) but only where their terms were clear and unambiguous.

   Finally, the court may be prepared to find an intention to create legal relations where there is 'mutuality'. In *Simpkins* v *Pays* (1955) three people living together were accustomed to enter a weekly newspaper competition, sending in the entry alternately in each name. When one of them won a monetary prize, the court held that the other two were entitled to share it.
2. Where the agreement is a commercial one, the court presumes that it was intended to be legally binding. However, as with the opposite presumption in relation to social and domestic agreements, it is rebuttable by clear evidence to the contrary.

   While evidence as to a contrary intention may be drawn from the surrounding circumstances (*Orion Insurance Co* v *Sphere Drake Insurance* (1992); *Evans* v *Merzario Ltd* (1976)), more often the words of the contract itself will rebut the presumption. In *Jones* v *Vernons Pools* (1938) a football pools agreement was stated to be 'binding in honour only' and the plaintiff was therefore unable to sue. In *Rose & Frank Co* v *J R Crompton Bros* (1925), the contract itself contained the words 'This agreement is not entered into … as a formal or legal agreement, and shall not be subject to legal jurisdiction in the law courts.' These words were held sufficiently clear and unambiguous to negative the usual presumption. A further example is provided by *Edwards* v *Skyways Ltd* (1964) where, in an agreement to make a termination payment to an employee, the payment was stated to be 'ex gratia'. These words were held to indicate that the defendants did not intend to be legally bound by their promise to pay.
3. Consideration must have some value, and it has long been established that the value must be economic: *White* v *Bluett* (1853). The consideration, however, need not be adequate. That is to say, the court refuses to act as valuer and, provided there is some consideration of economic value, will not judge whether it reflects the true value of what is promised in return.

Thus the practice has grown of giving nominal consideration: one peppercorn by way of annual rent or £1 in return for the transfer of shares or other property. This may lead to the enforcement of what are, in effect, gratuitous promises. Atiyah suggests that the nominal consideration can be regarded as a form to make the contract binding. This does not, however, accord with some of the reasons for non-enforcement of gratuitous promises, eg rashness of the promisor, or prejudice to creditors (although there may be more effective ways of dealing with these situations in modern times).

Rather than nominal, the consideration may be trivial but can nevertheless still be valuable. In *Chappell & Co Ltd* v *Nestlé Co Ltd* (1960) delivery of chocolate wrappers which were then thrown away was held to be valuable consideration. However, most recently in *Lipkin Gorman* v *Karpnale Ltd* (1991) the House of Lords held that gaming chips supplied by a club to one of its member were not consideration for the money paid to them. This decision sits uneasily beside *Chappell*, although a number of distinguishing points were noted. Perhaps, as Atiyah has suggested, the refusal to find valuable consideration was based on the context - ie the money paid by the member had been stolen, and the club was arguing against liability to the true owner - and the case may therefore be confined to its facts.

SUGGESTED ANSWER TO QUESTION ONE

General Comment

This requires discussion of the equitable doctrine of promissory estoppel. The particular issue here is whether, and to what extent, the promisor can resile from his promise.

Key Points

- The common law rules with regard to the payment of a lesser sum
- The origin and development of the doctrine of promissory estoppel
- The operation and limits of the doctrine
- The effects of the doctrine, in particular whether it is suspensive or extinctive and when it would be inequitable for the promisor to resile from his promise

Suggested Answer

At common law the payment of a lesser sum in payment of a larger sum does not discharge the debt in the absence of consideration for the creditor abandoning the balance owing to him. This derives from the rule in *Pinnel's Case* (1602), affirmed by the House of Lords in *Foakes* v *Beer* (1864) and more recently by the Court of Appeal in *Re Selectmove Ltd* (1995). Thus, at common law Les's promise to accept the reduced sum would be unenforceable, no consideration having been furnished for that promise, and he would be entitled to claim full implementation of Morgan's obligations.

The common law has, however, been modified by the doctrine of promissory estoppel and we are required to examine the effects of that doctrine on the rights of the parties.

The origin of the doctrine lies in the decision of the House of Lords in *Hughes* v *Metropolitan Railway Co* (1877), where Lord Cairns LC stated the principle of equity that

> '... if parties ...enter upon a course of negotiation which has the effect of leading one of the parties to suppose that the strict legal rights arising under the contract will not be enforced, or will be kept in suspense, or held in abeyance, the party who otherwise might have enforced those rights will not be allowed to enforce them where it would be inequitable having regard to the dealings which have thus taken place between the parties.'

(The earlier case of *Jorden* v *Money* (1854), where the House of Lords had held that estoppel related to statements of existing fact, not to promises as to the future, was not quoted.)

The equitable principle enunciated by Lord Cairns was applied by the House of Lords in the context of a landlord's claim for forfeiture of a lease. It was developed by Denning J in obiter dicta in *Central London Property Trust Ltd* v *High Trees House Ltd* (1947) to extend to the payment of money. His Lordship said that 'a promise to accept a smaller sum in discharge of a larger sum, if acted upon, is binding notwithstanding the absence of consideration.'

Denning J's judgment has been criticised as being in conflict with *Foakes* v *Beer* and *Jorden* v *Money*, but the doctrine of promissory estoppel has been accepted by the courts at all levels.

It is now necessary to apply the criteria for the doctrine to operate and its effects to the facts of the present problem.

Les's promise must have been clear and unequivocal: *Woodhouse A C Israel Cocoa SA* v *Nigerian Produce Marketing Co Ltd* (1972). It appears to have been so.

Morgan must have acted on the promise. It is not entirely certain what this requirement entails. It does not appear that he must have necessarily acted to his detriment. There is no clear authority, but there are obiter dicta stating that it is not necessary to show detriment: per Lord Denning MR in *W J Alan & Co Ltd* v *El Nasr Export & Import Co* (1972); per Goff J in *The Post Chaser* (1982). Lord Denning stated that all that is necessary is to show that the promisee must have been led to have acted differently from what he would otherwise have done. We must assume that Morgan was so led and that he acted differently by continuing with the rental of the lorry and paying the reduced sum.

That the doctrine suspends, rather than extinguishes, the promisor's rights was emphasised by the Privy Council in *F A Ajayi* v *R T Briscoe (Nigeria) Ltd* (1964) and by the House of Lords in *Tool Metal Manufacturing Co Ltd* v *Tungsten Electric Co Ltd* (1955). In the former case Lord Hodson said that: 'the promisor can resile from his promise on giving reasonable notice, which need not be a formal notice, giving the promisee reasonable opportunity of resuming his position'.

Les intended that his rights to the full instalments should be suspended. When he agreed that Morgan could pay the reduced sum until Morgan recovered from his illness, he must have intended that to mean until Morgan was financially able to resume payment of the full amount. Morgan's financial ability to do so is not affected by his wife

Noreen's winnings. Although they had agreed to share any winnings, she has refused to do so and Morgan has no claim upon them. However, Morgan is clearly financially able to resume payment of the full instalments as from the time he received the bequest from his uncle. Les is therefore entitled to demand the resumption of the full payment of the remaining instalments.

With regard to the arrears the situation is more problematical. Is the effect of the doctrine of promissory estoppel extinctive with regard to the right to the arrears? In *High Trees* Denning J held the view that the landlord's claim for the arrear rentals would have been extinguished, but this view was unnecessary for the decision in that case as the landlord was not claiming the arrears. In the absence of authority I must submit that it is more consistent with the doctrine to hold that Les's rights to the arrears would have been extinguished, but this is subject to the equity of the situation, to which we must now turn attention.

It is central to the doctrine that the promisor will only be estopped from resiling from his promise when it would be inequitable to allow him to do so. The effect of the operation of promissory estoppel is that it raises an equity in favour of the promisee, Morgan. In this context Morgan's conduct is relevant: he failed to disclose to Les his receipt of the bequest from his uncle, and continued to pay the reduced sum for some weeks after he had received it. Does this debar him from raising the equitable defence? The only guidance we have is in the judgement of Lord Denning in *D & C Builders Ltd* v *Rees* (1966). There his Lordship held that where the promise to accept the lesser sum had been obtained by a threat, by intimidation, the equity was not raised in the promisee's favour. The question is whether mere dishonesty would have the same effect. In my view it should. I conclude that on the facts presented Les would be entitled to resile completely from his promise and would also be entitled to claim the arrears.

It is, however, difficult to see on what basis Les could at this stage claim the return of the lorry. he could hardly maintain that the failure to pay the full instalments should be treated as a breach of condition which would justify termination of the contract.

SUGGESTED ANSWER TO QUESTION TWO

General Comment

This question requires discussion of the common law rules of consideration in relation to the payment of a lesser sum, and the modification of the common law rules by the equitable doctrine of promissory estoppel.

Key Points

- The common law
- The rule in *Pinnel's Case*
- The origin and development of the doctrine of promissory estoppel
- Limitations of the doctrine

Suggested Answer

At common law the rule in *Pinnel's Case* (1602) is that 'Payment of a lesser sum on the day in satisfaction of a greater sum cannot be any satisfaction for the whole.' This rule was affirmed by the House of Lords in *Foakes* v *Beer* (1884) and more recently by the Court of Appeal in *Re Selectmove Ltd* (1995). But even at common law there were certain limitations on the rule, if there was deemed to be accord and satisfaction. Thus, the debt could be discharged by payment in kind, or by earlier payment, or by payment elsewhere: *Couldrey* v *Bartrum* (1881); *Vanbergen* v *St Edmunds Properties Ltd* (1933). Payment of a lesser sum could also discharge the debt if if were made by a third party: *Hirachand Punamchand* v *Temple* (1911).

However, the protection that has been afforded to the person who has paid the lesser sum stems from the development of the equitable doctrine of promissory estoppel. The origin of this doctrine lies in the decision of the House of Lords in *Hughes* v *Metropolitan Railway Co* (1887) where Lord Cairns LC stated that it was a clear rule of equity that where one person, by his words or conduct, had led the other party to believe that his strict rights under the contract would not be enforced, or would be held in suspense or abeyance, then that person would not be entitled to enforce those rights where it would be inequitable to allow him to do so. (The earlier, and possibly conflicting, decision of the House of Lords in *Jorden* v *Money* (1854) was not quoted.)

In *Hughes* v *Metropolitan Railway Co* the landlord was estopped from claiming the forfeiture of a lease, but the equitable principle was applied by Denning J (as he then was) to the payment of a lesser sum of money in obiter dicta in *Central London Property Trust Ltd* v *High Trees House Ltd* (1947). The effect of this development was that where a creditor had promised to accept a lesser sum in discharge of the (larger) debt he could be estopped from claiming the balance. This doctrine of promissory estoppel is in conflict with the decision in *Foakes* v *Beer*, and represents an equitable modification of the common law principle.

The scope and limits of the doctrine of promissory estoppel must now be examined,

First, there must have been a clear and unambiguous promise; it is not sufficient that the creditor merely failed to enforce his contractual rights: *Woodhouse A C Israel Cocoa SA* v *Nigerian Produce Marketing Co Ltd* (1972).

Second, the doctrine provides 'a shield, not a sword', that is, it operates as a defence, it does not create a cause of action where none existed before: *Combe* v *Combe* (1951). (There is a different application of the doctrine by the High Court of Australia in *Walton Stores (Interstate) Ltd* v *Maher* (1988).)

Third, the promisee must have relied on the promise, he must have acted on it in some way. It is not entirely clear what this involves. There are obiter dicta to the effect that it is not necessary for the promisee to have acted to his detriment, he must merely have done something he would not otherwise have done: per Denning LJ in *W J Alan & Co Ltd* v *El Nasr Export & Import Co* (1972); and per Goff J in *Société Italo-Belge* v *Palm and Vegetable Oils, The Post Chaser* (1982). However, in *Goldsworthy* v *Brickell* (1987) Nourse LJ rejected the application of the doctrine because he could find no evidence of detriment.

Fourth, it must be inequitable for the promisor to go back on his promise: see the judgment of Lord Denning MR in *D & C Builders Ltd* v *Rees* (1966).

Fifth, it appears that the doctrine operates so as to suspend the creditor's rights, not to extinguish them. The Privy Council in *F A Ajayi* v *R T Briscoe (Nigeria) Ltd* (1964) and the House of Lords in *Tool Metal Manufacturing Co Ltd* v *Tungsten Electric Co Ltd* (1955) emphasised that the promisor could resile from his promise by giving the other party reasonable notice, allowing him to resume his former position. This represents a curtailment of the doctrine as originally formulated in High Trees. But in that case Denning J held the view that the estoppel had permanent effects because the lessors would not have been able to demand the arrear rentals.

To hold that the operation of the doctrine is suspensory is satisfactory where the contractual obligation involves payment by instalments, but less so where it involves a single, lump sum, payment. To hold, however, that the operation of the estoppel can be extinctive would clearly be in conflict with *Foakes* v *Beer*.

Difficulties remain. In *Woodhouse A C Israel Cocoa SA* (above) Lord Hailsham LC said:

> 'I desire to add that the time may soon come when the whole sequence of cases based on promissory estoppel since the war beginning with *Central London Property Trust Ltd* v *High Trees House Ltd*, may need to be reviewed and reduced to a coherent body of doctrine. I do not mean to say that any are to be regarded with suspicion. But as is common with an expanding doctrine they do raise problems of coherent exposition which have never been systematically explored.'

The time has still not come.

SUGGESTED ANSWER TO QUESTION THREE

General Comment

This involves an examination and application of the doctrine of promissory estoppel, a particular point being whether it would be inequitable for H to go back on his promise.

Key Points

- The common law principle regarding the payment of a lesser sum in satisfaction of a larger sum
- The modification of the principle by the equitable doctrine of promissory estoppel
- Origin and development of the equitable doctrine
- Application of the doctrine, in particular how and when the promisor may go back on his promise

Suggested Answer

Since *Pinnel's Case* (1602) and its affirmation by the House of Lords in *Foakes* v *Beer* (1884) it has been an established principle of the common law that payment of a lesser sum than the amount of a debt cannot be satisfaction of the debt, unless there is some additional benefit to the creditor so that there is an accord and satisfaction. More recently the Court of Appeal has refused to accept a submission that would endanger the common law principle: *Re Selectmove Ltd* (1995).

Clearly at common law H would be entitled to insist on the full rental for the future and to claim payment of the arrears, his promise to accept half rent being unenforceable for want of consideration.

This principle of the common law has, however, been modified by the equitable doctrine of promissory estoppel. The origin of this doctrine stems from the decision of the House of Lords in *Hughes* v *Metropolitan Railway Co* (1877), where Lord Cairns LC enunciated the equitable principle that where the parties to a contract enter into negotiations which have the effect of leading one of the parties to believe that the strict legal rights arising under the contract will not be enforced, or will be held in suspense or abeyance, the party who might otherwise have enforced those rights will not be allowed to enforce them where it would be inequitable for him to do so.

This statement of the equitable principle was extended by Denning J in *Central London Property Trust Ltd* v *High Trees House Ltd* (1947) where his Lordship uttered the dictum that 'a promise to accept a smaller sum in discharge of a larger sum, if acted upon, is binding notwithstanding the absence of consideration.'

The correctness of the dictum has been the subject of controversy: it was said to be inconsistent with *Foakes* v *Beer* (above) and with the earlier decision of the House of Lords in *Jorden* v *Money* (1854). But the principle of promissory estoppel has been recognised in a number of cases and its scope will now be examined in relation to the facts of the problem before me.

H's promise must have been clear and unequivocal: *Woodhouse AC Israel Cocoa SA* v *Nigerian Produce Marketing Co Ltd* (1972). This requirement is satisfied.

The promisee, P, must have relied on the promise. It does not seem that he must have acted to his detriment. There is no clear authority, but there are a number of obiter dicta to the effect that all that is required is that the promisee must have been led to have acted differently from what he would otherwise have done: per Lord Cohen in *Tool Metal Manufacturing Co Ltd* v *Tungsten Electric Co Ltd* (1955); per Lord Denning MR in *W J Alan & Co Ltd* v *El Nasr Export & Import Co* (1972); per Robert Goff J in *Société Italo-Belge* v *Palm and Vegetable Oils, The Postchaser* (1982). Perhaps it can be assumed that, by paying the half rent, P fulfilled this requirement.

H may be allowed to go back on his promise. Lord Hodson said in *F A Ajayi* v *R T Briscoe (Nigeria) Ltd* (1964) that 'the promisor can resile from his promise on giving reasonable notice, which need not be a formal notice, giving the promisee reasonable opportunity of resuming his position ...'. H's insistence would probably be considered notice, although it appears informal. However, it must not be inequitable to allow him to do so.

H agreed to accept half rent until P's financial state improved. It was improved by his national lottery win. H can require P to pay the full rent for the future on giving reasonable notice of this requirement: *High Trees House* (above). What is less easy to decide is whether H can claim payment of the arrears. There are two issues here: first, whether H's promise was suspensory or extinctive of his rights; second, whether P, having concealed the fact of his win, has deprived himself of the equity that might otherwise have been raised in his favour.

Although in most of the cases in which promissory estoppel has featured the effect of the doctrine has been suspensory, it appears from High Trees House that the promise there extinguished the promisor's rights to claim the rental arrears. That it can have an extinctive effect was also assumed in the New Zealand case of *P* v *P* (1957) and by Lord Denning in *Brikom Investments Ltd* v *Carr* (1979).

On balance, therefore, H might have been estopped from demanding the rental arrears, were it not for P's conduct. He had continued to pay half rent after his lottery win, without informing H of his good fortune. A deliberate act, such as the threat in *D & C Builders Ltd* v *Rees* (1966), was held by Lord Denning to deprive the promisee of the equitable defence. A failure to honour a promise to make a future payment would have also been held to have this effect: *Re Selectmove Ltd* (above).

In view of the uncertainty as to whether H's promise was extinctive of his rights in any event, coupled with P's less than honest conduct, I am led to the conclusion that it would not be inequitable of H to go back on his promise and consequently he would be entitled to claim the arrears as well as the future rental.

SUGGESTED ANSWER TO QUESTION FOUR

General Comment

Although this may seem as a somewhat 'open' question, more is required than a mere exposition of the principles of the doctrine of consideration. The focus should be on where, if at all, the doctrine causes complications, and whether it could be abolished.

Key Points

- Define consideration
- Areas of difficulty in the application of the doctrine
- Is there an alternative to determine what promises should be enforced?

Suggested Answer

It is trite law that for a simple contract to be enforced it must be supported by consideration. There are exceptions, notably contracts under seal, but these are beyond the scope of this question.

The traditional definition of consideration is that of Lush J in *Currie* v *Misa* (1875), namely:

> '... a valuable consideration in the sense of the law may consist either in some right, interest, profit or benefit accruing to one party, or some forbearance, detriment, loss or responsibility given, suffered or undertaken by the other.'

Pollock, in his *Pollock on Contracts* (13th edn), p133, defined it as:

> 'An act or forbearance of the one party, or the promise thereof, is the price for which the promise of the other is bought, and the promise thus given for value is enforceable.'

These words were adopted by Lord Dunedin in *Dunlop Pneumatic Tyre Co Ltd* v *Selfridge & Co Ltd* (1915).

In the application of the doctrine, one area is open to particular criticism, namely the principle that, whilst the consideration must be sufficient, it need not be adequate. This makes it possible to evade the doctrine by holding that what was in effect a gratuitous promise will be enforceable by the furnishing of nominal consideration. An extreme example of this would be the payment of £1 for a valuable property. But this is beyond the bounds of probability.

What does require further discussion is the question of inadequate consideration. Nominal consideration is one that is only of token value; inadequate consideration is one that does have some value, but is clearly less, even substantially less, than the performance rendered in return. Thus, in *Midland Bank Trust Co Ltd* v *Green* (1981), where a husband sold a property, reputedly worth £40,000, to his wife for £500, this payment was held to constitute good consideration. In *Chappell & Co Ltd* v *Nestlé & Co Ltd* (1960) chocolate wrappings were held to form part of the purchase consideration: this was perhaps an unusual case.

Acts of forbearance constitute good consideration. It is, of course, unexceptionable that giving up a good claim should be regarded as valuable consideration. Where a claim is doubtful in law, giving it up does involve a possible detriment to the potential claimant, or a possible benefit to the other party, and does also constitute good consideration: *Haigh* v *Brooks* (1839). What is perhaps less justifiable is that giving up a bad claim may also be held to be good consideration. Clearly the abandonment of a claim known by the claimant to be bad in law cannot be good consideration. But what if the claim is in fact bad, although the claimant believes it to be good? There is authority that the abandonment of such a claim does constitute good consideration: *Callisher* v *Bischoffsheim* (1870). This appears difficult to understand. If the claimant pursues a bad claim through the courts, he would (or should) lose, and be mulcted by an award of costs against him. It is, therefore, hard to see what detriment he has sustained by abandoning an invalid claim. However, in *Pitt* v *PHH Asset Management Ltd* (1993) the Court of Appeal held that the plaintiff had provided valuable consideration by abandoning the threat of an injunction, although this was only of nuisance value, as it had no chance of succeeding.

It is arguable that a further area of complication is in the rules relating to the performance of an existing duty. With regard to the performance of a duty imposed by law there is old authority to the effect that merely to perform (or promise to perform) a duty already imposed by law does not constitute good consideration: *Collins* v *Godefroy* (1831). It is submitted, however, that this case is now of doubtful authority: there are dicta of Denning LJ to the contrary in *Ward* v *Byham* (1956) and *Williams* v *Williams* (1957). Moreover, this former view appears inconsistent with the acceptance by the courts that the performance of an existing duty to a third party can constitute good consideration: *Scotson* v *Pegg* (1861); *Shadwell* v *Shadwell* (1860); *New Zealand Shipping Co Ltd* v *AM Satterthwaite & Co Ltd, The Eurymedon* (1975); *Pao On* v *Lau Yiu Long* (1980).

With regard to the performance of an existing contractual duty to the promisor there has also been development. The ruling that such performance did not constitute good consideration in the early nineteenth century case of *Stilk* v *Myrick* (1809) has been 'modified' and 'refined' by the Court of Appeal in *Williams* v *Roffey Bros & Nicholls (Contractors) Ltd* (1990), in which it was held that good consideration is furnished when the promisee performs an existing duty, where the promisor derives a factual benefit from such performance.

Even if one accepts that, as in the instances outlined above, the requirement of consideration impose complications in the formation of contracts, it does not follow that this requirement could easily be dispensed with. Professor Atiyah argues in his essay *Consideration: A Restatement (Essays on Contract* (1998)) 'that to talk of abolition of the doctrine of consideration is nonsensical'. Clearly, not all promises should be enforced and, as the learned author says, consideration provides a reason for the enforcement of a promise. Were consideration to be abolished the courts would have to find some other method of determining which promises should be enforced. The one that suggests itself is to find an intention to create legal relations. But this might well create considerable uncertainty, and there is no reason to believe that it would be less likely to cause complications.

SUGGESTED ANSWER TO QUESTION FIVE

General Comment

A two-part question with the first raising the question whether an additional promise on an existing obligation provides good consideration, and the second requires consideration of the principles of promissory estoppel.

Key Points

a)
- Whether performance of, or the promise to perform, an existing duty can constitute good consideration
- The three possible existing duties: a public duty, that is one imposed by law - a contractual duty to the promisor - a duty to a third party

b) An application of the principles of promissory estoppel to the problem posed

Suggested Answer

a) A person may already be under an existing obligation, arising from a public duty, a contractual duty to the promisor, or a duty to the third party. Whether the performance of such obligation, or the promise to do so, can constitute good consideration must be considered in relation to each of these duties.

The performance of an existing public duty
There is old authority to the effect that the promise merely to perform a duty already imposed by law does not constitute good consideration: *Collins* v *Godefroy* (1831). But this case is of doubtful authority in view of subsequent decisions. In *Williams* v *Williams* (1957) Denning LJ said: 'a promise to perform an existing duty is, I think, sufficient consideration to support a promise, so long as there is nothing in the transaction which is contrary to the public interest'. He had expressed the same view earlier in *Ward* v *Byham* (1956). In both cases, however, the Court of Appeal had

found that the promisee had furnished consideration additional to the existing duty. This was the majority view in the latter case, on somewhat tenuous grounds. If the promisee does do more than his existing duty he thereby furnishes fresh consideration for the promise: *Glasbrook Brothers Ltd* v *Glamorgan County Council* (1925). Support for the view that a promise merely to perform the existing duty can be good consideration, when the promisor thereby derives a practical benefit, appears from *Williams* v *Roffey Bros & Nicholls (Contractors) Ltd* (1990). This however, according to the Court of Appeal in *Re Selectmove* (1995), will not discharge the entire contractual obligation.

The performance of a contractual duty owed to the promisor

The old authority here is that of *Stilk* v *Myrick* (1809), which held that mere performance of an existing contractual duty did not constitute fresh consideration for the promise. This was held to be good law by Mocatta J in *North Ocean Shipping Co* v *Hyundai Construction Co, The Atlantic Baron* (1979). Again, if more than the contractual duty is done or promised, fresh consideration is furnished: *Hartley* v *Ponsonby* (1857).

The seminal case in this context is *Williams* v *Roffey Bros & Nicholls (Contractors) Ltd* referred to above. The Court of Appeal held that the defendant had obtained a practical benefit from the plaintiff's promise to perform the work on time (which he was already contractually obliged to do), and that practical benefit was sufficient to constitute consideration. (Glidewell LJ said that this 'modified and refined' the decision in *Stilk* v *Myrick*.) The Court of Appeal, however, in Re Selectmove declined to extend this principle to the payment of money. Further reference to this is made in part (b) of this question.

The performance of a duty to a third party

It is clear that the promise to perform an existing duty to a third party can be good consideration. Authority for this is found in two early cases (*Shadwell* v *Shadwell* (1860); *Scotson* v *Pegg* (1861)), and in two much more recent Privy Council decisions: *New Zealand Shipping Co Ltd* v *AM Satterthwaite & Co Ltd, The Eurymedon* (1975); *Pao On* v *Lau Yiu Long* (1980).

b) E has agreed to accept a lesser payment than the one to which he is contractually entitled. At common law payment of a lesser sum in satisfaction of a larger sum does not discharge the debt, because no consideration has been furnished by the debtor for the creditor promising not to claim the balance due to him: *Pinnel's* Case (1602); *Foakes* v *Beer* (1884). In *Re Selectmove Ltd* (see above) the company had promised to pay the sum already due to the Inland Revenue by instalments. It was argued that this would provide a practical benefit to the Inland Revenue, as the company would otherwise be forced into liquidation. The Court of Appeal refused to apply the principle in *Williams* v *Roffey Brothers & Nicholls (Contractors) Ltd* to that situation, holding that if it did apply it to the payment of money there would be very little left of *Foakes* v *Beer*.

At common law, therefore, E would have been entitled to claim both the arrears and full payment for the future. The common law has, however, been modified by the equitable doctrine of promissory estoppel.

The origin of the doctrine is in *Hughes* v *Metropolitan Railway Co* (1877), which involved the forfeiture of a lease. The equitable principle in that case was developed and applied to the payment of money by Denning J in *Central London Property Trust Ltd* v *High Trees House Ltd* (1947). The principle of promissory estoppel, as so developed, is that when one party to a contract in the absence of fresh consideration agrees not to enforce his rights an equity will be raised in favour of the other party, and the promisor will not be allowed to go back on his promise where it would be inequitable to allow him to do so. This equity is, however, subject to the qualifications: (i) that the other party has altered his position, that is relied on the promise; (ii) that the promisor can resile from his promise on giving reasonable notice, giving the promisee reasonable opportunity of resuming his position; and (iii) the promise only becomes final and irrevocable if the promisee cannot resume his position. I have derived this formulation from the decision of the House of Lords in *Tool Metal Manufacturing Co Ltd* v *Tungsten Electric Co Ltd* (1955) and the speech of Lord Hodson in *F A Ajayi* v *R T Briscoe (Nigeria) Ltd* (1964).

In applying the principle of promissory estoppel to the present problem two questions in particular must be addressed. First, has F relied on the promise? Second, to what extent is E's promise extinctive of his rights or merely suspensive of such rights? A conclusion may then be drawn as to whether it would be inequitable to allow E to resile from his promise.

The balance of authority would suggest that F need not have acted to her detriment in reliance on the promise: *W J Alan & Co Ltd* v *El Nasr Export & Import Co* (1972); *The Post Chaser* (1982) (but cf *Goldsworthy* v *Brickell* (1987)). I assume that by paying the reduced rent for six months F has relied on the promise.

It seems clear that E's promise is merely suspensive of his rights to the extent that he can demand the full rent for the future: *Hughes* v *Metropolitan Railway Co*; *Tool Metal Manufacturing Co* v *Tungsten Electric*; and the *High Trees* case itself.

I submit that F could not plead the equity with regard to the arrears that fell due after she had received the payment from social services, because of her failure to disclose this. E is entitled to demand those arrears. With regard to the rent due before she received this payment the position is not so clear. There is a paucity of direct authority on this point. In the light, however, of Denning J's obiter observations in *High Trees* I conclude, although not without doubt, that the rights to those amounts have become extinguished.

SUGGESTED ANSWER TO QUESTION SIX

General Comment

A problem-type question which considers the doctrine of consideration, and whether consideration has been sufficient.

Key Points

- The doctrine of consideration: definition of the doctrine

- Una's promise to Trevor: whether there has been sufficient consideration for that promise
- Una's promise to Vernon: whether that promise is supported by good consideration

Suggested Answer

In English law the general rule is that a promise, in order to be enforceable, must be supported by consideration. (The exceptions to this rule are not germane to the present question.) The most useful definition of consideration, in my submission, is that given by Sir Frederick Pollock (*Pollock on Contracts*, 13th edn, p133) and adopted by the House of Lords in *Dunlop Pneumatic Tyre Co Ltd* v *Selfridge & Co Ltd* (1915), namely:

> 'An act or forbearance of one party, or the promise thereof, is the price for which the promise of the other is bought, and the promise thus given for value is enforceable.'

In the light of this definition I shall examine each of Una's promises.

The promise to Trevor

The above definition recognises that a forbearance, or the promise thereof, can be good consideration. The question here is whether Trevor's agreement not to seek the injunction is sufficient forbearance so as to constitute good consideration for the promise Una made to him. Only if it is will Una's promise be enforceable.

Trevor has threatened a claim for the injunction. Whilst a promise to enforce a valid claim is clearly good consideration for the promise given in return, it appears that, as the fence was perfectly lawful, his claim is invalid. If Trevor knew that his claim was invalid the promise not to enforce it does not constitute good consideration: *Jones* v *Ashburnham* (1804). In that event Trevor would have no redress. I shall proceed on the assumption that he believed, albeit wrongly, that his claim was valid.

There is authority for the proposition that a promise to abandon a claim is good consideration, even though the claim is bad in law, if the promisor believes it to be valid: *Cook* v *Wright* (1861); *Callisher* v *Bischoffsheim* (1870). In the latter case, the reason given for the rule was that otherwise 'in no case of a doubtful claim could a compromise be enforced'. Treitel (*Treitel: The Law of Contract*, 9th edn, p34) says that this explanation does not cover the situation where the claim is not merely 'doubtful' but clearly bad. The learned author also points out that a promisor can hardly be considered to have suffered a detriment by abandoning a clearly bad claim. If he pursued such a claim he would lose the action and the costs.

Despite this criticism the rule survives, and in *Pitt* v *PHH Asset Management Ltd* (1993) the Court of Appeal held that the abandonment of the threat of an injunction constituted valuable consideration, although the threat was only of nuisance value, as it had no chance of succeeding.

Accordingly I would advise Trevor that, if he reasonably believed his claim for an injunction to be valid, Una's promise to him would be enforceable.

The promise to Vernon

Implicit in the doctrine of consideration is the element of reciprocity: a promise in exchange for a promise; an act performed in reliance on a promise. Logically, this entails that a promise given after the performance of the act cannot constitute good consideration. This finds expression in the rule that 'past consideration is not good consideration'. Strict applications of this rule appear from *Eastwood* v *Kenyon* (1840), *Roscorla* v *Thomas* (1842) and *Re McArdle* (1951).

The rule has, however, been modified. In an early case, that of *Lampleigh* v *Braithwait* (1615), the principle was established that a promise made after the performance of an act could be enforceable, if the act had been preceded by a request for the performance of it, and the promise could be linked to the prior request.

This principle was made the subject of interpretation by the Court of Appeal in *Re Casey's Patents, Stewart* v *Casey* (1892), where Bowen LJ said:

> 'Now the fact of a past service raises an implication that at the time it was rendered it was to be paid for for, and, if it was a service which was to be paid for, when you get in the subsequent document a promise to pay, that promise may be treated either as an admission which evidences or as a positive bargain which fixes the amount of that reasonable remuneration on the faith of which the service was originally rendered.'

This modifying principle received the consideration of the Privy Council in *Pao On* v *Lau Yiu Long* (1980). Lord Scarman set out the requirements for past consideration to be held good. These are, in Lord Scarman's words,

> 'The act must have been done at the promisor's request: the parties must have understood that the act was to be remunerated either by a payment or the conferment of some other benefit: and payment, or the conferment of a benefit must have been legally enforceable had it been promised in advance.'

It remains to apply this principle to the facts before me.

Una's promise to pay Vernon was made after he had given her the advice. The consideration for her promise was, on the face of it, past. The question is whether it can be held to be good consideration in the light of the principle just expounded. I shall apply the criteria set out by Lord Scarman.

I assume, although this is not self evident, that Vernon gave the advice at Una's request. It is extremely doubtful, however, that the parties understood that this act was to be remunerated in any way. They were neighbours, and Vernon was not a practising lawyer, but a lecturer who no doubt frequently gave such advice to students, friends and acquaintances.

As this essential requirement is not satisfied, I conclude that there has not been good consideration for Una's promise, and it is, therefore, unenforceable.

SUGGESTED ANSWER TO QUESTION SEVEN

General Comment

The question is short but it concerns a fundamental issue: it is not always clear why the courts insist on consideration before they will enforce a contract. The decisions which the courts have made concerning consideration and the often fine distinctions make this a rather difficult topic to grasp. Considering the answer to this question may lead to an understanding of why the courts appear at some times to have applied the rule harshly and at others leniently.

Key Points

- Original reason for the doctrine – protection for the defendant
- The idea of reciprocity: *Thorp* v *Thorp* – *Currie* v *Misa*
- Apparent changes in the court's attitude: *Lampleigh* v *Braithwait* – *Pao On* v *Lau Yiu Long* – *Stilk* v *Myrick* – *Hartley* v *Ponsonby* – *Williams* v *Roffey Bros & Nicholls (Contractors) Ltd*
- The adequacy of the consideration: *Brett* v *J S* – *Thomas* v *Thomas* – *White* v *Bluett* – *Chappell & Co* v *Nestlé Co Ltd* – *Lipkin Gorman* v *Karpnale Ltd*

Suggested Answer

It has long been a fundamental principle of English law that a contract is unenforceable without consideration unless it is under seal. The main reason is that the law once believed that people must be protected from the rashness with which they might make promises. The formality required of a contract under seal provided some pause for thought and showed, furthermore, that the parties had a strong intention to be legally bound. Thus, even if a promise is gratuitous, if it has been made under seal the courts will enforce it.

The requirement for consideration is based on a similar view. The requirement for consideration at least provides some protection for the defendant who will not be held to his promise unless he has been given something in return. This may be an act or a promise:

> 'Where the doing a thing will be a good consideration, a promise to do that thing will be so too': Holt CJ in *Thorpe* v *Thorpe* (1701).

An accepted definition of consideration is to be found in *Currie* v *Misa* (1875):

> 'A valuable consideration, in the sense of the law, may consist in some right, interest, profit or benefit accruing to one party or some forebearance, detriment, loss or responsibility, given, suffered or undertaken by the other.'

This definition embodies the idea of reciprocity: a promise will only be enforceable if it is given in return for a promise or act. Thus the promise is not gratuitous.

However, over the centuries which have seen the development of the doctrine of consideration, the courts have evolved fine distinctions which have given rise to much criticism. Certain acts which would not in the past have been regarded as constituting consideration have been in more recent times subject to exceptions. The first example is past acts or promises, ie made prior to the promise on which the action is brought. These were held in *Lampleigh* v *Braithwait* (1615) not to be good consideration, but in the more recent case of *Pao On* v *Lau Yiu Long* (1980), an earlier promise not to break a contract was held to be good consideration. Similarly, acts which the promisor was already legally bound to do were not good consideration: *Stilk* v *Myrick* (1809). However, an inroad was made into this principle as early as 1857 (*Hartley* v *Ponsonby*), where it was held that something over and above what the promisor was legally bound to do would provide good consideration, and it has had doubt cast upon it recently in *Williams* v *Roffey Bros & Nicholls (Contractors) Ltd* (1991) where consideration for additional payments to a builder was provided by the work he had already contracted for on the basis that his client had reason to believe the builder might not complete the work in time because of financial difficulties.

The best support for the view put forward by the question, however, comes from that line of cases where the court has consistently refused to act as valuer of consideration. It was clearly established by the mid-nineteenth century that consideration must have some economic value. Feelings of natural love and affection (*Brett* v *J S* (1600)), the natural desire to benefit someone (*Thomas* v *Thomas* (1842)), and a promise not to complain (*White* v *Bluett* (1853)) are all examples of consideration which has no economic value and therefore cannot be 'good' or 'valuable' consideration sufficient to support a contract. However, once a value has been established, the courts will not concern themselves with whether or not it was adequate in relation to what was being promised in return.

The consideration may therefore be quite trivial. In *Chappell & Co Ltd* v *Nestlé Co Ltd* (1960) chocolate wrappers were held to be consideration, even though they were only to be thrown away by the company, for a special offer to purchase records. Lord Somervill said in that case:

> 'It is said that, when received, the wrappers are of no value to the respondents, the Nestle Co Ltd. This I would have thought to be irrelevant. A contracting party can stipulate for what consideration he chooses. A peppercorn does not cease to be good consideration if it is established that the promisee does not like pepper and will thrown away the corn.'

A peppercorn has, of course, long been considered good consideration for the grant of a lease. More recently perhaps, it has become the practice for valuable shares in a business to be transferred for £1. The practical reason for this is that a deed takes more time and cost to prepare and it is easier to draw up a simple agreement, and the use of such 'nominal' consideration is now quite widespread. In such cases, gratuitous promises are in effect being enforced and the consideration is merely the formality which seals the bargain.

Certainly, recent cases have shown a trend in the courts to find valuable consideration more readily in cases where they might not previously have done so. The modern view seems to be that the technical absence of this formality will not permit a fully consenting adult to renege on his promises. The reason may be that the courts no longer feel the need to protect a defendant from the consequences of his own rashness and consider that there are sufficiently adequate means of dealing with preferment of creditors and duress without bringing consideration into the matter.

However, one should not assume that the courts will always find consideration when asked to do so. In the case of *Lipkin Gorman* v *Karpnale Ltd* (1991) the House of Lords refused to accept that gaming chips supplied to a club member could be consideration for the money paid for them. Atiyah points out that, while Lord Goff states that where a department store provides tokens in exchange for cash the store 'does not for the present purposes give valuable consideration for it', he also accepts that a contract is made when the customer obtains them at the cash desk. The question to be decided 'for present purposes' was not breach of contract, but the ownership of stolen money. Atiyah concludes that:

> 'The question whether a party has provided consideration may thus receive one answer when it arises for the purpose of determining the enforceability of a promise, and a different and narrower one when it arises for the purpose of determining whether a transaction has adversely affected the rights of a third party.'

The purposes for which the question is being decided ought to be irrelevant, however, and, if they are not then this would support the view that consideration is no more than a mere formality which will be found in those bargains which the courts wish to enforce.

SUGGESTED ANSWER TO QUESTION EIGHT

General Comment

Students should not write all they know about consideration given the nature of this question. What is required is a brief discussion of the doctrine, followed by its governing rules and an examination of the existence of the doctrine. Finally, mention must be made as to the justification of having the doctrine as a contractual element.

Key Points

- The nature of the doctrine
- The rules relating to consideration
- The purpose of the doctrine
- The justification for its existence

Suggested Answer

The doctrine of consideration has been developed by English law in order to determine which agreements should be legally binding. Traditionally, the basis of the idea has been one of reciprocity: the law, it is said, enforces bargains, and not bare or gratuitous promises. The classic definition of the doctrine was aptly expressed by Lush J in *Currie* v *Misa* (1875):

> '... a valuable consideration in the sense of the law may consist either in some right, interest, profit or benefit accruing to one party, or some forbearance, detriment, loss or responsibility given, suffered or undertaken by the other.'

The idea of reciprocity is also evident in the definition given by Sir Frederick Pollock (*Pollock on Contracts* (13th edn, p133)):

> 'An act or forbearance of one party, or the promise thereof, is the price for which the promise of the other is bought, and the promise thus given for value is enforceable.'

This definition was then adopted by the House of Lords in *Dunlop Pneumatic Tyre Co Ltd* v *Selfridge & Co Ltd* (1915) where it was held that where a promise is exchanged for performance, or where there has been a mutual exchange of promises, the traditional theory of consideration presents no difficulties. Where, however, consideration has been found in a forbearance, compromise or performance of an existing duty, the traditional theory becomes harder to justify. Treitel (*The Law of Contract* (9th edn, p67)) suggests that the courts have regarded an act of forbearance as the consideration for a promise even though the promisor had not intended to secure it. He terms this practice as 'invented consideration'.

The compromise of a claim, or a forbearance to sue on it, can constitute good consideration. A promise not to enforce a valid claim is clearly good consideration for a promise given in return, but a promise not to enforce a claim known to be invalid is not, according to *Jones* v *Ashburnham* (1804). The rules of doubtful claims, or claims wrongly believed to be valid, are less satisfactory. In *Haigh* v *Brooks* ((1839) the consideration involved the surrender of a document believed to be a guarantee which turned out to be of doubtful validity. A promise not to abandon a claim, even though it is clearly bad in law, is good consideration if the promisor believes it to be valid. That was the court's opinion in *Callisher* v *Bishoffsheim* (1870), subsequently applied in *Miles* v *New Zealand Alford Estate Co* (1886).

With regard to promises to perform an existing legal duty, the present state of the law appears to be somewhat confused. Three types of legal duty present themselves for discussion: an existing public duty (that is one imposed by law); an existing contractual duty to the promisor; and an existing duty to a third party.

There is old authority to the effect that the performance of, or the promise to perform, an existing public duty, is not good consideration: *Collins* v *Godefroy* (1831). Lord Denning, however, has consistently held that the performance of, or the promise to perform, a duty imposed by law can constitute good consideration: *Williams* v *Williams* (1957).

The promise to perform an existing contractual duty was held not to constitute good consideration in *Stilk* v *Myrick* (1809). However, the scope of that early decision has been curtailed by the Court of Appeal in *Williams* v *Roffey Bros & Nicholls (Contractors) Ltd* (1990), where it was held that a promise to perform an existing obligation can amount to good consideration provided that there are practical benefits to the promisee. In *Re Selectmove Ltd* (1995) the Court of Appeal refused to extend the principle of the *Williams* case to an obligation to make payment. To have done so would be to leave the principle in *Foakes* v *Beer* (1884) without any application.

It, appears, however, to be settled law that the promise to perform an existing duty to a third party can be good consideration. This has been held in the early cases of *Shadwell* v *Shadwell* (1860) and *Scotson* v *Pegg* (1861), and subsequently affirmed by the Privy Council in *New Zealand Shipping Co* v *A M Satterthwaite & Co Ltd, The Eurymedon* (1975), as well as the celebrated case of *Pao On* v *Lau Yiu Long* (1980).

The strict application of the rules of the doctrine of consideration with regard to part payment of a debt - the principle enunciated in *Foakes* v *Beer* - can lead to injustice, an injustice which equity has attempted to mitigate by the development of the doctrine of promissory estoppel, stemming from the judgment of Denning J in *Central London Property Trust Ltd* v *High Trees House Ltd* (1947). But a discussion on the doctrine of promissory estoppel is beyond the scope of this question.

The purpose of the doctrine of consideration is to determine what promises should be legally enforceable. Clearly not all promises can be held to be so. Professor Atiyah states that 'consideration means the reason for the enforcement of a promise, or, even more broadly, a reason for the recognition of an obligation'. Atiyah dismisses as 'nonsensical' the notion of the abolition of the doctrine. If the doctrine of consideration was to be abandoned, the courts would have to employ an alternative method of deciding what promises should be enforced. The question suggests that this could be evidence of intention to be bound by a clear promise. This, however, is questionable as a suitable or satisfactory alternative. It could lead to more uncertainty. Hence the justification for the retention of the doctrine of consideration.

3

Form and Contents of Contracts

Introduction

This chapter covers the diverse areas connected with the terms of a contract, other than excluding and limiting clauses, which are dealt with in Chapter 5.

A question on terms may appear in a number of different forms. First, there is the question of formalities required for a contract. When must the terms - or at least a memorandum of them - be in writing? What contracts must be made by deed? Such a question merely requires a candidate to summarise factual knowledge, but in such a way as to show a clear understanding.

Second, when the terms of a contract have been written down, to what extent will the courts allow in other evidence to add to, vary or contradict those terms? Again factual knowledge is required, together with examples which must, of course, be supported by case law.

The third area, which lends itself most readily to problem questions, but may also form the topic of a discussion question, is categorisation of terms. This naturally leads to a discussion of breach and remedies (see further, Chapter 12, where combined questions of this nature may also be found). Implied terms have sufficient scope to appear as a lone topic but may also be combined with a question which primarily concerns exemption clauses (see Chapter 5). Candidates should be aware of terms implied by statute and the circumstances under which a court would be likely to imply a term. Additionally, it is necessary to be able to categorise terms into conditions, warranties and intermediate terms in such a way as to reflect an understanding of the consequences of a breach of each. Examples of recent decisions include *Equitable Life Assurance Society* v *Hyman* (2000), *Bank of Credit and Commerce International SA* v *Ali* (2001) and *Actionstrength Ltd* v *International Glass Engineering IN GL EN SpA* (2002).

Questions

INTERROGRAMS

1. 'Form is not a necessary requirement under English Law.' Explain, giving examples.
2. How do the courts apply the rule that an agreement must be certain?
3. How has the Law of Property (Miscellaneous Provisions) Act 1989 affected the law relating to contracts for the sale of land?

QUESTION ONE

'In mercantile contracts, time clauses must always be given the force of conditions in the strict sense.'

Discuss.

University of London LLB Examination
(for external students) Elements of the Law of Contract June 1997 Q2

QUESTION TWO

a) 'The parties decide what is to be a condition of the contract. The law defines the consequences of that decision.'

Discuss.

b) In March X engaged Miss Y for 3 years as his research assistant at a salary of £25,000 under a written agreement which included the following clauses:

'6. The research assistant will dress smartly at all times. It is understood that trousers are not an acceptable form of dress under any circumstances.
7. The research assistant will work whatever hours are necessary to complete the assignments given to her.'

On 1 June X asked Y to produce certain statistics for a meeting with an important client at 9 am on 2 June. In spite of staying in the office until midnight, Y was not able to complete the statistics on 1 June. She returned to the office at 7 am on 2 June but had still not quite finished the work when X arrived at 8.30.

X was angry. He then noticed that Y was wearing trousers and told her, in front of several colleagues, that her contract was terminated. Y was extremely upset and humiliated: she is now receiving medical treatment for depression.

Advise Y.

University of London LLB Examination
(for external students) Elements of the Law of Contract June 1994 Q7

QUESTION THREE

Xavier manufactures photocopying machines designed for customers with special requirements. It is his practice not to sell the machines, but to lease them to customers. His standard leasing contract contains the following provisions:

1) Punctual payment of the agreed monthly rent is deemed to be of the essence of the contract.
2) It is a condition of the contract that the lessee will disconnect the power supply to the machine at the close of business each day.
3) The lessee will notify Xavier immediately of any fault in the machine and will not permit repairs to be carried out by another person other than Xavier's authorised representative.

In March 1989, Linus leased a photocopier from Xavier for three years on the above terms at a monthly rental of £200. Xavier has recently discovered that Linus sometimes allows the power supply to remain connected overnight and has repaired minor faults himself on a few occasions. Linus was also two days late in paying last month's rent.

Advise Xavier, who could now charge £300 a month rent, if the same photocopier were leased to a new customer.

University of London LLB Examination
(for external students) Elements of the Law of Contract June 1990 Q2

QUESTION FOUR

'The nineteenth century distinction between "conditions" and "warranties" has given way to a more flexible test.' (*Anson's Law of Contract.*)

Consider in the light of the existing case law.

University of London LLB Examination
(for external students) Elements of the Law of Contract June 1987 Q3

QUESTION FIVE

'When a contract is reduced to writing, the courts assume that this includes all the terms the parties intended to agree.'

Discuss.

Written by the Editor

QUESTION SIX

Peter runs his own accounting business. He recently entered into a contract with Efficient Business Equipment for the hire of a computer. His brother, Geoff, had offered to loan him a printer so Peter stipulated for a clause to be written into the contract of hire as follows:

> 'It is a condition of this contract that the computer will be compatible with a SmartPrint 11X printer and be able to run the SuperAccounts software package.'

Otherwise the contract is Efficient Business Equipment's standard terms and conditions of hire which provide that the hire is for a fixed period of three years at a rental of £50 per month.

Peter took delivery of the computer two months ago. It proved to be incompatible with Geoff's printer and Peter had to buy a new printer at a cost of £500. It has also now run into difficulties with the SuperAccounts package, which it ran quite well at first, but now that Peter has transferred all his records to it, frequently produces errors of a very serious nature. Peter has been told that he was badly advised. He could have bought a better quality computer which would have run his software and been compatible with the printer for only £1,000. On informing Efficient Business Equipment of this, he has been told that they only deal on their standard conditions which do not include the additional condition and that they will only release him from the contract on payment of the entire balance of the hire fee, ie £1,700.

Written by the Editor

QUESTION SEVEN

At the end of November, Anthony decided he needed a holiday as he had not taken any holiday that year. There is a custom in Anthony's trade that an employee is entitled to four weeks' holiday a year, although his contract of employment is silent on the subject of holidays, and so Anthony told his manager he would be away for the last four weeks in December. His manager was displeased by this as he said Anthony had too much work to do, and said he was forbidding Anthony to go.

Nevertheless, Anthony went to Buckett's Travel Agents and told them he wanted to go somewhere hot and sunny for four weeks. They booked him onto a package holiday in Tenerife, having shown him a picture in their brochure of the hotel at which they said he would be staying, which showed a fully-built hotel with a swimming pool. Anthony was pleased because his favourite hobby was swimming. Anthony then went to his local department store and bought a suitcase, having told the salesman he was flying to Tenerife.

Anthony's holiday turned out a disaster. The hotel at which he had expected to stay was fully booked and he was located in a hotel which had not been fully built. There was no swimming pool and Anthony was awoken at 6 o'clock every morning by the sound of bulldozers and other heavy machinery. His hotel room looked out over the building site. The weather was cold and it poured with rain every day. Anthony came home after a week. On the flight home, Anthony's suitcase proved not to be up to the baggage handling and split, losing most of the clothing and personal effects it contained. When he returned to work at the beginning of January, his employers claimed he had broken his duty of good faith to them and they intended to withhold his salary and sue him for extra fees they had to pay to an agency to provide a substitute for him.

Advise Anthony.

Written by the Editor

Answers

ANSWERS TO INTERROGRAMS

1. English law does not generally require contracts to be in a particular form or for any particular formalities to be observed in their execution. This is in contrast to other jurisdictions, where writing or notarisation may be a requirement. A contract may be made in writing, orally or by conduct or by any combination of these. Even though writing or a deed may be required Equity regards 'that as done which ought to be done' and will perfect the transaction where a contract has been made.

   There are, however, a number of exceptions to the general rule. This is where there is a need for certainty, or to create a written record or to avoid recklessness on the part of one or other of the parties. The exceptions may conveniently be divided into three categories: contracts required to be made by deed, contracts required to be in writing and contracts required to be evidenced in writing.

Contracts required to be made by deed

The execution of a deed - a contract under seal - is very rarely required, although any contract may be made under seal if the parties wish. The courts will not enforce gratuitous transactions and so any contract for which there is no consideration (ie something of value - an act, forbearance or promise - given in return for the promise on which the action is brought) will be unenforcable unless under seal. The formality prevents parties from entering into transactions rashly and evidences an intention to be legally bound.

There is one category of contract which the law specifically requires to be made by deed and that is a lease for a term of more than three years.

Contracts required to be in writing

While many people believe that a contract may not be made orally, this is not the case. Contracts may be oral or in writing or partly oral and partly in writing. Even where a contract is in writing, the court may agree to admit oral evidence to add to, vary or contradict its terms. Contracts of employment are often thought to be required to be in writing, but the law merely provides that the employer should, within a certain period, give the employee written notification of its terms.

The contracts for which the law requires writing are surprisingly few. Bills of exchange and promissory notes under the Bills of Exchange Act 1882 and bills of sale under the Bills of Sale Act (1878) Amendment Act 1882 have long been required to be in writing. In 1974 these were joined by consumer credit agreements subject to the Consumer Credit Act 1974. These agreements are required to be in writing for the consumer's protection, and the Act also contains detailed rules about the provision of copies, method of execution and a 'cooling off' period to permit the debtor to reconsider what might be a rash decision.

In 1989, the Law of Property (Miscellaneous Provisions) Act reformed the law relating to the sale of land and interests in land. It redefined the requirements for the execution of a deed - which was no longer required to be under seal. It also provided that a contract for the sale of land or any interest in land must incorporate express terms expressly or by reference.

Contracts required to be evidenced in writing

While there is no other requirement for contracts to be in writing, there may be a requirement for a memorandum. A memorandum is not intended to contain all the terms of a contract, merely to provide evidence that a contract was made and of its main terms.

The Statute of Frauds 1677 was originally conceived as a protective measure but it was discovered that the less scrupulous would hide behind the lack of written evidence to avoid their contractual obligations. Now the Statute applies only to guarantees (note, it does not apply to indemnities). A guarantee is where a third party promises to pay a debt owed by the debtor should that debtor fail to perform his obligation. There are some provisos to the requirement for writing: the guarantee must be a stand-alone contract and not part of a larger transaction and it must not be for the protection of some proprietory interest of the guarantor.

The contents of a memorandum required by the Statute are the identity and capacity of the parties, all material terms (except consideration) and the signature of the party to be charged (ie the guarantor).

In conclusion, therefore, while formality is not an absolute requirement, there are certain circumstances where formality must be observed.

2 The general rule is that the court will not enforce a contract which is vague or ambiguous: *Scammel & Nephew* v *Ouston* (1941). However, judges are always loath to defeat the parties' contractual intentions and will try to find a meaning wherever possible. In *Hillas & Co* v *Arcos* (1932) the court resorted to the general meaning in the trade to affix the definition of timber 'of fair specification'. In the recent case of *Lambert* v *HTV Cymru (Wales) Ltd* (1998), the defendant undertook to use all reasonable endeavours to obtain first rights of negotiation of book publishing for the plaintiff, who held the copyright in certain cartoon characters. They failed to do so and were held liable for breach.

Another possibility, illustrated by the case of *Nicolene* v *Simmonds* (1953), is to delete a meaningless phrase if this would give efficacy to the contract.

Often the court will glean the meaning of the phrase from other documents (*Punjab National Bank* v *De Boinville* (1992)), or the surrounding circumstances, or will enforce the agreement which it thinks to be reasonable in the circumstances (*Neilson* v *Stewart* (1991)).

It may be that the words are not ambiguous but that there is an essential term which has not been agreed. The courts will not enforce such a contract unless there is some provision for a solution: *British Bank for Foreign Trade* v *Novinex* (1949); *May and Butcher* v *R* (1934). However, if there is a provision for solution, eg a means of fixing an omitted price, the court will enforce the contract: *Campbell* v *Edwards* (1976).

3 Prior to the passing of the Act, contracts for the sale or disposition of land or an interest in land had to be evidenced in writing: s40 Law of Property Act 1925. Generally speaking, however, such sales or dispositions were made by deed (a contract executed under seal) and the parties and their agents would avoid any contract inadvertently being made during negotiations by including in their letters and other documents the words 'subject to contract'. Generally this was thought to be sufficient to avoid the operation of s40: *Tiverton Estates Ltd* v *Wearwell Ltd* (1975); *Cohen* v *Nessdale* (1982); *Alpenstow Ltd* v *Regalian Properties Ltd* (1985). However, there were decisions which cast doubt upon this principle at least where there appeared to be a contrary intention: *Law* v *Jones* (1974); *Griffiths* v *Young* (1970).

Section 2 of the Law of Property (Miscellaneous Provisions) Act 1989 provides that a contract for the sale or disposition of land or an interest in land must be in writing, signed by each party and must contain all the agreed terms, otherwise it is unenforceable. Section 2 is to be construed restrictively: *Firstpost Homes Ltd* v *Johnson* (1995). Section 1 of the same Act abolishes the requirement for a deed to be sealed by individuals and, instead, it is required to be signed and attested by a witness. It must also be clear on the face of the document that it is intended to be a deed.

Contracts which were made before 27 September 1989 are still subject to the provisions of s40.

SUGGESTED ANSWER TO QUESTION ONE

General Comment

Quite a straightforward question requiring discussion of 'conditions', particularly the effect of inserting a time clause in commercial contracts.

Key Points

- What is meant by a 'mercantile contract'?
- The nature and effect of a 'condition'
- The importance of 'time clauses' in the relevant contracts

Suggested Answer

I would define a 'mercantile contract' as one entered into for profit in a business context, that is where one or both of the parties conclude the contract in the course of business.

The word 'condition' is used in more than one sense (for example, as in condition precedent), but in the present context it means a promise in a contract of so essential a nature that a failure to perform it entitles the other party to terminate the contract, as well as being able to sue for damages. It is to be contrasted with a 'warranty' for breach of which the innocent party is only entitled to damages and not the right to terminate the contract. There is a third category, 'innominate terms'. In *Hongkong Fir Shipping Co Ltd* v *Kawasaki Kisen Kaisha Ltd* (1962) Diplock LJ said:

> 'There are, however, many contractual undertakings of a more complex character which cannot be categorised as being "conditions" or "warranties" ... Of such undertakings all that can be said is that some breaches will and others will not give rise to an event which will deprive the party not in default of substantially the whole benefit which it was intended that he should obtain from the contract ...'

A term is a condition if statute so provides as, for example, in ss12–15 Sale of Goods Act 1979, or where the parties have expressly so stipulated as, for example, in *Lombard North Central plc* v *Butterworth* (1987). What has to be examined is how the courts have, in the absence of statutory provision or express stipulation, characterised time clauses in mercantile contracts as conditions and not as innominate terms.

'In ordinary commercial contracts for the sale of goods the rule clearly is that time is prima facie of the essence with respect to delivery': per McCardie J in *Hartley* v *Hymans* (1920). If the time for delivery is fixed by the contract, then failure to deliver at that time will thus be a breach of condition which will entitle the buyer to refuse to take the goods. In contrast, s10(1) Sale of Goods Act 1979 provides: 'Unless a contrary intention appears from the terms of the contract stipulations as to time of payment are not of the essence of a contract of sale.' There are clear reasons for this difference. If payment is not made on the due date the seller can be adequately compensated by an award of interest; whereas, if the goods are not delivered on the due date the buyer may well be severely prejudiced with regard to a chain of transactions due to follow the original sale.

The rule that time is of the essence has been applied by the courts in other mercantile contracts. In *The Mihalis Angelos* (1971) in a charterparty a shipowner undertook that the ship would be 'expected ready to load ... about 1 July 1965 '. Megaw LJ, in discussing the term, said:

> 'In my judgment such a term in charterparty ought to be regarded as being a condition of the contract, in the old sense of the word "condition"; that is when it has been broken, the other party can, if he wishes, by intimation to the party in breach, elect to be released from performance of his further obligations under the contract ...'

In *Bunge Corporation* v *Tradax Export SA* (1981) a contract for the sale of soya bean flour required the buyers to give at least 15 consecutive days' notice of probable readiness of vessel(s). The Court of Appeal held that this term was a condition and, the buyers having given less than the required notice, the sellers were entitled to repudiate the contract. Megaw LJ pointed out the obvious commercial reasons why advance notice was required. His Lordship also observed that:

> 'I think it can fairly be said that in mercantile contracts stipulations as to time not only may be, but usually are, to be treated as being "of the essence of the contract" even though this is not stated in the words of the contract.'

The decision of the Court of Appeal in the above case was affirmed by the House of Lords where, in his speech, Lord Wilberforce noted that a time clause in a mercantile contract was of a totally different character to an innominate term. As to such a clause, his Lordship said there was only one breach possible, namely to be late.

The strictness of this approach is graphically illustrated by the decision of the Privy Council in *Union Eagle Ltd* v *Golden Achievement Ltd* (1997). In that case the contract for the sale of a flat provided that completion was to take place before 5 pm on a certain day, that time was of the essence in every respect of the contract, and that if the purchaser failed to comply with any of the terms of the contract the deposit was absolutely forfeited. The purchaser was ten minutes late in tendering cheques for the purchase money and relevant documents for completion. The vendor having rescinded the contract, the purchaser sought equitable relief. Their Lordships stressed need for a firm restatement of the principle that in cases of rescission of an ordinary contract of sale of land for failure to comply with an essential condition as to time, equity would not intervene.

In *The Naxos* (1990) the principle that a stipulation as to time in a mercantile contract would usually be interpreted as a condition was applied by the House of Lords to a clause requiring the seller of sugar to have it available immediately on the arrival of the ship. Their Lordships held that the clause could properly be described as a time clause, since it imposed on the sellers an obligation to have the goods available for loading at a definite point in time. It provided commercial certainty to a mercantile contract that loading would be promptly commenced and speedily carried out, thus enabling the buyers to perform their own onward delivery obligations to their customers punctually. It was to be regarded as a condition, breach of which entitled the buyers to treat the contract as at an end. Recently, the House of Lords implied certain terms to give the contract business efficacy: see *Bank of Credit and Commerce International SA* v *Ali* (2001).

SUGGESTED ANSWER TO QUESTION TWO

General Comment

A two-part question. The first requires a general survey of terms, ie conditions, warranties and innominate terms. The second is a problem calling for an analysis of the law on terms, particularly the classification of terms.

Key Points

a)
- The definition of 'condition', warranty' and 'innominate term'
- The consequences of a breach of condition as distinct from a breach of warranty
- When a term becomes a condition

b)
- Analysis of the two clauses, whether either of them can be classified as conditions
- Consequences of Miss Y's breach of the clauses
- The possible breach of contract by X and its consequences

Suggested Answer

a) A party must perform, or be willing to perform, all his obligations under the contract. But English law has long recognised that not all the obligations are of equal importance. In the Court of Appeal, in *Wallis, Son & Wells* v *Pratt and Haynes* (1910), Fletcher Moulton LJ described some obligations as going to the substance of the contract, so that a failure to perform them would be regarded as a substantial failure to perform the contract at all. Other obligations, though they must be performed, are not so vital that they go to the substance of the contract. Those obligations that go the substance of the contract have been classified as 'conditions', the latter obligations as 'warranties'. Breach of condition entitles the injured party to treat the contract as repudiated, and he can elect to terminate it. For breach of warranty, there is no right to terminate, the injured party's remedy is confined to a claim for damages. There are certain terms which it may be difficult to classify as either a condition or a warranty; breaches of them may be serious or trivial. Such terms, though previously recognised by the courts (compare, for example, the decisions in *Poussard* v *Spiers & Pond* (1876) and *Bettini* v *Gye* (1876)) were first categorised as 'innominate terms' by Diplock LJ in *Hongkong Fir Shipping Co Ltd* v *Kawasaki Kisen Kaisha Ltd* (1962). Whether a breach of such term is treated as a breach of condition or only as a breach of warranty 'depends on the nature, consequences and effect of the breach' - per Lord Scarman in *Bunge Corporation* v *Tradax Export SA* (1981).

When does a term of a contract become a condition? In *Bentsen* v *Taylor Sons & Co* (1893) Bowen LJ said:

> 'There is no way of deciding that question except by looking at the contract in the

> light of the surrounding circumstances, and then making up one's mind whether the intention of the parties, as gathered from the instrument itself, will best be carried out by treating the promise as a warranty sounding only in damages, or as a condition precedent by the failure to perform which the other party is relieved of his liability.'

Thus his Lordship stressed the paramountcy of the intention of the parties. The statement in the question before me that – 'The parties decide what is to be a condition of the contract' is, however, less than complete. Certain terms are, by statutory implication, conditions of the contract: inter alia ss12–15 Sale of Goods Act 1979; ss8–11 Supply of Goods (Implied Terms) Act 1973; ss2–5, 7–10 Supply of Goods and Services Act 1982.

The courts, too, have ruled that certain terms are to be construed as conditions. In mercantile contracts there is binding authority that 'time is of the essence': *The Mihalis Angelos* (1971); *Bunge Corporation* v *Tradax Export* (above); *The Naxos* (1990). Here the intention of the parties is imputed rather than actual. Recently, in *Re Coslett (Contractors) Ltd* (1996) the Chancery Division held that conditions must be construed in the light of the contract as a whole and not on its individual meaning, so as to effectively ascertain the parties' obligations under the contract in the event of a breach.

It can be suggested, also, that the courts do not always give effect to the intention of the parties. In *L Schuler AG* v *Wickman Machine Tool Sales Ltd* (1974) one clause in the contract was described as a 'condition'. No other clause was so described. In the light of the circumstances and the contract as a whole the majority of the House of Lords decided that despite employing the term 'condition' it could not have been the intention of the parties that the clause would operate as such. But see the speech of Lord Wilberforce, dissenting.

The consequences of a term being a condition have been set out above.

b) In this problem, in order to determine Y's rights, it is necessary to examine the relevant clauses in the contract. Clearly she has been in breach of both these clauses. Are either of them to be treated as a breach of condition entitling X to terminate the contract? I shall consider each clause in turn.

Clause 6

Although the clause provides that 'trouser are not an acceptable form of dress *under any circumstances*', I find it difficult to construe this as a condition. It is a term capable of a range of breaches, from serious to trivial. In my view it is an innominate term, and one must, therefore, look at 'the nature, effect and consequences of the breach'. Adopting the words of Diplock LJ in *Hongkong Fir Shipping* (above), does the breach deprive X of 'substantially the whole benefit which it was the intention of the parties as expressed in the contract that he should obtain'? I do not believe that the breach can be considered as doing so. Consequently it cannot be treated as a breach of condition. X cannot terminate the contract on this ground.

Clause 7

This term may well be a condition. Applying *Re Coslett* it appears to go to the root of the contract. If it is regarded as an innominate term, the nature of the breach in, apparently, not completing the assignment in time for an important meeting, would entitle X to treat it as a breach of condition. I conclude, though not without some doubt, that X would be entitled to terminate the contract on this ground.

If X is entitled to terminate the contract Y has no redress. As, however, I have expressed some doubt as to whether he is so entitled, I must consider the possibility that the termination was unlawful. In this event X would be in breach of contract, and Y would have an action for wrongful dismissal. She could claim for her pecuniary loss. But she could not claim for the distress and subsequent depression that she suffered: *Bliss* v *South East Thames Regional Health Authority* (1987).

SUGGESTED ANSWER TO QUESTION THREE

General Comment

Another problem question that requires analysis of terms with regard to their classification and the consequences of such classification in the event of a breach of contract.

Key Points

- Terms of contract
- Conditions or warranties
- Innominate terms
- Breach of contract, consequences

Suggested Answer

The issue raised by this question is the relative importance of contractual terms. Traditionally the terms of a contract were classified as conditions or warranties. A condition has been defined as an 'essential term' of the contract; or one where 'performance of the stipulation (went) to the very root ... of the contract': *Bentsen* v *Taylor Sons & Co* (1893). A breach of condition can be regarded by the injured party as a repudiation of the contract and entitles him to terminate it and thereby discharge himself from further obligations. A warranty is a less important term, its breach does not entitled the injured party to terminate the contract, but confines him to a remedy in damages. Warranty is defined in the Sale of Goods Act 1979 in s61(1) as a term 'collateral to the main purpose of [the] contract, the breach of which gives rise to a claim for damages, but not a right to reject the goods and treat the contract as repudiated.'

A further category has, however, been recognised. Certain terms cannot be classified as conditions or warranties, but whether they are to be treated as conditions or warranties depends on the nature of the breach. Such terms are called 'innominate terms'. This approach was adopted in the earlier cases of *Bettini* v *Gye* (1876) and *Poussard* v *Spiers* (1876). A further example is the case of *Aerial Advertising Co* v *Batchelor's Peas Ltd* (1938). But the concept of the innominate term was first expressly recognised by the Court of Appeal decision in *Hongkong Fir Shipping Co Ltd* v

Kawasaki Kisen Kaisha Ltd (1962). In the course of his judgment Diplock LJ (as he then was) said that many contractual undertakings could not be classified as conditions or warranties.

> 'Of such undertakings all that can be predicated is that some breaches will and others will not give rise to an event which will deprive the party not in default of substantially the whole benefit which it was intended that he should obtain from the contract'.

In *Bunge Corporation* v *Tradax Export SA* (1981) Lord Scarman said that

> 'Unless the contract makes it clear, either by express provision or by necessary implication arising from its nature, purpose and circumstances ... that a particular stipulation is a condition or only a warranty, it is an innominate term the remedy for a breach of which depends on the nature, consequences and effect of the breach.'

A contractual term is then a condition if the parties expressly intended it to be so, or if it is classified as such by statute, or judicial decision; otherwise whether it is treated as a condition or merely as a warranty depends on the nature, extent and consequences of the breach.

In the present problem Xavier wishes to terminate the contract. Linus has clearly been in breach of the provisions set out. The question is: are any of these breaches to be regarded as a breach of condition? Each of the provisions must be considered in turn.

The provision for punctual payment

It is provided that this 'is deemed to be of the essence of the contract'. The actual breach of this provision is trivial – Linus was two days late in paying last month's rent – but if the term is a condition any breach, however trivial, would justify Xavier in treating it as a repudiatory breach, and entitle him to terminate the contract.

Time is often of the essence in commercial contracts: see, for example, *The Mihalis Angelos* (1971). But a failure to make a punctual payment would not necessarily be considered to be repudiatory in a contract such as the present one: *Financings Ltd* v *Baldock* (1963). Clearly the nature of the breach here is not one that could be regarded as depriving Xavier of the substantial benefit of the contract. However, in *Lombard North Central plc* v *Butterworth* (1987) where there was a similar clause, the Court of Appeal held that even though the failure to pay promptly was not repudiatory, the clause had the effect of making failure to pay on time a breach of condition. In view of that decision, whilst it is harsh, it seems inescapable that Xavier would be able to rely on the breach by Linus as constituting a breach of condition, and thus entitling him to terminate the contract. A more recent case concerning a time stipulation is *Glencoe Grain Rotterdam BV* v *Lebanese Organisation for International Commerce* (1997). Here the buyers agreed to buy 25,000 tonnes of wheat at a set price with a stipulation for additional payments if the buyer did not take this quantity. The buyers' vessel was late arriving and the seller refused to load the wheat without prepayment of the additional amount. The court held that the breach could not be put right and the seller was justified in his action from the time the buyer had broken the contract. It did not matter that the seller had claimed a different justification at the time.

The provision with regard to disconnecting the power supply
This clause is described as a 'condition'. This is not conclusive; the court would have to be satisfied that the parties intended to use the word in the technical sense. In *L Schuler AG* v *Wickman Machine Tool Sales Ltd* (1974) one particular clause was called a condition and no other term in the 20 clauses was described as a condition. It was urged that because that particular clause was described as a condition any breach of it by the one party entitled the other party to terminate the contract. This argument was rejected by the House of Lords. Lord Reid held that the use of the word 'condition' was perhaps a strong indication that the parties intended the clause to be a condition in the technical sense, but it was not conclusive evidence. Their Lordships were able to come to the conclusion that the technical use of the word was not intended by a consideration of the contract as a whole. A further clause in the contract provided for notice to be given as a 'material breach'. This enabled the House of Lords to interpret the word in a non-technical sense. Lord Reid did say, however, that, but for this further clause, he would have found difficulty in reaching this conclusion.

The question here is not without difficulty. It seems unreasonable for Xavier to be held entitled to terminate the contract because of one failure by Linus to disconnect the power supply. But this would follow if this provision is interpreted as a condition, and it is so described. There is not the escape from that conclusion by a clause similar to the one in Schuler. There does not appear to be any provision for notice to Linus requiring him to remedy or desist from the breach. Accordingly it is submitted that this provision too would be regarded by the court as a condition, the breach of which would entitle Xavier to terminate.

The provision regarding faults and repairs
This provision appears to be one which cannot be categorised as being a condition or a warranty. It is typically a clause which would require consideration of - in Lord Scarman's words - 'the nature effect and consequences of the breach'. It is therefore an innominate term. The breaches of this provision that have occurred are not of sufficient gravity to justify treating them as breaches of condition. Xavier would not be able to rely on them to justify termination.

In conclusion it is submitted that although Xavier cannot rely on the third provision as entitling him to terminate he can do so by virtue of the breaches of the first two provisions. It must be admitted that this conclusion could be regarded as over-technical, but the authorities do not appear to allow for any alternative.

SUGGESTED ANSWER TO QUESTION FOUR

General Comment

Yet another question on the distinction between conditions and warranties and the consequences of classifying terms as one or the other. The discussion of innominate terms as a possible third category should not be omitted.

Key Points

- Classification into conditions/warranties was the orthodox division: apparently nineteenth century lawyers recognised no other
- Appearance of innominate term – *Hongkong Fir* case
- Earlier case law reflects development leading up to *Hongkong Fir* shows concept of something like innominate term had appeared a lot earlier
- Classifications possible now – definitions
- Is there more flexibility? – is Anson correct?

Suggested Answer

First it is necessary to define the subject matter of this answer. The distinction referred to between conditions and warranties is the apparent approach of nineteenth century contract lawyers to the classification of contractual terms. They appear generally (the reason for their qualification is given later in this answer) to have regarded the categories of conditions and warranties as being exhaustive: a contractual term had to be either one or the other. It is clear now, however, that English law recognises not two but three different types of terms: conditions, warranties and innominate terms (sometimes called intermediate stipulations).

A condition may be defined as a term, any breach of which entitles the innocent party not only to recover damages but also to terminate the contract if he so chooses, irrespective of the consequences of the breach. The right to terminate, which is an option not an obligation, arises because of the nature of the term broken, not because of the consequences which flow from the breach: *Hongkong Fir Shipping Co Ltd* v *Kawasaki Kisen Kaisha Ltd* (1962); *Bunge Corporation* v *Tradax Export SA* (1981); and *Lombard North Central plc* v *Butterworth* (1987).

An innominate term is a term, a breach of which entitles the innocent party to recover damages and may, in addition, entitle him to terminate the contract. The right to terminate is not always available, as with a condition, but only where the actual and prospective consequences of the breach are such as to deprive the innocent party of substantially the whole of the benefit of the consideration he bargained to receive under the contract (in short, where the breach goes to the root of the contract): *Hongkong Fir Shipping* v *Kawasaki Kisen Kaisha*. Thus in the case of an innominate term, the existence of the right to terminate depends upon the severity of the consequences of the breach.

A warranty is a term, any breach of which is remediable in damages only: *Bettini* v *Gye* (1876). No matter how serious the breach or its consequences, if the term broken is only a warranty then there is never a right to terminate the contract. Although this may seem harsh at first sight, to hold otherwise would so blur the distinction between innominate terms and warranties as to render it unworkable.

The reason for the qualifying remarks at the beginning of this answer can now be stated. Although this threefold classification of contractual terms has been accepted and applied in practice since *Hongkong Fir Shipping* v *Kawasaki Kisen Kaisha* in 1962, it has been suggested in some of the cases that innominate terms were recognised in earlier decisions in the twentieth century and in the nineteenth century too. The Court of Appeal made this point very forcibly in *Cehave* v *Bremer* (1976) and in *Bunge Corporation* v *Tradax Export SA* the House of Lords expressed similar views. For example, Lord Scarman spoke of innominate terms being 'rediscovered' in *Hongkong Fir Shipping* v *Kawasaki Kisen Kaisha* but of always having been part of English law.

If these views be accepted, then Anson is wrong to suggest that a twofold classification only existed in the last century. However it is fair to say that even if innominate terms were known to English law before 1962, they were largely (though perhaps not entirely) overlooked by both judges and academics alike.

The threefold classification is in any event now established. Taken out of context, though, Anson's proposition could be read as meaning that the classification of terms (albeit into three rather than two categories) is no longer important. It is respectfully submitted that this is not so, nor did the editor of Anson intend so to suggest.

The classification of terms is important. For the parties to know their legal rights and liabilities, the nature of the term is crucial, particularly as regards the availability or otherwise of the rights of termination. Further, the character of all terms is ascertainable at the moment the contract is concluded. Nothing that happens after its formation can alter the status of a term, although in the case of an innominate term it will determine the availability of the right of termination. To hold otherwise would lead to unacceptable uncertainty: a contract term cannot have a status capable of changing from one day to the next.

The flexibility to which Anson refers is introduced into the law by the innominate term. Instead of saying that the innocent can, in the case of a condition, always terminate, or in the case of warranty, never terminate is manifestly inflexible. Innominate terms allow the courts to permit termination where the circumstances justify it and the consequences are sufficiently serious. It is for this reason that innominate terms were regarded with obvious favour in cases such as *Hongkong Fir Shipping* v *Kawasaki Kisen Kaisha*; *Cehave* v *Bremer*; *L Schuler AG* v *Wickman Machine Tool Sales Ltd* (1974) and *Reardon Smith Line* v *Hansen-Tangen* (1976).

Nevertheless innominate terms are only one of the three categories and the other two cannot be ignored. It may be, for example, that the term in question is expressly designated a condition as a warranty by statute, such as the Sale of Goods Act 1979, or has already been judicially classified, as was the case in *The Mihalis Angelos* (1971). Further, it is open to the parties themselves expressly to classify the term, in which case providing their intention is clear the courts will give effect to it: *The Chikuma* (1981) and *Lombard North Central plc* v *Butterworth*. Lastly, the courts may be of the view that the parties must have intended the term to be a condition, even though they did not bother so to call it. The most obvious examples here are stipulations as to time in mercantile contracts: *United Scientific Holdings* v *Burnley Borough Council* (1978) and *Bunge* v *Tradax*. In all these cases, there is no flexibility. The right to terminate for breach (or not, in the case of warranty) follows on from the classification of the term.

In conclusion, whilst Anson is right to suggest that there is now greater flexibility in this area of the law, the distinction between the different types of contractual terms remains of considerable importance. This is evident in the light of two recent decisions of the House of Lords where their Lordships showed no reluctance to imply certain terms to salvage the contract and give it business efficacy: see *Equitable Life Assurance Society* v *Hyman* (2000) and *Bank of Credit and Commerce International SA* v *Ali* (2001).

SUGGESTED ANSWER TO QUESTION FIVE

General Comment

The good candidate will instantly recognise this quotation to be a statement of the parol evidence rule. The rule has a long history and, as is the case with such ancient common law rules, has over the years collected a significant number of exceptions. It is not always easy to categorise the exceptions made in individual cases and the case law contains some fine distinctions. Success in answering this question demands excellent recollection of case law together with an understanding of the historical background against which the cases were decided and the development of judicial thought.

Key Points

- The question refers to the parol evidence rule as stated in *Jacobs* v *Batavia and General Plantations Trust*
- The rule is based on certainty: *Rabin* v *Gerson Berger Association Ltd*
- The rule is still applied: *W F Trustees Ltd* v *Expo Safety Systems Ltd*
- It does not apply where the document was not designed to contain all the terms
- Where the contract is contained in more than one document: *Shearson Lehman Hutton Inc* v *Maclaine Watson & Co* – *Edwards* v *Aberayon Insurance Society Ltd* (1876)
- Where the written document is merely a memorandum and oral warranties or representations were given: *Hutton* v *Watling* – *Allen* v *Pink* – *Couchman* v *Hill* – *Routledge* v *McKay* – *Harling* v *Eddy*
- Where there is a collateral contract: *City and Westminster Properties (1934) Ltd* v *Mudd*
- Oral terms may be implied into a contract: *Produce Brokers Co Ltd* v *Olympia Oil and Cake Co Ltd* – *Smith* v *Wilson* – *The Moorcock* – *Shirlaw* v *Southern Foundries (1926) Ltd*
- Oral evidence may be allowed to prove the contents (but not the validity) of a contract: *Pym* v *Campbell* – *Newell* v *Radford* – *Scarfe* v *Adams* – *Turner* v *Forwood*

Suggested Answer

This presumption by the courts results from the parol evidence rule which was stated in *Jacobs* v *Batavia and General Plantations Trust* (1924) to be as follows:

> '... parol evidence cannot be admitted to add to, vary or contradict a deed or other written instrument. Accordingly it has been held that ... parol evidence will not be admitted to prove that some particular term, which had been verbally agreed upon, had been omitted

(by design or otherwise) from a written instrument constituting a valid and operative contract between the parties.'

The rule does not exclude merely oral evidence and it does not apply only to contracts and, although there are a number of exceptions (see below) it is still very much alive: *WF Trustees Ltd* v *Expo Safety Systems Ltd* (1993). The basis of the rule was confirmed in 1986 to be certainty: *Rabin* v *Gerson Berger Association Ltd* (1986).

The presumption is however, rebuttable and extrinsic evidence may be admitted in a number of situations.

Where the document was not designed to contain all the terms

The first situation under this heading is where the contract is contained in more than one document. Where the second document is incorporated by express reference, the courts will usually give effect to its terms: *Shearson Lehman Hutton Inc* v *Maclaine Watson & Co* (1989). Even without express reference, a further document may be admitted if it appears to have been the parties' intention that its terms should be incorporated: *Edwards* v *Aberayron Insurance Society Ltd* (1876).

Secondly, the written agreement may not and may not have been intended to contain all of the terms of the agreement. In *Hutton* v *Watling* (1948) a written document was held to be no more than a memorandum of the agreement, other terms having been agreed orally.

Examples abound where oral warranties have been given. It must be pointed out here that it was not until 1964 in *Hedley Byrne & Co Ltd* v *Heller & Partners Ltd* that oral representations which were not fraudulent became actionable as misrepresentations. There was therefore a greater need to find that these statements formed terms of the contract, breach of which could lead to damages or rescission. The cases of *Allen* v *Pink* (1838) and *Couchman* v *Hill* (1947) are both examples of oral warranties given in relation to the sale of animals which the court considered were actionable for breach. A more modern case, *Routledge* v *McKay* (1954), concerned the sale of a motor cycle.

The question is to ascertain the parties' intentions. The court must ask at what stage of the transaction the statement was made - if at the time of sale it is liable to be a term of the contract. Secondly, they must ask whether the statement was followed by a reduction of the terms to writing, for the exclusion of the oral statement suggests that it was not intended to be a contractual term. Finally, the court will ask whether the person who made the statement had special knowledge and skill: *Harling* v *Eddy* (1951). If so, the statement is again more likely to have been a term of the contract.

There is a third category of cases which again may be seen as remedying a deficiency prior to the actionability of oral statements as misrepresentations, where the court has found a collateral contract: a subsidiary contract which is dependent on the main contract and for which entry into the main contract may itself be consideration. An example is *City and Westminster Properties (1934) Ltd* v *Mudd* (1959) where the defendant accepted a term in a new lease restricting the use of the premises to 'showrooms, workrooms and offices only' on the basis of an oral assurance that he would be allowed to sleep on the premises. The oral assurance was held to be a collateral contract which protected the defendant from forfeiture for breach of covenant.

Implied terms

Terms may be implied into oral or written contracts by statute, by custom or by the courts themselves. There are many cases of evidence being admitted to prove a custom. In *Produce Brokers Co Ltd* v *Olympia Oil and Cake Co Ltd* (1916) Lord Sumner said:

> 'The custom, if any, is part of the bargain ... If the bargain is partly expressed in ink and partly implied by the tacit incorporation of trade customs, the first function of the arbitrators is to find out what it is: to read the language, to ascertain the custom, to interpret them both and to give effect to the whole ...'

Evidence may also be admitted to prove that certain words in a contract had a customary meaning different from the usual meaning (eg *Smith* v *Wilson* (1832) where '1000 rabbits' was proved to mean '1200 rabbits').

Terms may be implied by statute, a prime example being the implied terms as to satisfactory quality and fitness of purpose under the Sale of Goods Act 1979. It is not necessary to describe these further.

The court will imply a term where it is necessary to give 'business efficacy' to the contract: *The Moorcock* (1889). A term is usually required to pass the 'officious bystander' test described by MacKinnon LJ as follows:

> 'Prima facie that which in any contract is left to be implied and need not be expressed is something so obvious that it goes without saying; so that, if while the parties were making their bargain an officious bystander were to suggest some express provision for it in their agreement, they would testily suppress him with a common, "Oh, of course." ': *Shirlaw* v *Southern Foundries (1926) Ltd* (1939).

To prove the contents of a contract

There are a number of miscellaneous cases which come under the heading of proving the contents of a contract as opposed to its validity. These included evidence allowed in to show whether the contract operated (*Pym* v *Campbell* (1856)), who the parties were (*Newell* v *Radford* (1867)), the identification of the subject matter (*Scarfe* v *Adams* (1981)) and evidence of additional consideration (*Turner* v *Forwood* (1951)) or that it was executed by the parties under a common mistake.

In conclusion, therefore, it may be stated that while the courts do still maintain the presumption that the parties intended to include all the terms of the contract in their writing, this is a rebuttable presumption, and extrinsic evidence may be admitted in many and varied situations.

SUGGESTED ANSWER TO QUESTION SIX

General Comment

The problem posed by this question is the not unusual one of an additional term negotiated at the time a contract is made but not written into the standard terms and conditions imposed by one of the contracting parties. The main focus of the question is, however, not whether the term has been incorporated into the contract but what is the effect of breaching that term. What is needed here is an analysis of the term with regard to the classifications of warranty, condition and intermediate term, and suitable advice to Peter as to his remedies (if any) based on that analysis.

Key Points

- The term has almost certainly become an express term of the contract
- Whether Peter can rescind or merely claim damages for breach depends on the importance of the term which in turn depends on its classification as a condition or warranty
- The term may in fact be an intermediate or innominate term: *Hongkong Fir Shipping Co Ltd* v *Kawasaki Kisen Kaisha Ltd* - *Cehave* v *Bremer* - *Reardon Smith Line* v *Hansen-Tangen*
- That the term is described as a condition is not conclusive and the court will look at the substance of the agreement to determine the parties' intentions: *Schuler AG* v *Wickman Machine Tool Sales Ltd*
- The term must be evaluated at the time of contracting: *Bunge Corporation* v *Tradax Export SA*
- If the term is innominate, the court will examine the consequences of the breach
- If Peter relied on the salesman's advice, there may have been breach of an implied term of care and skill or a negligent misrepresentation on the part of Efficient Business Equipment

Suggested Answer

It is necessary first of all to dispose of Efficient Business Equipment's contention that the additional term negotiated by Peter is not included in the contract. Unless there is evidence to the contrary, it is clear that their salesman had at least apparent authority to negotiate the term and therefore it has become an express term of the contract which has been broken.

The question is whether Peter can rescind for breach of the term or whether he can only claim for damages for the losses he has suffered. This depends on the importance of the term. Terms have traditionally been classified as conditions or warranties. Breach of condition allows the injured party to rescind the contract, ie to be put back in the position he was in before the contract was made with no further liability under the contract. Breach of warranty merely allows him to sue for compensation for his loss.

In 1962, however, a third category of express term was recognised. In *Hongkong Fir Shipping Co Ltd* v *Kawasaki Kisen Kaisha Ltd* the Court of Appeal recognised that certain terms did not fit into these neat categories and that they could not effectively be classified until the effects of breach had been seen. Should the breach be so serious as fundamentally to destroy the basis of the contract, then rescission would be appropriate and the term could be classified as a condition. Otherwise it would be a warranty.

Those terms which are thus unclassifiable until breach have been termed 'intermediate' or 'innominate' terms, and this classification has been accepted both by a later Court of Appeal (*Cehave* v *Bremer Handelsgesellschaft mbH, The Hansa Nord* (1976)) and by the House of Lords: *Reardon Smith Line* v *Hansen-Tangen* (1976).

How then should the term in question be classified? It is necessary to ascertain the parties' intentions. The fact that it has been termed a condition is not conclusive, since no legal advice appears to have been taken and it is unlikely that the parties intended to use the word in its technical legal sense: *L Schuler AG* v *Wickman Machine Tool Sales Ltd* (1974). The court will then look at the substance of the agreement to try and ascertain the parties' intentions.

It is to be noted that there are two parts to the clause: first, that the computer be compatible with the printer and, second, that it be able to run the software. If the clause is to be either a condition or a warranty, it is to be evaluated at the time of contracting: *Bunge Corporation* v *Tradax Export SA* (1981). On the evidence in the question, the clause would be hard to evaluate as at that particular date. Evidence might be brought as to how important it was to Peter's existing business to use that software package and to what extent the Efficient Business Equipment salesman was aware of this. It is submitted that the compatibility of the printer is a lesser issue which would have been intended to be a warranty only.

If the terms are then innominate, the breach itself must be examined. The consequences of the breach of the part relating to the printer are clear. Peter has been forced to pay £500 for a new printer which he would not have had to pay had the other been compatible. This is a breach which could easily be dealt with by an award of damages and does not fundamentally affect Peter's business.

The breach of the part relating to the software is somewhat different. It would appear that the use of this particular program is fundamental to the running of Peter's business. Indeed, if this is the only piece of software which he uses, the computer may effectively be rendered useless to him. At any event, it is likely to have serious consequences for Peter's business if it is consistently producing errors. Whether or not Peter's records could be transferred without damage to another software program which the computer can run without difficulty is a factor which is likely to be taken into consideration. It seems, however, on the face of it that Peter may be able to rescind the contract on the basis of this failure. The court would have to be persuaded to see the two parts of the clause as separate clauses and not interdependent.

Finally, there is some suggestion in the question that Peter has been badly advised, although whether by Efficient Business Equipment themselves is not clear. There is too little detail about this to evaluate this part of the problem effectively, but it may be that, if Peter relied on their advice, there would be a breach of an implied condition as to the care and skill with which he was advised. If the salesman had warranted that the machine was compatible with either the printer or the software, and Peter had relied on this warranty, this would be an untrue statement of fact which might entitle Peter to rescind the contract for negligent misrepresentation.

SUGGESTED ANSWER TO QUESTION SEVEN

General Comment

The problems in this question centre almost entirely on terms which may be implied into a contract. The solution involves terms which may be implied by statute, by custom and by the court, all of which areas need to be thoroughly understood. A successful candidate will be able to demonstrate competent analytical powers, breaking down the question into its component problems and providing a coherent solution for each part.

With this type of question is is even more important than usual to organise one's thoughts into a plan before embarking on the answer.

Key Points

Holiday in Tenerife

- A duty of care and skill is implied by the Supply of Goods and Services Act 1982 as amended by the Sale and Supply of Goods Act 1994
- Anthony relied on the travel agent's advice
- Would the 'reasonable' travel agent have known it would be cold and wet in Tenerife?
- Showing Anthony the photograph may have been a negligent or fraudulent misrepresentation
- Damages may be recovered for loss of enjoyment in a holiday contract

Broken suitcase and lost effects

- Terms as to satisfactory quality and fitness for purpose implied in ss12–15 Sale of Goods Act 1979 as amended
- Suitcase was not fit for the purpose and it was not an unusual purpose
- Anthony may recover damages for the consequences of the breach

Employer's claim for breach of good faith

- A duty of good faith from the employee to the employee is implied in every contract of employment: *Hivac Ltd* v *Park Royal Scientific Instruments*
- A custom may be incorporated into a contract provided there are no inconsistent terms
- The right to take the holiday may be distinguished from the means of taking it, ie all at once and without reasonable notice
- Court might imply a term on behalf of the employer that the holiday should be taken with reasonable notice and at a time convenient to the employer: *Reigate* v *Union Manufacturing Co (Ramsbottom)* – *Shirlaw* v *Southern Foundries (1926) Ltd*

Suggested Answer

Contracts generally contain express terms, ie those which the parties agree orally, in writing or by conduct. However, in certain situations the law will imply terms into a contract which have not expressly been agreed by the parties. Such terms can be implied by statute, by custom or by the courts themselves, and it is with these terms that the question is concerned. The problem can be broken down into three separate elements which can be dealt with separately.

Holiday in Tenerife

The contract between Anthony and the travel agency is a contract for the supply of services. Terms are implied into such contracts by the Supply of Goods and Services Act 1982 (as amended by the Sale and Supply of Goods Act 1994). In particular, duties of care and skill are implied. Anthony expressed to the travel agents his desire to holiday somewhere hot and sunny and presumably relied on their advice as to where his destination might be. Whether or not the travel agents were in breach of their duty depends on whether or not the 'reasonable' travel agent could have been expected to know the weather would be cold and wet in Tenerife at that time. If this was a normal occurrence, they should at least have warned Anthony of this and suggested another destination. If, on the other hand, it was most unusual, they could not be held liable. So far as the hotel was concerned, by double-booking and not providing equivalent substitute accommodation, the agents were clearly in breach of their duty. Additionally, showing the picture of the hotel to Anthony in the brochure may have amounted to a negligent or even (if the agents already knew that the hotel was fully booked), a fraudulent misrepresentation (an untrue statement of fact which induced the contract), which would enable Anthony to rescind the contract and recover the money paid. Anthony's damages are, however, not limited to the amount he paid. It is well settled that damages may be recovered from a tour operator for loss of enjoyment if the holiday is spoilt as a result of the operator's breach of contract. This principle should apply here.

Broken suitcase and lost effects

Sections 12-15 of the Sale of Goods Act 1979 imply terms into contracts for the sale of goods. in particular, as to the satisfactory quality of those goods and the fitness for the purpose for which they were sold. The suitcase may have been of satisfactory quality but clearly it was not reasonably fit for the purpose for which it was sold. If this was an unusual purpose, this must have been made known to the supplier. However, a foreign holiday is hardly an unusual purpose in connection with a suitcase, and in any event Anthony told the salesman he was intending to fly to Tenerife. Anthony therefore has a claim of the return for the price of the suitcase and, as he may claim damages for all the consequences of the breach within the reasonable contemplation of the parties, damages for the loss of his clothing and other effects.

Employer's claim for breach of good faith

There is no doubt that every employee owes his employer a duty of good faith (*Hivac Ltd* v *Park Royal Scientific Instruments* (1946)) and this is implied into any contract of employment and need not be expressly stated. However, it appears that there is a custom to the effect that every employee in Anthony's trade should have an annual four-week holiday. The question is whether the parties intended this custom to be incorporated into Anthony's contract of employment. The more usual situation is where a collective agreement, made with a trade union, is incorporated by implication into individual employees' contracts, but there seems no reason why a term which is customary should not be implied into the contract.

Any contract may be deemed to incorporate a relevant custom of the market, trade or locality in which it is made unless inconsistent with the terms of of the contract. The contract of employment does not appear to deal with the question of holiday and, provided there are no inconsistent terms, there is no reason to exclude the term, if proven. If the contract is silent about holiday, given that an employee would hardly have agreed to it if there was not some agreement about holiday, it will be a difficult burden on the employers to show that Anthony was not entitled to take his holiday.

The method of taking it may pose some problem, since it could be argued that it would be implied that in order to give 'business efficacy' to the agreement, the employee should give reasonable notice of his intention to take a holiday and take it at a time convenient to the employer. Other than a term which is incorporated by statute or by usage, the courts will only imply a term to give 'business efficacy' to a contract (*Reigate* v *Union Manufacturing Co (Ramsbottom)* (1918)) and only if the term is so obvious as to pass the 'officious bystander' test as propounded by McKinnon LJ in *Shirlaw* v *Southern Foundries (1926) Ltd* (1939):

> 'Prima facie that which in any contract is left to be implied and need not be expressed is something so obvious that it goes without saying; so that, if while the parties were making their bargain an officious bystander were to suggest some express provision for it in their agreement, they would testily suppress him with a common, "Oh, of course." '

It would be for the court to decide whether this particular proviso was so obvious that it would naturally have been implied. Further, there would be a question of fact whether Anthony had had an opportunity of taking his holiday earlier and failed to take it or whether he simply had not been allowed the opportunity.

In summary, things are not as bleak for Anthony as they might at first seem. He has an action against the travel agents or the tour operators in respect of his holiday, an action against the department store in respect of his suitcase and lost effects, and a good defence against action by his employers.

4

Misrepresentation

Introduction

A further factor which may vitiate a contract is misrepresentation. Misrepresentation is such a common cause of action in the practical world that it ranks alongside mistake as one of the most popular areas for problem questions.

Misrepresentation involves an untrue statement of fact by one party to another which induces the other to enter a contract. A problem question on misrepresentation will therefore usually involve analysing pre-contractual statements with reference to the elements of this definition, illustrating the answer with suitable examples from recent case law such as *Kleinwort Benson Ltd* v *Lincoln City Council* (1999), *Clef Aquitaine Sarl* v *Laporte Materials (Barrow) Ltd* (2001) and *County NatWest Ltd* v *Barton* (2002).

Questions

INTERROGRAMS

1. What is the accepted definition of 'misrepresentation'?
2. How did the Misrepresentation Act 1967 improve the position of the plaintiff in a misrepresentation action?
3. What was the significance of the decision of the House of Lords in *Hedley Byrne & Co Ltd* v *Heller & Partners Ltd* (1964)?

QUESTION ONE

D was an antique dealer who specialised in selling china. E went to D's shop and agreed to buy a teapot for £400. It was described by D as a 'Peppermint' pattern piece. E, who was a specialist teapot collector, knew that such a teapot was worth at least £600 but said nothing to D about the fact that he had underpriced the piece. The written agreement of sale which was signed by D and E contained an exemption clause limiting D's liability to a maximum of £100 for all breaches of contract. Three months later the teapot was certified by an expert auctioneer to be a 'Buckle' teapot and worth only £50.

Advise E. What difference, if any, would it make to your advice if D had made no statement that it was a Peppermint piece but E believed it was Peppermint when he agreed to buy it?

University of London LLB Examination
(for external students) Elements of the Law of Contract June 2001 Q3

QUESTION TWO

'The remedies available to a person who has entered into a contract after the other party has made an inaccurate statement are complex. This makes advising clients difficult because the remedies available are purely a matter of historical accident.'

Discuss.

University of London LLB Examination
(for external students) Elements of the Law of Contract June 1999 Q5

QUESTION THREE

'It is difficult to see why the remedies should be so far-reaching remedies in respect of misrepresentation which has induced the plaintiff to enter into a contract, by comparison with those for breach of contract.'

Explain and comment.

University of London LLB Examination
(for external students) Elements of the Law of Contract June 1998 Q7

QUESTION FOUR

C advertised his bungalow, Hades, in the Upper Cwmtwrch for sale at £85,000. Subsequently, the estate agent's particulars, drawn up to C's specifications, described the bungalow as:

a) 'possessing a fine wide view with bracing air'. In fact, there was a view from the back of the house across a river estuary and there was a large power station on the river bank which belched out unpleasant fumes.
b) 'suitable as a retirement home'. In fact, it was not suitable for elderly residents because the house had a very narrow staircase and steps between different levels within the house.
c) 'in good decorative order'. In general this was true but the kitchen was in urgent need of modernisation.
d) 'not in need of planning permission to convert into a number of flats'. This was incorrect.

Though he had not viewed the property, D, having read the estate agent's particulars, wrote to C offering to buy Hades for £85,000 - completion within six weeks. C replied, 'Hades is yours at £85,000 though this agreement will have to be replaced by one drawn up by our solicitors.' D, who had paid a deposit of £10,000, decided not to buy Hades, which could have been worth £150,000 if it had a desirable view.

Advise the parties.

University of London LLB Examination
(for external students) Elements of the Law of Contract June 1997 Q4

QUESTION FIVE

In March, Bill, an estate agent, advised Charles to buy Donald's 'Fifty Acre Field' which was for sale. Bill gave Charles the particulars of the sale drawn up by Donald. These described the land as having a view over adjoining beautiful farm land. In fact, as Bill knew, the owner of this adjacent land was considering applying for planning permission to develop the land for a factory. Bill said, 'I am sure that the investment in the land is a good one.' Bill knew that the asking price for the land was very high by comparison with current market prices. Charles signed a contract to buy the land for £150,000, which was the asking price, and deposited this sum with Bill to await completion of the conveyance.

In May, Charles was advised by his accountant that the price was too high and that the neighbouring land was likely to be the subject of development. Charles then asked Bill not to pay any money over to Donald.

Advise Charles.

University of London LLB Examination
(for external students) Elements of the Law of Contract June 1996 Q7

Answers

ANSWERS TO INTERROGRAMS

1. Untrue, of course, means a deliberate lie (*Derry* v *Peek* (1889)) but a misleading statement or half-truth may also be a misrepresentation. Further, where the statement was true at the time it was made, there will still be a misrepresentation if circumstances change before the contract is concluded in such a way as to make the statement misleading, and the maker has not informed the party to whom it was made: *With* v *O'Flanagan* (1936).

   A statement of fact need not be made in words (*St Marylebone Property Co Ltd* v *Payne* (1994)) but statements as to law are excluded by the definition. Statements of opinion only are not misrepresentations (*Bisset* v *Wilkinson* (1927)) unless the maker does not genuinely hold that opinion or could not reasonably have held that opinion: *Smith* v *Land and House Property Corporation* (1884). Similarly, genuine statements of intention are not misrepresentations unless the party making the statement did not have or could not reasonably have had that intention (*Edgington* v *Fitzmaurice* (1885)) or did not intend keeping to it: *Esso Petroleum* v *Mardon* (1976).

   The statement must be made by a party to the contract or on his behalf and it must have induced the other to enter into the contract. Where the other party did not rely on the statement but made his own investigations, the statement, even if untrue, will not be a misrepresentation: *Attwood* v *Small* (1838). However, if a statement is made, he is entitled to rely on it and is not obliged to ascertain whether it is true even if the maker offers him the opportunity of doing so: *Redgrave* v *Hurd* (1881).
2. Prior to the enactment of the Misrepresentation Act 1967, a plaintiff who had been

induced to enter into a contract by a lie had only three courses of action. He could sue in the tort of deceit, prove that the statement formed part of the contract and sue for breach, or he could establish a claim for negligent misstatement.

Each of these possibilities had their pitfalls. In order to be able to establish a claim in deceit, the plaintiff must be able to show absolute dishonesty: *Derry* v *Peek* (1889). Clearly this was very difficult for 'the devil himself knows not the mind of a man'. The court was very often prepared to hold a statement or warranty to be a term of the contract, but this resulted in some rather complex rules and fine distinctions. The third possibility arose from the judgment of the House of Lords in *Hedley Byrne & Co Ltd* v *Heller and Partners Ltd* (1964) when it was held that, in certain circumstances, an untrue statement made without actual dishonesty could form the basis for a claim in negligence. However the plaintiff was required to prove that a 'special relationship' existed between himself and the defendant.

Section 2(1) of the Misrepresentation Act provides that if the defendant would have been liable to the plaintiff in fraud on the basis of his statement, then he will be liable even without fraud unless he can prove that he believed the statement and had reasonable grounds for doing so up until the time the contract was concluded. This means that the plaintiff need not prove fraud or a special relationship, nor that the statement had become a term of the contract. Instead the burden has passed to the defendant to prove that he believed the statement and that it was reasonable for him to do so.

3. The decision in *Hedley Byrne & Co Ltd* v *Heller and Partners Ltd* (1964) was something of a landmark. The facts of the case were that the plaintiffs had sought a banker's reference against a third party who was a client of the defendant bank. The reference was couched in misleading terms and the plaintiffs, believing the third party to be credit-worthy, did work on credit and thus incurred a loss.

The actual decision in the case was that the plaintiffs' claim in negligence must fail because the reference had included a disclaimer exempting the defendants from liability. However, the case is important for the dicta of the judges which established that, had there been no disclaimer, the plaintiffs would have succeeded in their claim. Prior to that, the plaintiffs would have had to prove either that the statement as to the third party's credit-worthiness was a term of a contract between themselves and the defendants (a course not open to them in this case as there was no contract) or that the reference was given fraudulently, which clearly was not the case.

The House laid down certain conditions for the operation of negligent misstatement:

a) there must be a special relationship between the parties;
b) this must arise from one party having a special knowledge or skill;
c) the plaintiff must have relied on that knowledge or skill; and
d) the statement must have been made in the course of a business.

While this was a welcome relaxation of the law, because of the conditions imposed it was somewhat restrictive and it was rare for plaintiffs to be able to take advantage of it. The position of the plaintiff was improved subsequently when the Misrepresentation Act 1967 removed the requirement to prove fraud, thus allowing a claim for misrepresentation on the basis of a negligent misstatement even where there was no special relationship.

SUGGESTED ANSWER TO QUESTION ONE

General Comment

A number of issues are raised by this question: the possible sale by description; misrepresentation; common mistake and unilateral mistake; and the effect of the exemption clause.

Key Points

- Whether the description invokes s13 Sale of Goods Act 1979
- Whether there has been an actionable misrepresentation
- Whether the contract is void at law for common mistake, and if not the possible remedy in equity
- The variation of the question suggesting unilateral mistake
- The effect of the exemption clause

Suggested Answer

The teapot was described as a 'Peppermint'. Under s13(1) Sale of Goods Act 1979 there is the implied term that the goods correspond with the description. But in *Harlingdon & Leinster Enterprises Ltd* v *Christopher Hull Fine Art Ltd* (1990) Nourse LJ said that 'The description must have a sufficient influence in the sale to become an essential term of the contract and the correlative of influence is reliance.' E could not be held to have reasonably relied on the description, as he was a specialist in the area and knew that such a teapot was worth considerably more than the price he paid. It would appear that E cannot invoke the statute, but I have some reservations about this view, as the facts here are not quite on all fours with those in the case cited, where the seller expressly disclaimed knowledge of the paintings in question.

It also seems doubtful whether E could successfully found a claim based on misrepresentation. Whilst the description of the teapot does constitute a representation, the difficulty would be in establishing that it induced him to enter into the contract for the reasons set out above.

On the assumption that both parties shared the mistaken belief that the teapot was a 'Peppermint', I must examine the effect of this common mistake, which is as to the quality of the subject matter.

At common law, where mistake is operative, the effect is to render the contract void. Operative common mistake at common law has been confined to very narrow limits by the decision of the House of Lords in *Bell* v *Lever Brothers Ltd* (1932). In his speech in that case, Lord Atkin held:

> '... a mistake will not affect assent unless it is the mistake of both parties, and is as to existence of some quality which makes the thing without the quality essentially different from the thing as it was believed to be.'

Lord Atkin would have applied this test somewhat restrictively. One of the examples his Lordship gave of a mistake that would not be operative is the sale of a picture which both parties believe to be the work of an old master and turns out to be a modern copy.

The speeches and decision in *Bell* v *Lever Bros* were analysed by Steyn J in *Associated Japanese Bank (International) Ltd* v *Credit du Nord SA* (1988), where the learned judge rejected the view that had been advanced by some commentators that the decision of the House of Lords made it virtually impossible to find a mistake as to quality which would render the contract void. His Lordship conceded that this would be rare, but he would have found that such mistake had this effect on the facts before him, but he decided the case on other grounds.

Whilst it is theoretically possible for a mistake as to quality to render the contract void, it is difficult to find a satisfactory case where this has been so. I must conclude that the present contract would not be void at common law. (In *Associated Japanese Bank* Steyn J advanced the proposition that a person could not rely on a mistake where he had no reasonable grounds for the belief: he referred to *McRae* v *Commonwealth Disposals Commission* (1951). This may be relevant here, considering E's knowledge and expertise.)

The next question is whether equitable relief would be available to E. In *Solle* v *Butcher* (1950) the Court of Appeal held that a contract although not void at law, was susceptible to being voidable in equity. Denning LJ held:

> 'A contract is also liable in equity to be set aside if the parties were under a common misapprehension either as to facts or as to their relative and respective rights, provided that the misapprehension was fundamental and that the party seeking to set it aside was not himself at fault.'

Some uncertainty attaches to this equitable principle. *Solle* v *Butcher* was followed in *Grist* v *Bailey* (1967) and in *Laurence* v *Lexcourt Holdings Ltd* (1978), but the correctness of these two decisions was doubted by Hoffmann LJ in *William Sindall plc* v *Cambridgeshire County Council* (1994). Moreover, it is doubtful whether equity would come to E's assistance, given that he was quite prepared to take advantage of D's considerable underpricing. Be that as it may, recently the Court of Appeal in *Great Peace Shipping Ltd* v *Tsavliris Salvage (International) Ltd, The Great Peace* (2002) observed that:

> 'In this case we have heard full argument, which has provided what we believe has been the first opportunity in this court for a full and mature consideration of the relation between *Bell* v *Lever Brothers Limited* and *Solle* v *Butcher*. In the light of that consideration we can see no way that *Solle* v *Butcher* can stand with *Bell* v *Lever Brothers Limited*. In these circumstances we can see no option but so to hold.'

I must submit, therefore, that the contract is neither void nor voidable.

I propose at this point to deal with the variation of the facts introduced in the last paragraph of the question. Here the mistake is unilateral. It is, I submit, clear on the authority of *Smith* v *Hughes* (1871) that this would not, in law, invalidate the contract. Nor would rescission in equity be available for the unilateral mistake: *Riverlate Properties Ltd* v *Paul* (1975).

E cannot, therefore rely on mistake. If I am correct that there has been no breach of sale by description, and no actionable misrepresentation, E has no remedy, and the exemption clause is irrelevant. But as I have conceded the possibility of there being either a breach of contract or a misrepresentation, I must consider the exemption clause in the light of those possibilities.

If there had been an actionable misrepresentation, the exemption clause would not apply, as it referred only to breaches of contract. The right of rescission would appear to be barred by the three months' delay. There is nothing to suggest fraud on D's part, but E would be entitled to damages under s2(1) Misrepresentation Act 1967. It is unlikely that D could discharge the onus imposed on him by the statute.The measure of damages, in tort, would be the difference between the price E paid for the teapot and its actual worth.

What would the effect of the clause have been if there had been a breach of contract? The clause had clearly been incorporated in the contract by E's signature thereto: *L'Estrange* v *F Graucob Ltd* (1934). But as the breach would have been of s13 Sale of Goods Act 1979, the clause would have been subject to the Unfair Contract Terms Act 1977. It can be assumed that E was dealing as a consumer, and s6(2) of that Act would render the clause totally ineffective. The clause would also fall foul of the Unfair Terms in Consumer Contracts Regulations 1999. E would have lost his right to reject, again because of the delay of three months, but would be entitled to damages, The measure being the difference between the actual value of the teapot - £50 - and the value it would have had if it had corresponded with the description - apparently at least £600: s53(3) Sale of Goods Act 1979.

SUGGESTED ANSWER TO QUESTION TWO

General Comment

This question could have framed with greater clarity. It requires an examination of the remedies for misrepresentation. In this area of the law it may indeed sometimes be difficult to advise clients, but this is not necessarily because of the manner in which the remedies have developed. To regard the development as 'purely a matter of historical accident' is perhaps a somewhat odd suggestion.

Key Points

- An outline of the remedies; rescission and damages
- Rescission: the availability and the bars to rescission - the discretion afforded to the courts by s2(2) Misrepresentation Act 1967
- Damages: fraudulent misrepresentation - damages under s2(1) of the Act - innocent misrepresentation

Suggested Answer

Remedies for misrepresentation have developed not perhaps in a logically coherent manner, but by the application of the principles of equity, the rules of the law of tort, and the provisions of the statute. Equity developed the remedy of rescission; for the rules as to damages for fraudulent misrepresentation we have to refer to the law of tort; and damages for non-fraudulent misrepresentation are provided for by the Misrepresentation Act (MA) 1967.

The common law failed to provide a remedy for misrepresentation, and it fell to the courts of equity to develop the remedy of rescission.

Rescission involves setting the contract aside prospectively and retrospectively, thus restoring the parties to the status quo ante, the position they were in before entering into the contract, as far as it is possible to do so.

Rescission may, in some circumstances, be a drastic remedy (see the discussion of s2(2) of the 1967 Act below). It may also provide an adequate remedy, but there are certain bars to rescission.

Affirmation

If by words or conduct the plaintiff affirms the contract the right to rescind it will be barred: *Long* v *Lloyd* (1958). However, the plaintiff will not be taken to have affirmed the contract if he had discovered the falsity of the representation, but did not know that he had the right to rescind it: *Peyman* v *Lanjani* (1985).

Restitutio in integrum not possible

Rescission will not be barred if it is not possible to restore the subject-matter of the contract: *Clarke* v *Dickson* (1858); cf *Armstrong* v *Jackson* (1917).

Third party rights

Section 23 Sale of Goods Act 1979 may bar rescission by conferring title to the goods on an innocent third party: *Lewis* v *Averay* (1972).

Delay

If the plaintiff delays in asserting his right to rescind he will lose that right: *Leaf* v *International Galleries* (1950).

Rescission may be a harsh remedy where the misrepresentation is innocent. This is mitigated by s2(2) MA 1967, which provides that where a party has a right to rescind for a misrepresentation, other than fraudulent, the court has a discretion to declare the contract subsisting and award damages in lieu of rescission. In *Thomas Witter Ltd* v *TBP Industries Ltd* (1996) Jacob J expressed the view, obiter, that the court had this discretion even where the right to rescind had been lost. But the contrary view was held by Judge Jack QC in *Zanzibar* v *British Aerospace (Lancaster House) Ltd* (2000).

It was originally thought that rescission was not available for innocent misrepresentation where the contract had been performed, but this rule was abrogated by s1 MA 1967.

The right to damages for misrepresentation stems from the law of tort. If it is fraudulent, the remedy is in the tort of deceit, and the measure of damages is accordingly tortious. There is a particular rule in relation to damages for fraud. The rule was stated in this way by Lord Denning MR in *Doyle* v *Olby (Ironmongers) Ltd* (1969):

> 'In contract, the damages are limited to what may reasonably be supposed to have been in the contemplation of the parties. In fraud, they are not so limited. The defendant is bound to make reparation for all the actual damage directly flowing from the fraudulent inducement.'

Thus, in *Smith New Court Securities Ltd* v *Scrimgeour Vickers (Asset Management) Ltd* (1997), where the plaintiffs had been induced to buy shares in a company by fraudulent misrepresentations, the defendants were held liable for a subsequent fall in the value of the shares for causes unconnected with their fraud.

At common law, in the absence of fraud, damages for misrepresentation were not obtainable. And fraud may be difficult to prove. In *Derry* v *Peek* (1889) Lord Herschell said:

> 'First, in order to sustain an action of deceit, there must be proof of fraud, and nothing short of that will suffice. Secondly, fraud is proved when it is shown that a false representation had been made (1) knowingly, or (2) without belief in its truth, or (3) recklessly, careless whether it be true or false.'

Liability in damages for non-fraudulent misrepresentation has been created by the Misrepresentation Act in s2(1). This provides that if a defendant would have been liable to damages if the misrepresentation had been made fraudulently, then even if it were not made fraudulently he shall be so liable as he 'would be liable to damages had the misrepresentation been made fraudulently'. In order to avoid such liability the defendant has the onus of proving 'that he had reasonable ground to believe and did believe up to the time the contract was made that the facts represented were true.' This may be a difficult onus to discharge: *Howard Marine & Dredging Co Ltd* v *A Ogden & Sons (Excavations) Ltd* (1978).

If the defendant succeeds in discharging this onus, the misrepresentation is wholly innocent and he will not be liable to damages, only on rescission of the contract, to indemnify the plaintiff for the expenses which the contract itself obliged him to incur: *Whittington* v *Seale-Hayne* (1900).

It is questionable why it was thought necessary to invoke this fiction of fraud. Applying it the Court of Appeal has held that the measure of damages under s2(1) is the same as for fraud: *Royscott Trust Ltd* v *Rogerson* (1991). The direct consequences rule applies. That the fraudster should be liable for all the direct consequences of his fraud is understandable, but is it fair under s2(1), where the fraud is entirely fictional? This makes mere carelessness equivalent to deliberate fraud.

The contractual, not the tortious, measure was suggested, obiter, by Hoffmann LJ for damages in lieu of rescission under s2(2) in *William Sindall plc* v *Cambridgeshire County Council* (1994). There had been a sharp decline in the value of the property concerned, but his Lordship held that damages in lieu of rescission could not include loss due to a general decline in market value subsequent to the sale. The proper measure of damages was the cost of remedying the defect in the property, or the reduced market value attributable to the defect.

That the remedies for misrepresentation are complex cannot be denied, nor can the difficulties this causes in advising clients be ignored.

SUGGESTED ANSWER TO QUESTION THREE

General Comment

It is not sufficient, in answering this question, merely to set out the remedies for misrepresentation, and then to add brief notes on the remedies for breach of contract. An analysis and comparison of the respective remedies is required.

Key Points

- A comparison of the right of the innocent party to terminate the contract for breach with the right to rescind it for misrepresentation
- A comparison of damages for breach and damages for misrepresentation

Suggested Answer

Termination and rescission

For breach of contract the innocent party is only entitled to terminate the contract if the breach is a breach of condition. For breach of warranty he is only entitled to damages. For breach of an innominate term, he is only entitled to termination where the breach is so serious as to deprive him of substantially the whole benefit of the contract. The contract is not automatically terminated by the breach: the innocent party must indicate his acceptance of the breach, otherwise he will be taken to have affirmed the contract, and his obligations under it will continue: *Photo Production Ltd* v *Securicor Transport Ltd* (1980). Termination for breach discharges the innocent party from any further performance, the contract is brought to an end prospectively.

For misrepresentation the remedy of rescission may be available to the innocent party. Rescission sets the contract aside both retrospectively and prospectively; the parties are put in the position - as far as possible - that they were in before they entered into the contract. Rescission may be available whether the misrepresentation is fraudulent, 'negligent' under s2(1) Misrepresentation Act (MA) 1967, or wholly innocent. (These categories are dealt with more fully below.)

There are, however, certain bars to rescission, namely: (i) where the innocent party has affirmed the contract; (ii) where restitutio in integrum is not possible; (iii) where third party rights have intervened; and (iv) where there is delay in exercising the right. Furthermore, under s2(2) MA 1967, where a party has the right to rescind for a misrepresentation, other than fraudulent, the court has a discretion to declare the contract subsisting and award damages in lieu of rescission, where it would be equitable to do so.

A particular point of comparison is worth noting. As noted above, the right to terminate is not available for breach of contract, where the breach is merely of warranty - only damages would be available. For misrepresentation, however, s1 MA 1967 provides that, if the innocent party would have been entitled to rescind the contract, he shall be so entitled notwithstanding that the misrepresentation has become a term of the contract. Thus, if the term, which the misrepresentation has become, would only be regarded as a warranty, the right to rescind remains. It is difficult to see why this should be so, but perhaps it would be mitigated by the application of s2(2).

Damages

The governing purpose of an award of damages for breach of contract is to put the plaintiff in the same position, as far as money can do so, as if the contract had been performed: *Robinson* v *Harman* (1848); *Victoria Laundry (Windsor) Ltd* v *Newman Industries Ltd* (1949). Thus the innocent party would be entitled to expectation loss. There is an important limitation to this: the damages must not be too remote. The contract-breaker is only liable for loss that was in the reasonable contemplation of the parties: *Hadley* v *Baxendale* (1854).

The right to damages for misrepresentation depends on the nature of the misrepresentation. If it is fraudulent, the remedy is in the tort of deceit, and the measure of damages is tortious, which is to put the plaintiff in the position he would have been in if the statement had not been made, not – as in the contractual measure – to put the plaintiff in the position he would have been in if the statement were true. Thus, there would not be entitlement to expectation loss.

But there is a particular rule in relation to damages for fraud. The rule, and its contrast with the contractual measure, was put thus by Lord Denning MR in *Doyle* v *Olby (Ironmongers) Ltd* (1969).

> 'In contract, the damages are limited to what may reasonably be supposed to have been in the contemplation of the parties. In fraud, they are not so limited. The defendant is bound to make reparation for all the actual damage directly flowing from the fraudulent inducement.'

For a striking example of the application of this rule, see *Smith New Court Securities Ltd* v *Scrimgeour Vickers (Asset Management) Ltd* (1997), where the defendants were held liable for a fall in the value of shares for causes unconnected with their fraud.

Fraud may be difficult to prove: it was somewhat rigorously defined by the House of Lords in *Derry* v *Peek* (1889). However, even if the representation was not fraudulent, the defendant may incur liability for misrepresentation under s2(1) MA 1967. This has the effect of imposing liability for 'negligent' misrepresentation. It says that he shall be so liable as he 'would be liable to damages had the misrepresentation been made fraudulently'. In order to avoid such liability the defendant has the onus of proving 'that he had reasonable grounds to believe and did believe up to the time the contract was made that the facts represented were true'. This may be a difficult onus to discharge: *Howard Marine & Dredging Co Ltd* v *A Ogden & Sons (Excavations) Ltd* (1978). If the defendant succeeds in discharging this onus, the misrepresentation is wholly innocent and he will not be liable in damages, only for an indemnity: *Whittington* v *Seale Hayne* (1900).

It is not clear why it was thought necessary to invoke this fiction of fraud. Applying it the Court of Appeal has held that the measure of damages under s2(1) is the same as for fraud: *Royscott Trust Ltd* v *Rogerson* (1991). The direct consequence rule applies.

That the fraudster should be liable for all the direct consequences of his fraud is understandable, but it is questionable whether it is fair under s2(1), where the fraud is entirely fictional. This equates mere carelessness with deliberate fraud. There is a sharp contrast with the measure of damages suggested (obiter) by Hoffmann LJ for damages in lieu of rescission under s2(2) in *William Sindall plc* v *Cambridgeshire County Council* (1994). There had been a sharp decline in the value of the property concerned, but his Lordship held that damages in lieu of rescission could not include loss due to a general decline in market value subsequent to the sale. The proper measure of damages was the cost of remedying the defect in the property, or the reduced market value attributable to the defect.

SUGGESTED ANSWER TO QUESTION FOUR

General Comment

This question requires consideration of the legal principles relating to an actionable misrepresentation. Emphasis must be paid to whether all the essential elements required to sustain an action for misrepresentation have been established.

Key Points

- Has a contract been concluded?
- On the assumption that it has been concluded, analyse the various particulars: whether this amounts to a misrepresentation - whether this induced D to enter into the contract - the truth or falsity of this statement - statement of fact or statement of law?
- If there have been actionable misrepresentations, the remedies available to D

Suggested Answer

The possible effect of C's reply that 'this agreement will have to be replaced by one drawn up by our solicitors' is that the agreement will not be legally binding until the formal document is duly executed. If this is so, no binding contract has been concluded, and D's only claim is for the return of his deposit. The other possibility is that the formal document is intended only as a record of an already binding agreement as in *Branca* v *Cobarro* (1947). I am proceeding on the latter assumption in order to discuss the law relating to misrepresentation.

A misrepresentation is a statement of fact made by one party to the contract to the other, which, although not a term of the contract, induced that other to enter into the contract, and is false. Clearly the statements are not contractual terms; they are not intended so to be: *Heilbut, Symons & Co* v *Buckleton* (1913). An analysis of the various statements must now be made in the light of the above definition in order to determine whether they (or any of them) amount to actionable misrepresentations. For them to be so, they must be: (i) statements of fact, not of opinion, intention or law; (ii) have been addressed to D; and (iii) induced D to enter into the contract. One can assume that the statements were addressed (inter alia) to D: the other two factors require consideration.

a) This statement might appear at first sight to be one of opinion. However, in view of the existence of the power station it is not an opinion that could reasonably have been held, and this amounts to a misrepresentation: *Smith* v *Land and House Property Corporation* (1884); *Brown* v *Raphael* (1958). It might also be regarded as a misleading half-truth, which also amounts to a misrepresentation: *Dimmock* v *Hallett* (1866). It can be assumed that this statement would have induced a reasonable person to enter into the contract, and the onus would be on C to prove that it did not induce D: *Museprime Properties Ltd* v *Adhill Properties Ltd* (1990).

b) The phrase 'suitable as a retirement home' does imply that it was suitable for elderly residents, and an implication can constitute a misrepresentation: *Laurence* v *Lexcourt Holdings Ltd* (1978). However, it is not apparent that D was interested in the property as a retirement home, so the status of this statement as an inducing factor must be in doubt.

c) It is also doubtful whether this statement could constitute a mis-representation. That the property was 'in good decorative order' appears to be largely true. It is arguable whether or not that statement is consistent with the need for modernisation of the kitchen. I conclude, although not without doubt, that the statement might be regarded as a misleading half-truth and, therefore, a misrepresentation.

d) This statement appears to be one of law, not of fact. But the distinction is not always easy to draw – see the difference of opinion in the Court of Appeal in *Solle* v *Butcher* (1950). It might be a mixed statement, partly of law and partly of fact, in which case it would constitute a misrepresentation. But, in the absence of information to this effect, I must conclude that it is a statement of law, and not, therefore, a misrepresentation. It is also not clear that this was an inducing factor.

It appears to me that only statement (a) can confidently be regarded as an actionable misrepresentation (although statements (b) and (c) might also be so), but that would be sufficient to afford D remedies, the nature of which must now be considered.

D would be entitled to rescind the contract. Rescission is available whether the misrepresentation is fraudulent, falls within s2(1) Misrepresentation Act 1967, or is wholly innocent. None of the bars to rescission would appear to operate here; there is no question of affirmation, impossibility of restitution, third party rights or delay. Nor are there any grounds for suggesting that the court would exercise its discretion under s2(2) of the Act and award damages in lieu of rescission. In the event of rescission D would, of course, recover his deposit.

It remains to consider D's entitlement to damages. There is insufficient evidence on the facts before me that any of the statements were made fraudulently. If there was, then damages would include all losses flowing naturally out of the fraud, as illustrated in *Smith New Court Securities Ltd* v *Citibank NA* (1997). D would rely on s2(1) of the Act in order to found a claim for damages. It appears highly unlikely that C could discharge the onus imposed on him by s2(1) to avoid liability in damages. This measure of damages by the Court of Appeal was affirmed in the recent case of *Clef Aquitaine Sarl* v *Laporte Materials (Barrow) Ltd* (2000).

Despite earlier suggestions to the contrary it is now clear that the measure of recovery under s2(1) is the reliance measure, not the expectation measure: *Royscott Trust Ltd* v *Rogerson* (1991).

That being so, D has no claim in respect of what the property could have been worth if it had a desirable view; that would be expectation loss, the contractual measure of damages. D would be entitled to his reliance loss and, as for fraud, D would be entitled to recover for all the loss directly following from the misrepresentation(s), whether or not such loss was reasonably foreseeable: *Royscott Trust Ltd* v *Rogerson*. In the absence of information I am called upon to speculate as to what that loss might be. It would include any expenses D incurred in entering into the transaction, loss of interest on his deposit and possibly for loss of the chance of investing his money in some other property: *East* v *Maurer* (1991).

SUGGESTED ANSWER TO QUESTION FIVE

General Comment

Another question requiring examination of whether all the elements needed to mount a successful action for misrepresentation have been satisfied.

Key Points

- The assumption that Bill was acting as Donald's agent
- The grounds for an actionable misrepresentation
- Analysis of the relevant statements
- The remedies that might be available to Charles and his possible liabilities
- On the assumption that Bill was not Donald's agent, Bill's liability for negligent misstatement or for breach of a collateral contract

Suggested Answer

I am assuming, in the first instance, that Bill was acting as Donald's agent by virtue of his capacity as an estate agent, who normally acts on behalf of the seller of property.

Charles wishes to rescind the contract, and I must examine his grounds for doing so.

There are two relevant statements to be considered: one relating to the view from the property; the other with regard to the investment. On the basis of the assumption I have made, I am attributing both these statements to the seller of the property, Donald.

The two statements (in so far as Donald is concerned) were not, in my submission, intended as terms of the contract: *Heilbut, Symons & Co* v *Buckleton* (1913). They were, if anything, 'mere' representations.

The requirements for an actionable misrepresentation are: a statement of fact (which is false); addressed by one party to another; and which induces that other to enter into the contract. The statements must be examined in the light of these requirements.

The first statement is with regard to the view from the property. Donald has made this statement and I am attributing knowledge of its falsity to him. The statement could be regarded as a mere 'puff', or as an expression of opinion. A mere 'puff' is not construed as a representation (*Dimmock* v *Hallett* (1866)), nor is a simple expression of opinion: *Bisset* v *Wilkinson* (1927). On the facts before me I do not consider that the statement can be dismissed as a mere 'puff'. Nor do I consider that it is no more than an expression of opinion. An opinion is regarded as a representation if that opinion could not reasonably have been held: *Smith* v *Land & House Property Corporation* (1884); *Brown* v *Raphael* (1958). In view of Bill's knowledge of the proposed development of the adjacent land - knowledge which I have attributed to Donald - I submit that the opinion could not reasonably have been held and the statement must be regarded as one of fact, and therefore a representation.

The statement that the investment in the land was 'a good one' might at first sight be regarded as no more than an opinion. But in view of Bill's knowledge that the asking price of the land was very high, I submit that this opinion could not reasonably have been held. There were no grounds for this belief: see *Brown* v *Raphael* (above). I am again attributing the statement, and knowledge of its falsity, to Donald.

The statements were clearly addressed to Charles and there can be no doubt but that they induced him to enter into the contract. They did not have to be the sole factors which persuaded him to conclude the contract in order to ground an actionable misrepresentation: *Edgington* v *Fitzmaurice* (1885).

Charles, by his request to Bill not to pay over any money to Donald, is seeking rescission of the contract. On the basis of the assumption I have made as to agency, he is entitled to rescind. Rescission is the available equitable remedy for misrepresentation. He is obliged to communicate his decision to rescind to Donald, but his instruction to Bill can be so regarded.

As Charles does not appear to be seeking damages from Donald, it is not relevant to discuss, at length, entitlement to damages for misrepresentation either at common law or under the Misrepresentation Act 1967. I would note, however, that it is unlikely that Charles could establish that the statements were fraudulent under the strict criteria of *Derry* v *Peek* (1889). But Donald would be liable in damages under s2(1) of the Act. The measure of damages would be tortious and the same as for fraud: *Royscott Trust Ltd* v *Rogerson* (1991).

I must enter a caveat. If it appears that Bill was not acting as Donald's agent, there could be no liability for misrepresentation on Donald's part. In that event Charles' purported rescission would be wrongful and Donald would be entitled to bring an action for breach of contract. As the contract is one for the sale of land he might well obtain an order for specific performance.

If there was no agency relationship between Donald and Bill, and Donald has not incurred any liability, I must consider the possible redress that Charles may have against Bill. There are two possible claims: an action for negligent misstatement; and an action based on the existence of a collateral contract. Both these actions would be a claim for damages, if Charles is unable to rescind the contract, or is compelled to perform it, or is found liable in damages himself if he fails to do so.

A claim for negligent misstatement against Bill might well be open to Charles on the basis of the principle in *Hedley Byrne & Co Ltd* v *Heller & Partners Ltd* (1964). The essential of a 'special relationship' between the parties is, I submit, clearly present.

The further possibility is that Charles may have an action against Bill on the basis of a collateral contract. In assessing Bill's responsibility for the statements regard must be had to the profession in which he is engaged. He must be deemed to have had special knowledge both with regard to the view and, more particularly, with regard to the quality of the investment. In Bill's special position of knowledge the statements must be regarded as having been made with contractual intent: *Esso Petroleum Co Ltd* v *Mardon* (1976).

It is clear that there may be a contract, the consideration for which is the making of some other contract: *Heilbut, Symons & Co* v *Buckleton* (above). It is also clear that there may be a contractual promise, the consideration for which is the making of a contract with a third party, thus incurring the promisor with liability for breach of the collateral contract: *Shanklin Pier Ltd* v *Detel Products Ltd* (1951); *Wells (Merstham) Ltd* v *Buckland Sand and Silica Ltd* (1964).

The statements made by Bill were collateral promises, the consideration for which was Charles' conclusion of the contract with Donald. I therefore submit that Bill would be liable for breach of the collateral contract.

5

Exclusion Clauses

Introduction

Excluding or limiting clauses in contracts is a very popular area indeed, with examiners tending to favour a problem question approach. Often the effect of a number of clauses is required to be considered within the same question. Candidates should approach this area in a methodical fashion, demonstrating an ability to apply first the common law rules for incorporation of exclusion clauses into a contract and their general construction, and then the effect of the relevant clauses when the Unfair Contract Terms Act 1977 is applied, especially when the liability sought to be excluded concerns liability for negligence. Thirdly, the effect (if relevant) of the Unfair Terms in Consumer Contracts Regulations 1999 must be evaluated. Recent cases include *O'Brien* v *MGN Ltd* (2001), *Paragon Finance plc* v *Nash* (2001) and *Director General of Fair Trading* v *First National Bank plc* (2002).

Questions

INTERROGRAMS

1. What is the situation when the clause upon which the defendant relies to relieve him of liability is an indemnity?
2. What is the significance of an exclusion clause being printed on the back of a ticket?
3. Does a fundamental breach deprive the defendant of the right to rely on clauses which exclude or limit his liability?

QUESTION ONE

D, who was deaf, went to an auction run by E. D had a copy of the catalogue and had intended to bid for a picture attributed to Lowry. When the lot came up, E explained that there was some doubt about the authenticity of the picture and that E could not guarantee that it was genuine. However, D did not hear this qualification and bought the picture for £26,000. An expert later confirmed that it was probably a very good copy worth £3,500. D sought to return the painting and recover compensation. The conditions of sale which were posted on the walls of the auction rooms stated,

> 'There is no warranty about the condition of goods. Goods sold subject to errors of description.'

Advise D. What difference, if any, would it make to your advice if D were an art dealer who had bought the painting to sell on in the course of D's business?

University of London LLB Examination
(for external students) Elements of the Law of Contract June 2000 Q3

QUESTION TWO

R, a car dealer, agreed to sell a car to S for £5,000 after S had examined the car on the garage forecourt. The document on the car windscreen indicated the price and in large letters said, 'All our cars are in tip top condition!' Later in small print was a clause which read, 'we accept no legal responsibility for the condition of the vehicle. For terms of sale see the notice in the office and the details in the sale agreement.' In the office, where there was a large notice on the wall indicating all the major provisions, S signed the agreement to purchase the car. It contained the following provisions:

> 'It is agreed that there is no warranty, condition, or statement about the condition of the car and that no statement was made which persuaded the purchaser to enter into the contract.'
>
> 'It is agreed that the maximum damages payable for breach of contract shall be £2,500.'
>
> 'There is no express term, implied term (statutory or otherwise) or warranty or statement about the vehicle which is to have any legal effect. There is no promise about the condition of the vehicle.'

Two days later, when S's wife was driving the car which S had given to her as a birthday present, the car crashed because the brakes were defective. Mrs S was injured and off work for six months causing her to lose £14,000 in wages. The car was a write-off.

Advise S.

University of London LLB Examination
(for external students) Elements of the Law of Contract June 1998 Q6

QUESTION THREE

Hugh, a stockbroker and keep fit enthusiast, bought an exercise machine from Steve's sports goods shop. The sales note contained the following clauses:

> '11. The seller accepts no responsibility for loss or injury caused by defects in the manufacture or design of the equipment.
> 12. It is for the buyer to ensure that the equipment is suitable for his personal needs.
> 13. No complaints will be entertained unless notified to the seller in writing within six weeks of the date of purchase.'

Hugh used the machine regularly for four weeks. He then noticed that he was experiencing back pain, which he had never had before, and telephoned Steve about this. Steve said there was nothing to worry about.

Hugh continued to use the machine for another month, but then suffered serious back injury when the saddle on the machine collapsed while he was exercising. The defect in the saddle could not have been discovered on examination, but it has now been established that the dimensions of the machine are totally unsuitable for a person of Hugh's height and build.

Advise Hugh. Would your advice be different if Hugh was a professional athlete and had bought the machine for the purposes of his athletic training?
University of London LLB Examination
(for external students) Elements of the Law of Contract June 1996 Q3

QUESTION FOUR

F, an experienced sailor, agreed to buy a boat from G for £22,000. Subsequently, the agreement entered into between F and G contained, inter alia, the following clauses:

> '(9) It is agreed that there is no undertaking of quality, fitness for purpose or of description.
> (10) It is agreed that there is no express or implied condition or warranty, express, statutory or otherwise, fundamental or otherwise in this contract of sale.'

Two months later, on the first occasion F took the boat out to sea, the boat proved not to be seaworthy and nearly sank. The members of F's family who were acting as crew were seriously frightened for their lives and H, F's 14-year-old daughter, was mentally ill for two years.

Advise F who wants to return the boat and recover the price he has paid. What difference, if any, would it make to your advice if the boat had sunk?
University of London LLB Examination
(for external students) Elements of the Law of Contract June 1995 Q4

Answers

ANSWERS TO INTERROGRAMS

1. An indemnity clause is a contractual provision that one party will reimburse the other for any losses sustained by him. Indemnities may be as onerous as exclusions and, in some cases have been used in an attempt to circumvent the law on exclusion clauses by providing that the defendant will be reimbursed costs of action and even damages.

   Section 4 Unfair Contract Terms Act 1977 applies to indemnity clauses. It provides relief where the indemnity is against business liability and the person who provides the indemnity is a consumer. The clause will not be effective in respect of any liability incurred by the other for negligence or breach of contract unless it satisfies the requirement of reasonableness. The section applies whether the liability is that of the person to be indemnified or vicarious or whether it is to the person dealing as a consumer or to someone else.
2. Where an exclusion clause is printed on the back of a ticket, the question is whether or not it has been incorporated into the contract. Reasonable steps must be taken to bring an exclusion to the notice of the other party before the contract is made. It therefore follows that if the ticket in question is issued after the conclusion of the contract, this rule will not have been satisfied.

   There are a number of cases on the point. In *Chapleton* v *Barry UDC* (1940), the plaintiff was injured when a deckchair collapsed. He had paid for the deckchair and had been given a ticket. A clause excluding the Council from liability was printed on the reverse. It was held that the contract had been concluded before the plaintiff received the ticket. Similarly, in *Thornton* v *Shoe Lane Parking Ltd* (1971) the customer at the entrance to an automatic car park put money into a machine which issued a ticket to him. It was held that the contract was concluded at that point and that terms printed on the ticket and displayed at the exit were not part of the contract. In contrast, however, are cases where the taking of a ticket has been held to be acceptance of the offer, for example *Thompson* v *London Midland & Scottish Railway Co* (1930). The explanation of the distinction, given by Lord Denning in the *Thornton* case, is that the contract is concluded when the plaintiff is committed.

3. A fundamental breach is a breach which defeats the main purpose of the contract. It may or may not also be a breach of a fundamental term. At one time, the courts considered that there was a rule of law that an exclusion clause could not protect a party against liability for a fundamental breach. However, the House of Lords in *Suisse Atlantique Société d'Armament Maritime SA* v *NV Rotterdamsche Kolen Centrale* (1967) established that this was merely a rule of construction and that an exclusion clause could be effective to cover a fundamental breach, provided that there were clear words.

   The later case of *Harbutt's Plasticine Ltd* v *Wayne Tank and Pumps Co Ltd* (1970) took the older viewpoint that a breach of contract by one party accepted by the other as discharging him from further obligation brought the contract to an end including any exclusion clause in it. However, in *Photo Production Ltd* v *Securicor Transport Ltd* (1980), the principle in *Suisse Atlantique* was reaffirmed. In *George Mitchell (Chesterhall) Ltd* v *Finney Lock Seeds Ltd* (1983), Lord Bridge confirmed that this had given 'the final quietus to the doctrine that a "fundamental breach" of contract deprived the party in breach of the benefit of clauses in the contract excluding or limiting his liability.'

SUGGESTED ANSWER TO QUESTION ONE

General Comment

Discussion of different possibilities is required here: the statement in the catalogue, whether it is a contractual term or a representation; the effect of E's explanation; the effectiveness of the exclusion clause; and the consequence of D having dealt in the course of business.

Key Points

- On the assumption that the statement in the catalogue is a contractual term, the possible breach of s13 Sale of Goods Act 1979, the effect of the exclusion clause where D is dealing as a consumer and in the course of business
- On the assumption that the statement is a representation, the question of inducement and the effect of the exclusion clause

Suggested Answer

I shall firstly consider the possibility that the statement attributing the picture to Lowry is a term of the contract. The first question is whether the sale of the painting falls within s13(1) Sale of Goods Act 1979 as being a 'sale of goods by description', it being an implied term (a condition) that the goods correspond with the description.

In order for a sale to fall within s13, the description must relate to the identity of the goods sold: *Reardon Smith Line* v *Hangsen-Tangen* (1976). Clearly that requirement is satisfied. There is, however, a further requirement, it must have been reasonable for the buyer to have relied on the description: *Harlingdon & Leinster Enterprises Ltd* v *Christopher Hull Fine Art Ltd* (1990). This creates a difficulty for D. The auctioneer, E, stated the doubt about the authenticity of the picture. (I consider the fact that D did did not hear this explanation, because he was deaf, irrelevant.) In the light of this explanation and the notice posted on the walls of the auction rooms, I submit that it would not have been reasonable for D to have relied on the description and that accordingly s13(1) does not apply. A fortiori this conclusion would be justified if D had bought the picture in the course of business.

Nevertheless, I should consider the possibility that the sale was one by description within s13, and the effect of the exclusion clause in that event. It may well be that, applying the contra profenterem rule, the clause does not cover the breach: it purports to exclude a warranty, whereas the breach is of a condition: *Wallis, Son & Wells* v *Pratt & Haynes* (1911). If it does cover the breach, then the provisions of the Unfair Contract Terms Act 1977 are relevant. If D was dealing as a consumer, then under s6(2) of that Act the clause would be void. If D was dealing in the course of business then under s6(3) it would have to meet the requirement of reasonableness. In view of E's explanation it seems that it might do so.

However, I have concluded that the attribution of the picture was not a contractual term. There is a further reason for doing so. The paramount factor in determining whether a statement is to be construed as a term is the intention of the parties: *Heilbut, Symons & Co* v *Buckleton* (1913). Clearly there was no such intention.

Although the statement attributing the painting to Lowry was not a term, it appears that it did amount to a representation and, being false, constituted a misrepresentation. It was clearly a statement of fact and addressed to D (amongst others). Did it induce D to enter into the contract? There is room for doubt about this in view of E's explanation (which I have assumed D should have heard). The question is one of onus of proof. Whilst the statement might not, in view of E's explanation, have induced a reasonable man to enter into the contract, D could argue that it did induce him; the onus of proof would be on D: *Museprime Properties Ltd* v *Adhill Properties Ltd* (1990). He would succeed in establishing inducement if he discharged that onus. I assume, although not without doubt, that he could do so. This might be more difficult for him if he was an art dealer.

Assuming that there was an actionable misrepresentation, further consideration must be given to the exclusion clause. This clause refers to 'warranty' and 'description' and does not expressly refer to a representation. Arguably it therefore does not apply. If it does, its effectiveness must be considered in the light of s3 Misrepresentation Act 1967, as amended by s8(1) Unfair Contract Terms Act 1997. Under this provision the clause would be of no effect unless it satisfied the requirement of reasonableness stated in s11(1) of the latter statute. Whilst E's explanation might be persuasive that it did so, I shall assume, for the purpose of further discussion, that the clause is ineffective.

It would appear, consequently, that D has an action for misrepresentation and the remedies available to him must now be considered.

D wishes to return the painting, thus seeking the equitable remedy of recission. He appears to be entitled to this. There do not appear to be any of the bars to rescission. Before 1967 the performance of the contract would have been a bar because of the doctrine in *Seddon* v *North Eastern Salt Co* (1905), but that bar was removed by s1 Misrepresentation Act 1967. There is no suggestion of the other bars applying, such as affirmation, impossibility of restitution, third party rights or delay.

Under s2(2) Misrepresentation Act 1967 the court has a discretion to award damages in lieu of rescission, but there is insufficient information to determine whether or not a court would exercise that discretion.

D also seeks compensation. No information is given as to the loss he might have sustained that would not compensated for by his being able to rescind. If he has sustained other loss, then his entitlement to damages must be briefly considered.

If the representation were fraudulent D would be entitled to damages for the tort of deceit. But there are no grounds for assuming fraud here. However, even in the absence of fraud, D would be entitled to damages under s2(1) Misrepresentation Act 1967 unless the representor proves both that he believed that the attribution of the picture was true and that he had reasonable grounds for that belief. It is difficult to see how that onus could be discharged. The measure of damages under s2(1) is the same as for fraud: *Royscott Trust Ltd* v *Rogerson* (1991).

SUGGESTED ANSWER TO QUESTION TWO

General Comment

An analysis of the effectiveness of exclusion clauses is required by this question. Discussion is also required of the position in relation to the damages suffered by S's wife, whether she or S has any contractual remedy in respect of those damages.

Key Points

- An analysis of the notice 'in tip top condition'
- Incorporation of the clause 'we accept no responsibility'
- Incorporation of the provisions in the sale agreement
- The nature of the breach of contract, whether covered by the exclusion clauses
- The effect of the relevant provisions of the Unfair Contract Terms Act 1977 and the Unfair Terms in Consumer Contracts Regulations 1999

Suggested Answer

The notice 'All our cars are in tip top condition!' appears to be sales talk, a mere puff, and therefore has no legal consequences. (I have some slight doubt about this, because R is a car dealer, and in *Andrews* v *Hopkinson* (1957) the scarcely more precise statement by a dealer about a car was 'It's a good little bus. I would stake my life on it. You will have no trouble with it.' – and this statement was held to constitute a collateral contract. However, it is probably distinguishable, as there the statement related to a specific car.)

The notice which read, 'we accept no legal responsibility for the condition of the vehicle' appeared in small print. This seems to be an unusual, even a harsh and onerous clause, and there is authority that, for such a clause to be effective, the party seeking to rely on it should have adopted special measures to bring it to the other party's attention: *Spurling* v *Bradshaw* (1956); *Thornton* v *Shoe Lane Parking Ltd* (1971); *Interfoto Picture Library Ltd* v *Stiletto Visual Programmes Ltd* (1988). I submit that this notice required special measures, and as it was buried in small print it would be ineffective.

The major provisions of the sale agreement appeared in a large notice. This may well have constituted reasonable notice to S, but in any event they also appeared in the agreement which S signed. This is sufficient to have incorporated the provisions: *L'Estrange* v *Graucob* (1934).

The breach of contract here is of the term implied by s14(2) Sale of Goods Act (SGA) 1979, 'that the goods are of satisfactory quality'. The section applies because R is a seller 'in the course of a business'. This provision is not excluded by s14(2C)(b), because although it appears that S examined the car, there is no indication that the examination ought to have revealed that the brakes were defective.

There was a fundamental breach of contract (the term implied by s14(2) is a condition) and the question whether the exclusion clauses apply to that breach is one of the true construction of the contract: *Suisse Atlantique Société d'Armament Maritime SA* v *NV Rotterdamsche Kolen Centrale* (1967); *Photo Production Ltd* v *Securicor Transport Ltd* (1980); *George Mitchell (Chesterhall) Ltd* v *Finney Lock Seeds Ltd* (1983). It is clear that here they do so apply.

Although, at common law, the exclusion clauses were incorporated and do apply to the breach, they do not survive the application of the Unfair Contract Terms Act (UCTA) 1977. S is a consumer as defined in s12(1) of the Act. As against a person dealing as a consumer liability for the obligation arising from (inter alia) s14 SGA 1979 cannot be excluded or restricted by reference to any contract term: s6(2) UCTA 1977.

The 'no statement' provisions in two of the clauses are somewhat puzzling. They are presumably intended to exclude liability for misrepresentation. But there does not appear to have been any representation apart from the 'tip top condition' notice which it has already been decided was mere sales talk. In any event, by virtue of s3 Misrepresentation Act 1967 (as amended by s8 UCTA 1977) the exclusion of liability for misrepresentation would have no effect unless it satisfied the requirement of reasonableness set out in s11(1) UCTA 1977. It is submitted that the 'no statement' provisions would not satisfy this requirement because they purported to exclude all forms of misrepresentation, including fraudulent misrepresentation: *Thomas Witter Ltd* v *TBP Industries Ltd* (1996).

The exclusion clauses would also be regarded as unfair terms under the Unfair Terms in Consumer Contracts Regulations 1999, but this does not take the matter any further.

Therefore S has a claim in respect of the loss of the car.

It remains to consider the position of S's wife. She was a third party, and therefore has no claim in contract against R. There is nothing to suggest that S was acting as her agent.

Does S have any claim in respect of this wife's injuries and loss of wages? It appears not. In *Woodar Investment Development Ltd* v *Wimpey Construction (UK) Ltd* (1980) the House of Lords held that the contracting party could not sue for the third party's loss, disapproving Lord Denning's view in *Jackson* v *Horizon Holidays Ltd* (1975).

(Note: This position is not changed by the Contracts (Rights of Third Parties) Act 1999.)

SUGGESTED ANSWER TO QUESTION THREE

General Comment

A problem question requiring consideration of whether the exclusion clauses have been properly incorporated, cover the loss in issue and whether they fall foul of statutory requirements.

Key Points

- The assumption that the clauses are incorporated in the contract
- The type of contract concluded and the nature of the possible breaches of contract
- The validity of the clauses under the Unfair Contract Terms Act (UCTA) 1977 and under the Unfair Terms in Consumer Contracts Regulations 1994, as amended by the Unfair Terms in Consumer Contracts Regulations 1999

Suggested Answer

We are informed that the sales note contained the clauses; it can be assumed, therefore, that the contract incorporated the clauses, and therefore no further discussion is required on this point.

As the contract is clearly one for the sale of goods, consideration must be given to the possible breaches of the terms implied by the Sale of Goods Act (SGA) 1979, as amended by the Sale and Supply of Goods Act (SSGA) 1994.

It appears that the collapse of the saddle was due to the dimensions of the machine being totally unsuitable for a person of Hugh's height and build. Under s14(2) SGA 1979, where the seller sells goods in the course of business, there is an implied term (a condition in England, Wales and Northern Ireland) that the goods are of satisfactory quality. As the seller here does sell in the course of business the section applies. As the defect in the saddle could not have been discovered on examination the limitation provided by s14(2C)(b) does not apply.

'Satisfactory quality' is defined in s14(2A), and aspects of quality are set out in s14(2B). Goods are now required to be fit for all the purposes for which they are commonly supplied: s14(2B)(a). Prior to the amendment it might have been possible to argue that goods were of merchantable quality if they were fit for one of those purposes.

But it is submitted that the defect would now fall within the amended provision. Section 14(2B) now also provides that aspects of quality include freedom from minor defects (s14(2B)(c)) and safety (s14(2B)(d)). It is further submitted, therefore, that the machine was not of satisfactory quality.

A further relevant provision in the Act must be considered. Under s14(3) where the buyer, expressly or by implication makes known to the seller any particular purpose for which the goods are being bought, there is an implied term (condition) that the goods are reasonably fit for that purpose. It is at least highly probable that the seller must have been aware of Hugh's height and build and was, therefore, impliedly made aware of the particular purpose. Thus the seller is also in breach of s14(3).

Brief mention must be made of the applicability of the exclusion clauses. It is settled law that the question whether such clauses are applicable, at common law, where there is a fundamental breach of contract (as in the present problem), is one of the true construction of the contract: *Suisse Atlantique Société d'Armament Maritime SA* v *NV Rotterdamsche Kolen Centrale* (1967); *Photo Production Ltd* v *Securicor Transport Ltd* (1980); *George Mitchell (Chesterhall) Ltd* v *Finney Lock Seeds Ltd* (1983). As a matter of construction, there appears to be no doubt but that clauses 11 and 13 are applicable at common law. The applicability of clause 12 is more questionable, and this is dealt with below.

The validity of the clauses under the Unfair Contract Terms Act (UCTA) 1977 must now be considered. In the first position presented Hugh is 'dealing as a consumer' as defined in s12 UCTA 1977; he did not make the contract in the course of a business - the seller did - and the goods are of a type ordinarily supplied for private use. In this situation liability for breach of s14 SGA 1979 cannot be excluded and the clauses are, in consequence, totally ineffective: s6(2)(a) UCTA 1977. The recent case of *Paragon Finance plc* v *Nash* (2001) lends support to this contention.

The exclusion of liability for injury contained in clause 11 might also be affected by s2(1) UCTA 1977. This is also discussed below.

As the clauses are ineffective under UCTA 1977 it is unnecessary to consider in detail the provisions of the Unfair Terms in Consumer Contracts Regulations 1994, save to state that they would also have the effect of rendering the clauses ineffective.

It follows that Hugh has an action against the seller, Steve, for breach of contract. His remedy would lie in damages for his personal injury. It appears that Hugh might have been deemed to accept the goods under s35 SGA 1979 but I do not have sufficient information in this regard. If he has not accepted the goods he would be entitled to reject them; if acceptance is deemed he would be confined to an action for damages for breach of warranty.

I am also asked to consider the position if Hugh had bought the machine for the purpose of his profession as a professional athlete. In this situation he would not have been dealing as a consumer, and in that context I shall consider each of the clauses in turn.

Clause 11

As previously indicated this clause would be ineffective under s2(1) UCTA 1977, whether or not Hugh was dealing as a consumer, if the defect in the machine could be attributed to the negligence of the seller. But there is no clear indication that this was so, although it might be suggested that Steve, in telling Hugh that there was nothing to worry about after the complaint, was, or should have been, aware of the defect, and was thus guilty of negligence. This is no more than a supposition and, on the information before me, cannot be pursued further.

If Hugh were dealing in the course of business (which includes profession: s14 UCTA 1977), the relevant provision of that Act is s6(3). This provides that a term excluding liability for breach of s14 SGA 1979 can only be excluded in so far as the term satisfies the requirement of reasonableness. The requirement of reasonableness is set out in s11 UCTA 1977, as read with Schedule 2 to that Act.

I submit that a clause which purports to exclude liability for loss or injury caused by defects would not pass the reasonableness test. The rigour with which the courts have applied the test is revealed in the judgments in *George Mitchell (Chesterhall) Ltd* v *Finney Lock Seeds* (above), *Smith* v *Eric S Bush* (1990) and *St Albans City and District Council* v *International Computers Ltd* (1996).

Clause 12

In so far as this clause purports to exclude liability for breach of s14(3) SGA 1979, the implied term of fitness for a particular purpose, it might well be deemed to meet the requirement of reasonableness. I would submit, however, that as a matter of construction it does not apply to a breach of s14(2) (satisfactory quality), and, if it does, it fails to meet that requirement.

Clause 13

This clause imposes a condition on the acceptance of liability. A relevant factor is whether compliance with that condition would be practicable - Schedule 2, para (d), UCTA 1977. On completely different facts, compliance with a time limit of three days imposed in *R W Green Ltd* v *Cade Bros Farms* (1978) was held not to be practicable. That decision has little bearing on the present problem and a time limit of six weeks might well be regarded as reasonable.

As, however, the seller cannot rely on clauses 11 and 12, Hugh would be entitled to the same remedies as mentioned above, even if he were not dealing as a consumer.

It remains to note that in this situation the Unfair Terms in Consumer Contracts Regulations would not apply.

SUGGESTED ANSWER TO QUESTION FOUR

General Comment

Yet another problem question that requires candidates to look at issues of incorporation and construction of exclusion clauses before being declared valid. Enforceability, of course, also depends on the statutory requirements being satisfied in addition to common law.

Key Points

- The effect of the exclusion clauses at common law

- The validity of the clauses under the Unfair Contract Terms Act 1977
- The validity of the clauses under the Unfair Terms in Consumer Contracts Regulations 1999
- The position in relation to the contract of F's daughter and the other members of his family
- The recoverability of damages for the fright occasioned to F's family and for the mental illness of his daughter

Suggested Answer

At common law for an exclusion clause to be effective it must be incorporated into the contract and the clause must cover the breach. If it is effective at common law, its validity must be examined under the provisions of the Unfair Contract Terms Act 1977. It is not necessary here to discuss incorporation as the problem states that the contract contains the clauses.

The contract is one of sale of goods. It is not stated whether or not G sold the boat in the course of a business. If he did, the fact that the boat was not seaworthy means that there were breaches of the implied terms (conditions in England, Wales and Northern Ireland) that the boat was of satisfactory quality under s14(2) of the Sale of Goods Act 1979 (as amended), and that it was fit for the purpose for which it was bought under s14(3) of the same Act. If G were a private seller these sections would not apply. However it is submitted that, at common law, a term must be implied into the contract that the boat was seaworthy, and that the implication would pass the 'officious bystander' test propounded by MacKinnon LJ in ***Shirlaw* v *Southern Foundries* (1926) *Ltd*** (1939).

The next question to be considered is whether the exclusion clauses cover the breach. The law on this point is set out in the trilogy of House of Lords' decisions in ***Suisse Atlantique Société d'Armament Maritime SA* v *NV Rotterdamsche Kolen Centrale*** (1967); ***Photo Production Ltd* v *Securicor Transport Ltd*** (1980); and ***George Mitchell (Chesterhall) Ltd* v *Finney Lock Seeds Ltd*** (1983). The principle that has been established is that whether an exclusion clause is applicable where there has been a fundamental breach of contract is one of the true construction of the contract.

Was the fact that the boat was not seaworthy a fundamental breach of contract? I am inclined to the view that there was a fundamental breach of contract, but in the absence of further information as to the condition of the boat and as to other relevant circumstances it is difficult to give a more definite answer. In any event it is submitted that the clauses, in particular clause (10) of the agreement, would cover the breach, even if it were fundamental.

One has next to consider the validity of the clauses under the Unfair Contract Terms Act (UCTA) 1977. The two possibilities have to dealt with: (1) that G was selling in the course of a business; and (2) that G was a private seller.

If G sold the boat in the course of a business then, as previously stated, the statutory implied terms would apply. As it can be assumed that F was dealing as a consumer, then by virtue of s6(2) UCTA 1977, the exclusion clauses would be totally ineffective. There having been breaches of conditions of the contract, F would be entitled to return the boat and recover the purchase price.

If G sold the boat as a private seller then, as the statutory implied terms would not be applicable, s6 would not afford F any protection. Nor could s3 UCTA 1977 be invoked, as that section would operate only if G were dealing in the course of a business. It should be noted that the Unfair Terms in Consumer Contracts Regulations would also not apply as reg 2(1) defines a seller as one who 'is acting for purposes relating to his business'. If G acted as a private seller, therefore, F would have no redress.

It also appears from the facts presented that members of F's family were seriously frightened and that F's 14-year-old daughter suffered mental illness. Whether they have contractual rights against G depends on two factors: (1) were they parties to the contract?; and (2) are damages recoverable for their distress?

In the light of *Jackson* v *Horizon Holidays Ltd* (1975), as explained by Lord Wilberforce in *Woodar Investment Development Ltd* v *Wimpey Construction (UK) Ltd* (1980), it could be argued that F, his daughter and the other members of his family were all parties to the contract or, alternatively, that any recoverable loss suffered by his family was also F's loss.

The next question is whether the fright sustained by the family and the mental illness suffered by F's daughter can be compensated by an award of damages. I must consider the circumstances in which damages for distress can be recovered.

The general rule is that damages are not recoverable for mental distress in an action for breach of contract: *Addis* v *Gramophone Co Ltd* (1909). However, in *Watts* v *Morrow* (1991) Bingham LJ stated as follows:

> 'But the rule is not absolute. Where the very object of a contract is to provide pleasure, relaxation, peace of mind ... damages will be awarded if the fruit of the contract is not provided or if the contrary result is procured instead.'

It follows that damages could be recoverable for the distress suffered by F's family. This, however, depends on whether the exclusion clauses are operative. If liability for breach of contract has been effectively excluded (if G were a private seller) then no liability can arise for the mental distress. Such liability could only arise if the exclusion clauses were held to be ineffective.

Lastly, I am asked to consider if my advice would be different if the boat had sunk.

I can only suggest possibilities. It may be that the sinking of the boat would be of such a serious, fundamental nature that the exclusion clauses could not be construed as covering the breach of contract. In this event G would incur liability for breach, even if he were a private seller. It may also be that the sinking of the boat would deprive F of the right to return it, and he would have to seek redress in damages.

6

Capacity

Introduction

This chapter is concerned with categories of persons who are deemed not to have full contractual capacity. The law views them as requiring protection, for consent with full knowledge and understanding is a prerequisite of any contract under English law and, because of specific characteristics, such persons may have entered the contract without sufficient understanding of the obligations which they were incurring.

The most popular topic for examination questions is the incapacity of minors (persons under 18 years of age). The Minors' Contracts Act 1987 is relevant in this respect. However, there are also special rules for persons who drink, mentally disordered persons and corporations. A recent case involving corporations was decided in the Court of Appeal: *Braymist Ltd* v *Wise Finance Co Ltd* (2002). See also *OTV Birwelco Ltd* v *Technical and General Guarantee Co Ltd* (2002).

Questions

INTERROGRAMS

1. How does statute now define 'necessaries' and does that definition differ in any way from earlier common law definitions?
2. What limitations does the law place on the capacity of a corporation to enter into a contract?
3. Why should one beware when making a contract with a person who may be drunk or mentally disordered?

QUESTION ONE

F was a prostitute who had just moved to London where she was not known. She leased a flat in a fashionable part of town from E, agreeing to pay £1,000 a week rent. E did not know that F was a prostitute: he guessed that she must either be a very highly paid executive or a prostitute, but he was not sure which. F arranged for G to refurbish the flat for £28,000: this included £12,000 for a luxurious bed. F bought food and wine from H which cost £4,500. F bought a large car with a specially constructed rear seat from J. J did not know that F was a prostitute, though the request for a large back seat was unusual. F has paid for none of these items. K paid £12,000 in advance for 48 'love sessions' at £250 each. After four sessions F refused either to perform with K or return his money.

Advise F. What difference, if any, would it make to your advice if F was only 17 years old?

University of London LLB Examination
(for external students) Elements of the Law of Contract June 1998 Q4

QUESTION TWO

Simon is seventeen. He lives in an isolated village and has recently been offered a job as a sales assistant in the nearest town, which is 15 miles from the village. As there is no bus service, he agreed to buy a used car from Finan Motors for £500. Two days later he discovered that he would be able to get a lift to work from a friend. He then told Finan Motors that he no longer needed the car and would not collect it or pay for it.

Simon also bought a personal stereo and a set of golf clubs from General Trading plc. He has paid for the stereo but not the clubs. Because of a fault the stereo has damaged an irreplaceable tape of great sentimental value.

Consider Simon's rights and liabilities in respect of the car, the stereo and the golf clubs.

University of London LLB Examination
(for external students) Elements of the Law of Contract June 1988 Q6

QUESTION THREE

G, aged 16 years, was left an orphan by a car crash which killed his parents. He took an evening job as a delivery boy at his local supermarket to supplement his income. He was owed sixteen weeks' wages amounting to £800 but the supermarket failed to pay. He arranged with Dr Manieri to have weekly piano lessons for six months at £50 per lesson. G was determined to complete his studies as he envisaged becoming a professional piano-player when he completed his education. After two lessons G decided that he did not want any more lessons and wrote to Dr Manieri to this effect. He arranged with his bank manager to borrow £15,000 till his parents' estates had been settled. He was to repay this loan at a rate of £500 per month. After two months he failed to keep up his payments. He had spent £5,000 on a piano. Also, he owed a bookmaker £300. When the estates of his parents were calculated it was found that as a result of debts there was no inheritance for G.

Advise G.

University of London LLB Examination
(for external students) Elements of the Law of Contract June 1994 Q3

QUESTION FOUR

Consider the rights and liabilities of Jason, who is 17, in respect of the following transactions:

i) he bought a pair of gold cufflinks costing £200 from Harold, but has not paid for them;
ii) he has bought an exercise bicycle from Kenneth and paid for it, but has now decided that exercise is a waste of time and wants to have his money back;
iii) he agreed to work as an assistant in Simon's shop but left after one week because the hours were too long. The contract with Simon provided that it could only be terminated by six months' notice on either side.

University of London LLB Examination
(for external students) Elements of the Law of Contract June 1990 Q7

Answers

ANSWERS TO INTERROGRAMS

1. Earlier definitions in case law were not substantially different. Necessary goods were defined in *Peters* v *Fleming* (1840) as: 'such articles as are fit to maintain the particular person in the state, station and degree … in which he is'. The substitution of 'condition' and 'actual requirements' does little to improve the rather vague and feudalistic definition.

   There is a paucity of modern authority as to the nature of necessaries. In *Peters* v *Fleming* itself, jewellery supplied to the son of a wealthy man was found to be necessaries, but in *Ryder* v *Wombwell* (1869) the court set aside the verdict of a jury that similar items were necessaries. In *Nash* v *Inman* (1908), 11 fancy waistcoats were considered 'necessaries' in relation to an undergraduate. It is, perhaps, doubtful whether these authorities could provide much guidance in the present day.

   It must first be shown that the class into which the goods fall is capable of being 'necessary' and then that the goods supplied were actually necessary at the time of the contract. It is generally considered that services as well as goods are capable of being necessaries (see Treitel, *Law of Contract*).

2. For many decades, the ultra vires rule applied to corporations. This stated that a company could not enter into any contract which was not envisaged in the objects written into its memorandum of association. If it attempted to do so, the contract was void: *Ashbury Railway Carriage and Iron Co* v *Riche* (1875). The rule also prohibited using a power which the company was given in its memorandum for an object which it was not (eg the borrowing of money (a power) for the purpose of pig farming (an object) in *Re Introductions Ltd* (1970)). The reasoning behind the strict application of the rule is that a company must register its memorandum of association at Companies House and so its contractual capacity is available for everyone to see. The ultra vires rule still exists but its practical effects have been all but extinguished by the provisions of the Companies Act 1985.

   Prior to this enactment, companies sought to give themselves greater contractual capacity by drafting the objects clause in their memorandum in the widest possible terms. The court also helped to soften the harshness of the rule as it applied to innocent third parties who might find that they had no redress against a company which reneged on its contractual obligations. (See, for example, *Rolled Steel Products* v *BSC* (1984).)

   Section 35 of the Companies Act 1985 provides that where a company enters into an ultra vires contract the innocent third party is not affected by the lack of capacity and can enforce the contract as if the company had that capacity. Instead the fault shifts to the directors, who may be sued by the company. Section 35 does not, however, protect the company itself.

3. The contractual capacity of both drunken persons and mentally disordered persons is less than for others. This is because their ability to freely consent to their obligations under the contract has been impaired.

   If one party was so drunk as not to be able to understand the transaction and the other party knew of this, the court may set the transaction aside. However, the drunken party may ratify the contract when sober. Further, even if the contract falls within this category, the drunken person is still liable to pay a reasonable prices for 'necessaries'.

Section 3(3) Sale of Goods Act 1979 defines necessary goods as goods 'suitable to the condition in life of the ... person ... and to his actual requirements at the time of the sale and delivery.' It is thought that necessary services must also be paid for.

There are two categories of mentally disordered person:

a) a person who has been certified under the Mental Health Act 1983, Part IV as being incapable of dealing with his property. Such persons are unable to dispose of their property and the court has control of it, although day-to-day management is usually carried out by a relative.
b) a person who has not so been certified.

As regards category (b), the contract may be set aside if the party did not understand the transaction by reason of his disorder and the other party knew of the disorder.

As with drunkards, the mentally disordered person may ratify the contract should the disorder cease temporarily or permanently. Also he will be liable to pay a reasonable price for necessaries.

SUGGESTED ANSWER TO QUESTION ONE

General Comment

This question is mainly on the area of illegal contracts, in particular the enforcement of such contracts. The reference to the situation if F was only 17 years old requires some discussion of contracts entered into by minors.

Key Points

- Enforcement of an illegal contract by the guilty party and the innocent party - the application of the rules to E, G, H and J
- Recovery of property passed or money paid under an illegal contract - the application of the in pari delecto rule to G and J and as between F and K
- Consideration of the effect of the above contracts if F was a minor: whether any of the contracts are for the supply of necessaries - whether G and J can obtain restitution under s3(1) Minors' Contracts Act 1987

Suggested Answer

The general rule is that a guilty party cannot enforce an illegal contract, the innocent party may be able to do so. With regard to the recovery of money paid or property passed under an illegal contract the general rule is that recovery is not possible - in pari delicto potior est conditio defendentis: to this rule there are a number of exceptions.

I shall consider these rules in relation to each of the parties involved.

The contract with E

A contract with a prostitute would be illegal as one promoting sexual immorality and therefore contrary to public policy. Thus, in *Pearce* v *Brooks* (1866) a contract to hire out a brougham to a prostitute for the use in her profession was held to be illegal, and the owner was not entitled to enforce. Here, however, the court stressed that the owner of the brougham knew of the use to which it was to be put. This case might be distinguishable from the lease with E. He might have suspected that F was a prostitute, but it is questionable whether mere suspicion, as distinct from certain knowledge, is sufficient to deny him a remedy. Nor is it entirely clear that he knew, or should have known, the use to which the flat would be put. A contract to let a room to a prostitute who practised her profession elsewhere was held to be valid 'because persons of that description must have a place to lay their heads': *Appleton* v *Campbell* (1826). It is also possible that the courts in this more permissive age might adopt a less censorious attitude to sexual immorality than they did in Victorian times. In *Armhouse Lee Ltd* v *Chappell* (1996) the Court of Appeal held that promotional material for telephone sex lines was not so immoral that the courts would decline to enforce the payments for the advertisements.

I conclude therefore, although not without some doubt, that E would be able to enforce the lease.

The contract with G

Here it appears that G is entirely innocent of any question of illegality. There is no suggestion that he was, or should have been, aware of the purpose to which F might put the flat. '£12,000 for a luxurious bed' does not necessarily have a sinister connotation. That being so, G is entitled to enforce the contract: *Archbolds (Freightage) Ltd* v *S Spanglett Ltd* (1961). Even if G is deemed to have constructive notice that F was a prostitute and was using the flat for that purpose, he would be entitled to recover possession of the bed under the exception to the pari delicto rule whereby recovery will be allowed where no reliance is placed on the illegal contract: *Bowmakers Ltd* v *Barnet Instruments Ltd* (1945).

The contract with H

H, again it appears an innocent party, can enforce the contract.

The contract with J

The suggestion here is that, although J did not know that F was a prostitute, the request for a specially constructed large back seat was so unusual as to put him on inquiry. If it appears that his suspicions were aroused, but that he deliberately chose to ignore them, he may well have forfeited the right to be deemed an innocent party. In this even he could not enforce the contract: *Pearce* v *Brooks* (above). Whether or not he is deemed innocent of the illegality, recovery of the car would be permitted for the reasons set out in relation to the contract with G.

The contract with K

A further exception to the in pari delicto rule is that a plaintiff is entitled to recover a payment made under an illegal contract if he repudiates the illegal purpose in time. The payer has a locus poenitentiae and may withdraw from the illegal contract and recover the payment he has made. Can K avail himself of this? There are two important qualifications to this entitlement. First, the repudiation must take place before the illegal purpose has been effected, as in *Taylor* v *Bowers* (1876), where recovery was allowed, but recovery will not be allowed when the repudiation takes place after performance of the illegal purpose has actually begun: *Kearley* v *Thomson* (1890). There is an element of doubt here. Genuine repentance is probably not required and whilst complete performance of the illegal purpose is a bar to recovery, apparently partial performance is not: *Tribe* v *Tribe* (1995). How partial the performance can be is uncertain.

Whilst there may be this suggestion of doubt as to whether the partial performance is a bar to recovery, the second qualification is fatal to K's claim: the repudiation must be voluntary; it must not be forced on the party claiming recovery by the other party's breach of contract: *Bigos* v *Bousted* (1951). This is precisely the situation here.

The situation if F was a minor

If F was only 17 years old she would have been a minor in law. A minor is only bound by contracts for necessary goods, defined in s3(3) Sale of Goods Act 1979 as 'goods suitable to the condition in life of the minor ... and to his actual requirements at the time of the sale and delivery.' There seems little doubt that the luxurious bed purchased from G, and the car purchased from J could not be regarded as necessaries. Payment for these items could not, therefore, be exacted from her. However, under s3(1) Minors' Contracts Act 1987 the court may require her to restore them to the respective parties.

With regard to the lease entered into with E, this falls within the category of contracts voidable at the instance of the minor. F could set aside this contract, provided she did so before attaining majority or within a reasonable time thereafter. By doing so she would avoid any further liability, but could not recover any payments made before that: *Steinberg* v *Scala (Leeds) Ltd* (1923).

SUGGESTED ANSWER TO QUESTION TWO

General Comment

This problem clearly concerns the contractual capacity of a minor. A good answer will analyse each of the transactions in turn and consider whether it is binding on Simon.

Key Points

The purchase of a secondhand car

- A minor is bound by a contract for necessaries: *Peters* v *Fleming* - s3(3) Sale of Goods Act 1979 - *Nash* v *Inman*
- It may be that he is only bound if he has actually been supplied with the goods: *Roberts* v *Gray*

The purchase of the stereo

- As it is not a necessary the infant is not bound but the other party is: *Bruce* v *Warwick*
- Liability under s14 Sale of Goods Act 1979

- Extent of damages: *Hadley* v *Baxendale* (1854) – *H Parsons (Livestock) Ltd* v *Uttley Ingham & Co Ltd* – *Bliss* v *South East Thames Regional Health Authority*

The purchase of the golf clubs

- Not necessaries but Simon may be forced to return them: s3(1) Minors Contract Act 1987

Suggested Answer

This question requires discussion of the contractual capacity of minors.

Simon, a minor, has entered into three contracts: first, for the purchase of a secondhand car; second, for the purchase of a personal stereo; and, third, for a set of golf clubs. It is necessary to examine each of these contracts in turn.

The purchase of a secondhand car

A minor is bound by a contract for necessary goods. Necessary goods were defined in the common law as 'such articles as are fit to maintain the particular person in the state, station and degree ... in which he is': *Peters* v *Fleming* (1840). Section 3(3) of the Sale of Goods Act 1979 defines necessaries as 'goods suitable to the condition in life of the minor ... and to his actual requirements at the time of the sale and delivery.' The onus would be on Finan Motors to prove that the car was not only capable of being a necessary but was so in Simon's particular case: *Nash* v *Inman* (1908).

There seems little doubt, in the circumstances, that the car is a necessary. If the car had actually been delivered to Simon he would be bound by the contract. However, Simon has repudiated the contract before the car has been delivered to him and the question is: can the minor be held to an executory contract? This question has not been finally resolved. In *Nash* v *Inman* Fletcher-Moulton LJ held that the minor was liable re, because he had been supplied, and not consensu, because he had contracted. His Lordship held further that a minor was incapable of contracting, and that the law only imposed an obligation upon him to pay if the necessaries had actually been delivered to him.

In the same case, however, Buckley LJ held that a contract for necessaries was one that a minor could make. He held that a minor had a limited capacity to contract. The contention that a minor is only bound if the goods have actually been delivered to him is also supported by the definition of necessaries in the Sale of Goods Act quoted above. Under s3(2) of the same Act the minor is only obliged to pay a reasonable price for the necessaries, which may not be the contract price.

These statutory definitions suggest that a minor is only bound if he has actually been supplied with the necessary goods, and that the minor would not be bound by an executory contract. However, there is authority to the contrary. In *Roberts* v *Gray* (1913) the defendant, who was a minor, desired to become a professional billiard player and made a contract with Roberts under which the parties agreed to accompany each other on a world tour and to play matches together. Roberts expended a great deal of time and trouble and incurred certain liabilities in the course of preparing for the contract. Gray repudiated the contract while it was still largely executory and Roberts obtained damages for breach of contract. In the Court of Appeal Hamilton LJ said:

> 'I am unable to appreciate why a contract which is in itself binding, because it is a contract for necessaries ..., can cease to be binding merely because it is executory ... If the contract is binding at all it must be binding for all such remedies as are appropriate of it.'

In Cheshire, Fifoot & Furmston's *Law of Contract* it is observed that the contract in *Roberts* v *Gray* (1913) was more closely analogous to beneficial contracts of service, which are binding even though not completely executed. It is also observed that all the authorities relied upon by the court in *Roberts* v *Gray* concern beneficial contracts of service. Treitel has the view that it is difficult to justify the distinction between necessary goods and beneficial contracts of service. Treitel considers that the reasons for holding a minor liable and for limiting his liability are the same in both cases.

The position is therefore still open to argument. However it is submitted that Treitel's view is the better one. If that is so, Simon would be bound by the contract and therefore liable in damages to Finan Motors for breach of contract. It is clear that the suppliers could not obtain an order for specific performance against him.

The purchase of the stereo

It seems clear that the stereo is not a necessary. Whilst Simon, therefore, would not be bound by the contract the other party, General Trading plc, is bound by the contract: *Bruce* v *Warwick* (1815). General Trading plc appear to be in breach of contract. More particularly they are in breach of s14(2) of the Sale of Goods Act – the implied condition that the goods supplied under the contract are of satisfactory quality. (The provision in the Infants Relief Act 1874 which made certain contracts with minors 'absolutely void' has now been repealed by the Minors Contract Act 1987.) General Trading plc are therefore liable in damages to Simon. They would therefore be liable for the cost of the tape that has been damaged: such damage would be reasonably foreseeable: see *Hadley* v *Baxendale* (1854). We are informed that the tape was of great sentimental value. Whether this would increase the damages available to Simon is however doubtful. It is not immediately apparent that such increased damages would have been reasonably foreseeable. It could be argued, though, that as General Trading plc could have foreseen the kind of damage, they are not absolved from liability merely because they could not foresee the extent of the damage: *H Parsons (Livestock) Ltd* v *Uttley Ingham & Co Ltd* (1978). It is also possible that Simon's claim for the loss of an article of sentimental value is closely akin to claiming damages for distress. In *Bliss* v *South East Thames Regional Health Authority* (1987) Dillon J stated that damages for distress were limited to cases

> '... where the contract which has been broken was itself a contract to provide peace of mind or freedom from distress.'

A similar view was taken by the Court of Appeal in *Hayes* v *James & Charles Dodd* (1990). It does not appear that the purchase of the stereo was such a contract and that therefore a claim in respect of the sentimental value of the tape could not be supported, as the damages would be too remote.

As the contract for the stereo has already been performed Simon cannot recover the money he paid for it: *Corpe* v *Overston* (1833).

The purchase of the golf clubs

It seems clear that the golf clubs are not necessaries. The supplier cannot therefore claim either the contract price or a reasonable price from Simon. Simon can, however, be held liable to restore the golf clubs to General Trading plc. Such liability was imposed in equity before the Minors Contract Act 1987. Section 3(1) of the Act now gives the court a discretion to order the minor to transfer to the adult party any property acquired by the minor under a contract which was not enforceable against him. There seems to be no reason why the court would not exercise its discretion in favour of General Trading plc and order Simon to transfer the golf clubs back to them.

SUGGESTED ANSWER TO QUESTION THREE

General Comment

A further problem concerning the enforceability of contracts entered into by a minor, this is a fairly complex question and requires separation out into three contracts. Once this has been done, it is quite straightforward and may be tackled with confidence.

Key Points

- Meaning of minor: s1 Family Law Reform Act 1969

The contract with the supermarket

- The supermarket is bound by the contract
- The minor cannot claim specific performance but can claim for an agreed sum: *Flight* v *Boland* (1828)

The contract with Dr Manieri

- Minors are bound by contracts for necessaries
- Definition of 'necessaries': *Chapple* v *Cooper* – *Peters* v *Fleming* – *Nash* v *Inman* – s3(3) Sale of Goods Act 1979
- The minor may not be bound if the contract is executory only: *Roberts* v *Gray*

The loan from the bank

- A minor is not liable on a loan contract even if to purchase necessaries: *Darby* v *Boucher*
- If he has purchased necessaries, the lender may be able to recover the part of the loan used for that purpose: *Marlow* v *Pitfield* – *Re National Permanent Benefit Building Society*
- The piano could be a necessary: s3(3) Sale of Goods Act 1979
- Even if the loan was obtained by misrepresentation, the bank could not sue: *R Leslie Ltd* v *Sheill*
- Payments made to the bank cannot be recovered: *Corpe* v *Overston*

The debt to the bookmaker

- Such debts are unenforceable whether against a minor or adult

Suggested Answer

G, being aged 16 years, is a minor in law: the age of majority is 18 years: s1 Family Law Reform Act 1969. The purpose of the law with regard to minors' contracts is to prevent minors from incurring liability for imprudent bargains because of their inexperience, but also to avoid causing hardship to adults who deal with minors in good faith. Certain contracts are binding on minors; contracts for necessary goods and services; and contracts of service, if for the benefit of the minor as a whole. Certain contracts are voidable at the instance of the minor, but these are not relevant to this problem. Even if a minor is not bound by a contract, the other party may be bound and the contract may have other effects.

The contract with the supermarket

G entered into a service contract with the supermarket. It is not necessary to discuss whether or not G was bound by that contract; in either event the supermarket is bound. Where a contract is not binding on the minor, but is binding on the other party, the minor's remedies are limited in that he cannot claim specific performance: *Flight* v *Boland* (1828). G's claim is, however, for the payment of an agreed sum; whilst it is a claim for the specific performance of the supermarket's obligation to pay the agreed wages, as it is simply a claim for money it is not subject to the restrictions which equity imposes on the enforcement of specific performance. Accordingly, G can claim the £800 owing to him.

The contract with Dr Manieri

Minors are bound by contracts for necessaries. Necessaries consist of necessary goods and necessary services; such services include education of either a liberal or a vocational nature: *Chapple* v *Cooper* (1844). Necessaries are defined in relation to goods as 'such articles as are fit to maintain the particular person in the state, station and degree ... in which he is': *Peters* v *Fleming* (1840). According to Treitel any service can be necessary if it satisfies the test in relation to necessary goods. As G is intent on becoming a professional piano-player it would appear that the piano lessons do fall within the category of necessary services. The question is, however, whether G is bound by an executory contract for these services. It is still a matter for dispute whether a minor is bound by an executory contract for necessary goods: see the differing views of Fletcher Moulton J and Buckley J in *Nash* v *Inman* (1908). The definition of necessary goods in s3(3) Sale of Goods Act 1979 suggests that goods can only be necessaries when they have been actually delivered; a minor would not be bound by an executory contract for such goods. On the authority of *Roberts* v *Gray* (1913), however, it is submitted that so far as necessary services are concerned a minor is bound by the contract for such services even though it is partly executory. G can, therefore, be held liable in damages to Dr Manieri.

The loan from the bank

A minor cannot be made liable on a loan, nor can he be made liable on a loan advanced to enable him to purchase necessaries: *Darby* v *Boucher* (1694). Where the minor has actually used a portion of the loan to discharge his liability for necessaries supplied to him, the lender can in equity recover that portion of the loan used for that purpose: *Marlow* v *Pitfield* (1719); *Re National Permanent Benefit Building Society* (1869). It appears that G has purchased, and paid for, a piano for the sum of £5,000 from the proceeds of the loan. Was the piano a necessary? This question is not without difficulty.

In s53(3) Sale of Goods Act 1979 necessaries are defined as 'goods suitable to the condition in life of the minor … and to his actual requirements at the time of sale and delivery.' In view of his ambition to become a professional piano-player, a piano might well be regarded as a necessary. What is questionable is whether an apparently expensive instrument, one costing £5,000, could be suitable to G's 'condition in life' and to 'his actual requirements at the time of sale and delivery'. At the time G obtained the loan from the bank, and presumably when he purchased the piano, G apparently believed that he was to receive a substantial inheritance – a belief that proved to be ill-founded. If the piano could be considered a necessary then the bank could recover the £5,000 expended on it. It is, however, arguable that, even if at the time of purchase G was potentially wealthy, a piano costing £5,000 was not suitable to the condition in life of a minor then having to supplement his income by working as a delivery boy; nor, at the commencement of his piano studies, was it suitable to his actual requirements.

There is the possible suggestion in the question that G may have misrepresented the position with regard to his parents' estate to the bank, perhaps fraudulently. Even if this were so the bank would not be able to sue G in tort for recovery of the loan made to him. To allow the bank to do so would be an indirect method of enforcing the invalid contract: *R Leslie Ltd* v *Sheill* (1914).

In conclusion, the bank can probably neither recover the loan, nor can it recover the £5,000 as expenditure made on a necessary. However, the bank is not without a remedy. Under s53(1) Minors' Contracts Act 1987 the court 'may, if it is just and equitable to do so, require (G) to transfer to the (bank) any property acquired by (G) under the contract, or any property representing it'. By virtue of this provision the bank may be able to obtain an order for the transfer of the piano to them.

It remains to note that, although G is not bound by the contract of loan, he cannot recover any payments he has made to the bank: *Corpe* v *Overston* (1833).

The debt to the bookmaker

There is no question of G being held liable for this debt as gambling contracts are unenforceable no matter who the parties are.

SUGGESTED ANSWER TO QUESTION FOUR

General Comment

This problem question on the enforceability of contracts made by a minor is neatly divided into three straightforward parts. It should be easily tackled by any candidate with a good knowledge of the topic.

Key Points

The purchase of the cufflinks

- A minor is bound by a contract for necessary goods: *Peters* v *Fleming* - s3(3) Sale of Goods Act 1979 - *Ryder* v *Wombwell* - *Nash* v *Inman*
- If the cufflinks are not necessaries, the seller may be able to recover the goods: s3(1) Minors' Contracts Act 1987

The purchase of the exercise bicycle from Kenneth

- A bicycle may be a necessary: *Clyde Cycle Co* v *Hargreaves*
- If not a necessary, Jason will not be able to recover the money paid: *Wilson* v *Kearse* - *Corpe* v *Overston* - *Ex parte Taylor*

The contract to work for Simon

- A minor is bound by beneficial contracts of service: *Clements* v *L & N W Ry* - *Doyle* v *White City Stadium Ltd* - *De Francesco* v *Barnum*
- Specific performance may not be awarded against Jason: s16 Trade Union and Labour Relations Act 1974

Suggested Answer

Jason, being under the age of 18, is a minor in law - s1 Family Law Reform Act 1969. This question, therefore, raises the issue of the contractual capacity of minors. Jason has entered into three contracts: (i) the purchase of the cufflinks from Harold; (ii) the purchase of the exercise bicycle from Kenneth; and (iii) the agreement to work as an assistant in Simon's shop. These three transactions will be considered in turn.

The purchase of the cufflinks

A minor is bound by a contract for necessary goods - described in *Peters* v *Fleming* (1840) as:

> '... such goods as are fit to maintain the particular person in the state, station and degree ... in which he is.'

Section 3(3) Sale of Goods Act 1979 defines 'necessaries' as:

> '... goods suitable to the condition in life of the minor ... and to his actual requirements at the time of the sale and delivery.'

There is a paucity of modern authority as to the nature of necessaries. In *Peters* v *Fleming* jewellery supplied to the son of a wealthy man were found to be necessaries, but in *Ryder* v *Wombwell* (1869) the court set aside the verdict of a jury that similar items were necessaries. It is, perhaps, doubtful whether these two mid-nineteenth-century cases can provide much guidance in the present day.

The onus is on Harold to show that the cufflinks were necessaries. He would have to prove not only that they were capable of being necessaries, but that they actually were necessaries in Jason's case: *Nash* v *Inman* (1908). It seems unlikely that Harold could discharge this onus - it is difficult to conceive that gold cufflinks costing £200 could be regarded as necessaries for a 17-year-old.

If they are not necessaries the contract is unenforceable against Jason. The purchase price cannot be recovered from him. However, Harold is not without a remedy. Equity provides the remedy of restitution where non-necessary goods were sold and transferred to a minor who was guilty of fraud. At common law restitution can also be ordered in certain cases of quasi-contract. This remedy is now also afforded by statute: s3(1) Minors' Contracts Act 1987 gives the court a discretion to order the minor to transfer to the plaintiff any property acquired by the minor under a contract which was not enforceable against him. There does not appear to be any reason why the court should not exercise its discretion in favour of Harold and order Jason to restore the cufflinks to him. The possibility should briefly be considered that, by virtue of Jason's particular circumstances, these articles are considered to be necessaries, although - as has been indicated - this is thought to be unlikely. If they are necessaries s3(2) Sale of Goods Act provides that the minor must pay a reasonable price for them. This may not be the contract price, but there is insufficient information to determine what it might be.

The purchase of the exercise bicycle from Kenneth

The question here again is whether this article can be considered to be a necessary. A helpful authority is, possibly, *Clyde Cycle Co* v *Hargreaves* (1898), which concerned the purchase of a racing bicycle by an apprentice. This was held to be a necessary. However, too much reliance should not be placed on that case. It is not conclusive with regard to the present problem; much depends on the price of the exercise bicycle and on Jason's particular requirements. Both possibilities must be considered: that the bicycle is not a necessary, and that it is. If it is not a necessary the contract would not be enforceable against Jason. But it appears that he has already paid for it. He cannot recover the money paid simply on the ground that he was not bound by the contract because of his minority. Treitel cites three authorities in support of this proposition: *Wilson* v *Kearse* (1800): *Corpe* v *Overston* (1883); and *Ex parte Taylor* (1856). The right to reject the goods and reclaim the purchase price would have to be based on grounds that were also available to an adult.

If the bicycle is a necessary then Jason is bound by the contract, subject to the aforestated provision in the Sale of Goods Act that he would have been required to pay only 'a reasonable price', not necessarily the contract price. But what a reasonable price might have been is of academic interest: he has made the payment and, as indicated by the above three authorities, once the minor has performed the contract, he cannot recover the money.

The contract to work for Simon

This is a contract of service, and the rule in this regard is that a minor is bound by beneficial contracts of service. The test is this: if the contract is to the minor's benefit as a whole, he will be bound by it, notwithstanding that it contains certain provisions that are to his disadvantage: *Clements* v *L & N W Railway* (1894); *Doyle* v *White City Stadium Ltd* (1935). He will not be bound by a service contract if it is on the whole harsh and oppressive: *De Francesco* v *Barnum* (1890). It is difficult to be certain whether or not Jason's contract with Simon would fall into the latter category. No information is given as to the hours of work, the other conditions of the employment and his remuneration. It is conceivable that the mere requirement of six months' notice from a minor performing a menial task would persuade the court that the contract is harsh and oppressive. In that event the contract would not be binding on Jason, and he would not incur any liability by leaving. Even if the contract is binding on Jason the remedy available to Simon is somewhat limited. He could not obtain an order which would have the effect of compelling Jason to return to work. The courts have long refused to order specific performance of contracts involving personal service, and such an order is prohibited by s16 Trade Union and Labour Relations Act 1974. Simon would be confined to a claim for damages for the breach of contract and, in view of the nature of the employment and the plaintiff's duty to mitigate his loss, such claim would only realise an extremely modest amount, and the damages might only be nominal.

7

Mistake

Introduction

Mistake is a topic which provides fertile ground for both problem questions, centring on the practical effects of a mistake, and discussion questions aimed at eliciting an analysis of the legal effects. It also combines well with other topics such as misrepresentation or, more rarely, offer and acceptance. This chapter provides examples of several types of question. This area features regularly in London Examinations.

The plethora of material on mistake derives from the classification of mistakes into distinct types and the treatment of the effect of a mistake differently at common law and in equity. This has given rise to abundant case law and fine distinctions.

For obvious reasons, there is no general principle that a mistake will nullify a contract. Candidates wishing to attempt a mistake question should therefore demonstrate a clear knowledge of the types of mistake which the law permits to affect a contract, and their respective effects, ie whether the contract is void or voidable in law and what the practical effects of that legal distinction are on the respective rights of the parties and any third party concerned. Some of the more important decisions affecting this doctrine include *Kleinwort Benson Ltd* v *Lincoln City Council* (1998), *Clarion Ltd* v *National Provident Institution* (2000) and, more recently, *Great Peace Shipping Ltd* v *Tsavliris Salvage (International) Ltd, The Great Peace* (2002).

Questions

INTERROGRAMS

1. Explain what is meant by a plea of non est factum.
2. Explain and comment upon the statement that a contract is not made void by a mistake as to the attributes of the other contracting party.
3. How does mistake affect the validity of a contract (if at all) when it leads to the parties being at cross purposes?

QUESTION ONE

'The present position where a party is mistaken about the identity of another contracting party is unsatisfactory.'

Discuss.

University of London LLB Examination
(for external students) Elements of the Law of Contract June 2001 Q7

QUESTION TWO

'When one or more parties to a contract are mistaken it is not always easy to advise about the remedies which are available.'

Discuss.

University of London LLB Examination
(for external students) Elements of the Law of Contract June 2000 Q2

QUESTION THREE

On Monday, R, agreed to sell her car to S for £6,000 after he had represented that he was the well known sports personality T. S asked R to accept a cheque but R refused. S produced an identification card with T's name on it below S's photograph. R rang up the number S gave and an accomplice answered and the accomplice misrepresented S's identity. R went to the library and checked that T lived at the address given.

R eventually allowed S to take the car in return for the cheque supposedly drawn on T's account. On Wednesday, it was dishonoured. On learning of this, R contacted the police and the local garages. On Thursday, S sold the car to X for £3,000. S cannot be traced.

Advise the parties

University of London LLB Examination
(for external students) Elements of the Law of Contract June 2000 Q7

QUESTION FOUR

A wrote to B offering to sell his car for £5,000. B assumed that A was referring to A's Austin car worth £6,000 whereas, in fact, A was referring to his Morris worth £4,500. B replied, 'I agree to buy it provided it is in good condition. I will be away from the UK for two weeks so I will not be able to come and see it but I will put a cheque in the post.' Two days later B sent a cheque for £5,000 to A. When B returned and came to collect the car from A's drive the mistake was discovered. B refused to take the Morris and A refused to return B's money. Two days later the Morris was taken from the drive and was written off by joyriders.

Advise the parties. What difference, if any, would it make to your advice if, instead of being taken by joyriders, the Morris car had a large number of minor defects?

University of London LLB Examination
(for external students) Elements of the Law of Contract June 1999 Q1

QUESTION FIVE

M, a well known antique dealer, offered a teapot with the label 'Gaudy Welsh' attached for £200. In fact, it was a Staffordshire piece and worth only £90.

M also offered for sale a cup and saucer which were on a shelf with other cups and saucers which were 'Gaudy Welsh' although M had not labelled the cup and saucer as such. N mistook it for a Gaudy Welsh cup and saucer, but it was in fact Torquay ware and worth only £10.

N bought the teapot for £200 and the cup and saucer for £78 cash.

A person calling himself O bought a tea service in 'bleeding heart' pattern for £1,000, paying by a cheque drawn on O's account. In fact, the purchaser was not O, but was a rogue who had stolen the cheque book from O's purse. The cheque was dishonoured; M told the police about this, and the next day the rogue sold the tea service to P for £650.

Advise M.

University of London LLB Examination
(for external students) Elements of the Law of Contract June 1998 Q5

QUESTION SIX

Advise H on the following:

a) G was engaged in 1994 as H's secretary on a five-year contract paid monthly. G is dishonest and has been systematically stealing from H for a number of years. H, who was unaware of G's dishonesty, decided to dispense with G's services and agreed to pay G £80,000. H has now discovered the facts and is demanding the return of the £80,000.
b) H bought a teapot from I's shop for £800 believing it to be a rare Delft teapot. I had not said anything about the pot. In fact, the pot was an excellent reproduction. At the time of the sale neither H nor I knew this. H wishes to recover the £800.
c) H bought a flat for £100,000 from J. Two years later H discovered that under a complex family settlement he beneficially owned the flat.
d) H bought a valuable picture which was known to be in the collection of Lord Kink from Lemon who was pretending to be Lord Kink. Lemon produced the receipt for the picture and a false passport containing Lemon's photograph which purported to be Lord Kink. H paid Lemon £100,000. A year later the real Lord Kink demanded the return of the painting and receipt which had been stolen by Lemon.

University of London LLB Examination
(for external students) Elements of the Law of Contract June 1997 Q7

QUESTION SEVEN

'Even though a party suffers because of a mistake with regard to the subject matter of the contract, the contract stands unless Equity can intervene.'

Discuss.

University of London LLB Examination
(for external students) Elements of the Law of Contract June 1996 Q2

Answers

ANSWERS TO INTERROGAMS

1. A plea of non est factum (meaning 'not my deed') will enable a party to avoid liability under a contract if he or she can prove that it was signed under a mistake as to the essential nature of the document. The relief is an equitable one and, because of the danger of abuse is construed very strictly.

   Some cases illustrate how the plea has evolved since it was first allowed. Originally, the mistake had to be as to the character of the document (ie not as to its contents): *Howatson* v *Webb* (1907). In *Foster* v *Mackinnon* (1869), the plea succeeded when an elderly man was induced to indorse a bill of exchange by being told that it was merely a guarantee. Equally, it was successful in *Lewis* v *Clay* (1898) when the promissory notes were signed under the mistaken impression that the signatory was merely witnessing another's signature.

   This distinction was, however, much criticised and was rejected in the leading House of Lords case: *Gallie* v *Lee* (1971). In that case, the plaintiff gave the deeds of her house to her nephew so that he could raise money on the property. L, a friend of P's, induced her to sign a conveyance of the property to him by telling her that it related to the deed of gift to her nephew. The plaintiff was unable to read the document for herself as she had lost her spectacles. L mortgaged the property to a building society who claimed possession for default. The test employed by the House of Lords was that the document must be 'fundamentally', 'radically' or 'totally' different to what the signatory believed it to be. In that case, the plaintiff was not held to have satisfied the test. The new test has also attracted criticism as being likely to lead to uncertainty.

   A further restriction on the plea is that it is only available to persons who, for some permanent or temporary reason, are incapable of both reading and sufficiently understanding the document to be signed, and must be unable to understand to the extent that they are unable to detect a fundamental difference between the actual document and the document they had believed it to be: Lord Pearson in *Gallie* v *Lee*. The reason for their inability to comprehend the nature of the document may be due to defective education, illness, innate incapacity, senility or some other cause. Non est factum is not available to someone who grants a power of attorney and then finds that the donee has abused it: *Norwich & Peterborough Building Society* v *Steed* (1992).
2. What falls to be discussed initially here is whether a distinction can be drawn between a mistake as to identity of the contracting party and a mistake as to the attributes of that party. This distinction was made in *King's Norton Metal Co Ltd* v *Edridge, Merrett & Co Ltd* (1897) where the Court of Appeal was constrained to distinguish the facts of that case from those present in the earlier case of *Cundy* v *Lindsay* (1878). In the latter case a party called 'Blenkarn' disguised his letter so as to make it appear to be from a respectable firm called 'Blenkiron & Co' whom the plaintiff knew. It was held by the House of Lords that the mistake was one as to identity which rendered the contract void. In *King's Norton Metal,* on the other

hand, where the rogue fraudulently misrepresented himself as the proprietor of a large business – which did not in fact exist – the mistake was held to be only one as to attributes. This rendered the contract merely voidable, not void.

In *Phillips* v *Brooks* (1919) the rogue obtained goods on credit by fraudulently misrepresenting himself as a well-known titled person. The mistake here was held to be only one as to attributes, that is the creditworthiness of the rogue, and again the contract was voidable only and not void. It is difficult to distinguish this case from that of *Ingram* v *Little* (1961) where the rogue in that instance obtained possession of a car from the sellers having persuaded them to accept a worthless cheque on the strength of his misrepresentation that he was some other person. In *Ingram* v *Little* the sellers were able to recover the car from an innocent third party to whom the rogue had 'sold' the car, the mistake here being regarded as one rendering the contract void.

In *Lewis* v *Averay* (1972) the rogue pretended to be a well-known film actor and gave a worthless cheque in the actor's name in return for the car. The plaintiff seller only allowed the car to be taken away when the rogue produced a special admission card to a film studio to prove that he was the actor. The Court of Appeal followed *Phillips* v *Brooks* and distinguished and disapproved *Ingram* v *Little* and held that the contract was voidable only. It appears therefore that *Ingram* v *Little* is no longer to be relied on although it has not yet been overruled.

Lord Denning stated in *Lewis* v *Avery* that the distinction between a mistake as to identity and a mistake as to attributes was a distinction without a difference. His Lordship also stated that he did not accept the theory that a mistake as to identity renders a contract void. This approach is in conflict with *Cundy* v *Lindsay,* but Lord Denning expressed the view that the case would not be decided in the same way today.

Professor Glanville Williams has also argued that the distinction between attributes and identity is based on a fundamental misconception. He states that what the courts have chosen to call a mistake as to identity is in fact a mistake as to attributes.

It is clear from the authorities cited that, if the distinction between attributes and identity is still valid, a mistake as to attributes does not make the contract void. What is less certain is whether this distinction can validly be made, and, if it can, the extent to which a mistake as to identity will make the contract void.

3. It is submitted that the statement in question refers to three quite different situations, namely:

   a) where the effect of the mistake is that offer and acceptance do not coincide and there is therefore no true agreement between the parties;
   b) where there is a mistake as to the terms of the offer known to the other party;
   c) where there is a mistake as to identity.

These will be considered in turn.

The classic example of (a) is *Raffles* v *Wichelhaus* (1864). Here the parties contracted for the sale and purchase of a cargo of cotton on board the ship Peerless from Bombay. There were two ships of this name, each of which had sailed from Bombay carrying cotton. The contracting parties each intended the contract to deal with a different ship. Since it was impossible for the court to say that the subject matter of the contract was either one cargo or the other, the contract was held to be void for mistake.

A less obvious example is *Scriven Bros & Co* v *Hindley & Co* (1913) where an auctioneer and bidder intended to deal with different subject matter. Here the court concluded the contract was void only because the auction catalogue was somewhat ambiguous: but for this the bidder would probably have been stuck with the lot knocked down to him, whether or not he wanted it.

These two cases are variously treated by commentators as being mistake cases or as being offer and acceptance cases. Their classification is probably not so important as the principle that they illustrate, namely that in exceptional cases where the parties are at cross purposes and it is impossible objectively to impute an agreement to them, consent will be negatived and no contract concluded.

Category (b) derives from the decision of the Court of Queen's Bench in *Smith* v *Hughes* (1871) and is best regarded as an exception to the caveat emptor rule and the general principle that one party is under no duty to correct a misapprehension the other may have (unless the former has caused or contributed to it). The rule in *Smith* v *Hughes* is that where one party makes a mistake as to the terms of the contract, and the other knows of that mistake, the contract is void. The rationale for this principle is that not only are the parties not ad idem, but one of them knows they are not ad idem. Thus in *Hartog* v *Colin and Shields* (1939), where negotiations for skins had been conducted on the basis of a price per piece, it was held that no contract was concluded where one party purported to accept an offer mistakenly made by the other at a price per pound.

Category (c), mistake as to identity, has given rise to a good deal of case law. With some diffidence, it is suggested that the following principles represent the present state of the law.

Where the parties are not physically in each other's presence (eg they are dealing by correspondence), and one party is mistaken as to the identity - not the attributes - of the other and intends instead to deal with some identifiable third party, and the other knows this, then the contract will be void for mistake: *Cundy* v *Lindsay* (1878) and *King's Norton Metal* v *Edridge, Merritt & Co Ltd* (1897).

However, where the parties are inter praesentes, there is a strong presumption which will rarely, if ever, be rebutted, that the parties intend to deal with the person physically present and identifiable by sight and sound, irrespective of the identity which one or other may assume: *Phillips* v *Brooks* (1919) and *Lewis* v *Avery* (1972). Nevertheless, there is some authority (*Lake* v *Simmons* (1927) and *Ingram* v *Little* (1961)) which suggests that in exceptional cases a mistake as to identity inter praesentes can negative consent so as to render a contract void.

SUGGESTED ANSWER TO QUESTION ONE

General Comment

This should not have been a difficult question to answer: there are well established cases. But a mere recital of the case law would not have been sufficient. For a good answer an analysis of the problem should have been attempted.

Key Points

- The nature of the problem
- Void and voidable contracts and the consequences of this classification
- The situation where the parties are negotiating at a distance, and where they are face to face
- The difficulties in distinguishing some of the cases from each other
- The solution to the problem?

Suggested Answer

Where one party is mistaken as to the identity of the other contracting party, this mistake can render the contract void, or merely voidable. In virtually all the cases we shall be considering, the contract involved the sale of goods by their original owner to a person who had misrepresented his identity and the latter's subsequent disposal of those goods to a third party. The courts are then faced with the task of deciding which of two innocent parties should bear the loss.

If the contract is void, no rights can flow from it, property did not pass to the imposter, and the owner can recover the goods from whoever has them in his possession. If, however, the misrepresentation merely renders the contract voidable, the original owner's claim for recovery of the goods might be defeated by the operation of s23 Sale of Goods Act 1979. Under this section, where the imposter sells the goods to a third party, the seller (the imposter) has a voidable title to the goods, but if his title had not been avoided at the time of the sale, the third party buyer acquires good title to the goods provided that he bought them in good faith and without notice of the seller's defect of title.

An early and perhaps unusual case (incidentally not involving disposition to a third party) is that of *Boulton* v *Jones* (1857). The defendant had a running account with a Mr Brocklehurst against whom he had a set-off. He addressed an order for goods to Brocklehurst which he sent to the latter's place of business. Unknown to the defendant Brocklehurst had disposed of his business to the plaintiff who substituted his own name on the order and supplied the goods. The contract between the plaintiff and the defendant was held to be void. Whilst this was a justifiable application of the principle that an offer addressed to one party cannot be accepted by another, the case had curious consequences. The plaintiff, who was apparently unaware of the set-off, could not recover the purchase price, nor the goods as they had been consumed, and the defendant obtained the benefit of the goods without having to pay for them and still retained his rights against Brocklehurst. This represents one unsatisfactory aspect of the law involving mistake as to identity.

In *Cundy* v *Lindsay* (1878) the rogue, when ordering goods, had sought to give the impression that he was the reputable firm Blenkiron & Co (known to the owner of the goods) by styling himself A Blenkarn and giving an address in the same street but at a different number from the reputable firm. The owners, believing that they were contracting with the firm they knew, dispatched the goods to the address given by the rogue, who then sold them to an innocent third party. The House of Lords held that the contract with the rogue was void for mistake. The owners' intention had been to contract with Blenkiron & Co, not with the author of the order at the address that had been given. In contrast in *King's Norton Metal Co Ltd* v *Edridge Merret & Co Ltd* (1897) the rogue placed an order, describing himself as trading as Hallam & Co - which was fictitious. The Court of Appeal held that as Hallam & Co did not exist the intention could only have been to contract with the writer of the order: the contract was therefore voidable and not void. These two cases are not all that clearly distinguishable.

Further uncertainties emerge from a consideration of the cases in which the parties contracted inter praesentes, in each others' presence. In *Phillips* v *Brooks Ltd* (1919) the rogue entered a jeweller's shop falsely announcing himself as a titled personage. This persuaded the shopkeeper to part with an item of jewellery for a worthless cheque. Before the fraud was discovered the rogue had sold the jewellery in question to an innocent third party who, by virtue of s23 Sale of Goods Act 1979, obtained good title. The jeweller's contract with the rogue had been merely voidable, not void.

On similar facts a contrary decision was reached in *Ingram* v *Little* (1961). In purchasing a car, the rogue had proffered a cheque in payment, which the plaintiff found unacceptable and declared that 'the deal was off'. Thereupon, the rogue falsely declared that he was a Mr Hutchinson and furnished certain addresses. After checking these addresses the plaintiff was satisfied and allowed the rogue to take the car in return for the cheque. Here the rights of the innocent third party, to whom the car was subsequently sold, did not prevail. The contract between the plaintiff and the rogue had been void for mistake. Pearce LJ held that *Phillips* v *Brooks Ltd* was a borderline case, decided on its own facts. Devlin LJ dissented, holding that there was a presumption 'that a person is intending to contract with the person to whom he is actually addressing the words of contract'.

A case similar to the above two is *Lewis* v *Averay* (1972), the facts of which are virtually indistinguishable from *Ingram* v *Little*. Here a cheque was accepted in payment for the purchase of a car after the rogue had produced a fraudulent document purporting to prove that he was Richard Greene (then a well known actor). The Court of Appeal held that this deceit rendered the contract voidable, and not void, and the innocent third party's rights prevailed. Lord Denning MR stated what he believed to be the true principle: his Lordship said:

> 'When two parties have come to a contract - or rather what appears on the face of it, to be a contract - the fact that one party is mistaken as to the identity of the other does not mean that there is no contract, or that the contract is a nullity and void from the beginning. It only means that the contract is voidable, that is liable to be set aside at the instance of the mistaken person so long as as he does so before third parties have in good faith acquired rights under it.'

Lord Denning had expressed a similar view in the Court of Appeal in *Gallie* v *Lee* (1969) when he said: 'I have long had doubts about the theory that, in the law of contract, mistake as to the identity of the person renders a contract a nullity and void.' He went on to express reservations about the decision in *Cundy* v *Lindsay* (above). Indeed it is questionable whether that case is reconcilable with Lord Denning's formulation of the law.

The effect of holding the contract void is to prejudice the third party, who might have acted in perfect good faith. The Law Reform Committee has recommended

> '... that contracts which are at present void because the owner of the goods was deceived or mistaken as to the identity of the person with whom he dealt should in future be treated as voidable so far as third parties are concerned' (Twelfth Report, *Transfer of Title to Chattels* (1966), Cmnd 2958, para 15).

If this recommendation were to be implemented by legislation it would bring a measure of certainty to this question. Admittedly it might cause hardship to owners of goods who have been deceived, but they are able to protect themselves by ensuring payment before surrendering possession of the goods: innocent third parties usually have no safeguard.

SUGGESTED ANSWER TO QUESTION TWO

General Comment

This is a somewhat wide-ranging question. Whilst the main issue is the doctrine of mistake, there are situations in which, although a party entered into a contact under a mistake, that mistake will not operate to make the contract void at common law, or render it liable to be set aside in equity. This involves consideration of the law relating to misrepresentation and the remedies for breach of contract.

Key Points

- Mistake at common law – the general rule – the effect of operative mistake, when the mistake renders the contract void – types of mistake
- Mistake in equity – when the mistake renders the contract liable to be set aside in equity
- Situations where the mistake neither makes the contract void, nor renders it voidable in equity
- Possible remedies for misrepresentation or for breach of contract

Suggested Answer

Mistake at common law

The general rule is that mistake does not affect the validity of a contract: *Smith* v *Hughes* (1871). There are, however, situations where a mistake will render the contract void at common law. The types of mistake that can occur are: where one party is mistaken (unilateral mistake); where the parties are at cross purposes (sometimes referred to as mutual or bilateral mistake); or where the parties share the same mistake (common mistake).

> 'If mistake operates at all, it operates so as to negative or in some case to nullify consent': per Lord Atkin in *Bell* v *Lever Brothers Ltd* (1932).

The fact that one party is (unilaterally) mistaken as to the terms of the contract will only affect its validity in exceptional circumstances as in *Hartog* v *Colin & Shields* (1939).

One party may be mistaken as to the identity of the other party. Where the contract is concluded inter praesentes that mistake will not usually negative consent and thus render the contract void: *Phillips* v *Brooks Ltd* (1919); *Lewis* v *Averay* (1972); but see *Ingram* v *Little* (1961). Where the parties are dealing with each other at a distance the situation may be different, if it appears that the intention was only to deal with a particular, designated person: *Boulton* v *Jones* (1857); *Cundy* v *Lindsay* (1878).

Where mistake as to identity does not render the contract void, the injured party may have an action for misrepresentation. This is dealt with further below.

Mistake may negative consent, thus rendering the contract void, where the parties are at cross purposes (mutual or bilateral mistake): *Scriven Bros & Co* v *Hindley & Co* (1913); *Raffles* v *Wichelhaus* (1864).

In the case of common (shared) mistake, the mistake may operate so as to nullify consent and render the contract void. But the operation of common mistake at common law was confined to very narrow limits by the decision in *Bell* v *Lever Brothers Ltd* (above). Mistake may so operate in exceptional circumstances, such as purchasing one's own property: *Cooper* v *Phibbs* (1867). Common mistake may also have this effect where the mistake is as to the existence of the subject matter: s6 Sale of Goods Act 1979: *Couturier* v *Hastie* (1856). But a party may not be able to rely on a mistake if he had no reasonable ground for that belief: *McRae* v *Commonwealth Disposals Commission* (1951).

A somewhat difficult question is whether a mistake as to the quality of the subject matter can render a contract void. It did not do so in *Bell* v *Lever Brothers Ltd*. But it is theoretically possible: see the propositions enunciated by Steyn J in *Associated Japanese Bank (International) Ltd* v *Credit du Nord SA* (1988).

Where a common mistake does not make contract void at law, it may render it voidable - liable to be set aside - in equity. The leading authority in this regard is *Solle* v *Butcher* (1950). This decision was followed in *Grist* v *Bailey* (1967) and *Laurence* v *Lexcourt Holdings Ltd* (1978), although the correctness of these two decisions was doubted by Hoffmann LJ in *William Sindall plc* v *Cambridgeshire County Council* (1994). Recently, it was noted by the Court of Appeal in *Great Peace Shipping Ltd* v *Tsavliris Salvage (International) Ltd* (2002) that:

> 'In this case we have heard full argument, which has provided what we believe has been the first opportunity in this court for a full and mature consideration of the relation between *Bell* v *Lever Brothers Limited* and *Solle* v *Butcher*. In the light of that consideration we can see no way that *Solle* v *Butcher* can stand with *Bell* v *Lever Brothers Limited*. In these circumstances we can see no option but so to hold.'

This equitable remedy of rescission is discretionary, and is not usually available for unilateral mistake, unless the party against whom it is sought has been at fault: *Riverlate Properties Ltd* v *Paul* (1975). In the case of unilateral mistake equity may operate to the extent of refusing an order for specific performance to the party seeking to enforce the contract: *Malins* v *Freeman* (1837).

It remains to consider the position where, although a party is mistaken, the mistake does not operate to make the contract either void or voidable.

The mistake may have been induced by a misrepresentation which induced the injured party to enter into the contract. Here the equitable remedy of rescission may be available, that is rescission for misrepresentation, not for mistake. Thus where one party misrepresents his identity, the innocent party may seek to have the relevant contract set aside.

In addition, the innocent party may be entitled to damages. If the misrepresentation is fraudulent, the innocent party will be entitled to damages for the tort of deceit. Even if the misrepresentation was not fraudulent he may be entitled to damages under s2(1) Misrepresentation Act 1967.

It may be that the false statement is not a 'mere' representation, but is a term of the contract. In that event the remedy will lie in an action for breach of contract. The precise remedy will depend on the nature of the term that has been breached. If the term is a warranty (or treated as such) the remedy will lie in damages. If the term is a condition (or treated as such) the innocent party will be entitled, in addition to a claim for damages, to treat the breach as a repudiation of the contract.

SUGGESTED ANSWER TO QUESTION THREE

General Comment

The one issue in this question is mistake as to identity, when it can operate so as to render the contract void and when it will merely render it voidable.

Key Points

- The effect of mistake as to identity, whether the contract is void or voidable
- The consequences of the distinction
- Analysis of the decided cases, and an attempt to derive a principle from those cases

Suggested Answer

The question at issue here is whether mistake as to identity renders the contract void, or merely voidable. The importance of the distinction is that if the contract is void, it is void ab initio, and no rights can flow from it. If it is merely voidable, an innocent third party might have acquired rights as a consequence of the contract.

I propose to discuss the decided cases in this area of the law, attempt to formulate a principle form those cases, and then apply that principle to the facts before me.

In *Boulton* v *Jones* (1857) the basis of the decision was that an offer addressed to a specific named person could not be accepted by another. In *Cundy* v *Lindsay* (1878) the finding was that the plaintiff had intended to deal only with a reputable firm of whom the plaintiff knew and not with anyone who might have placed the particular order. In both these cases the contracts were therefore held to be void. (In contrast, in *King's Norton Metal Co Ltd* v *Edridge, Merrett & Co Ltd* (1897) the mistake did not have this effect, because the plaintiff could only have intended to deal with the writer of the particular letter, who had fictitiously described himself as trading under the name of a firm which did not in fact exist.)

In the above-mentioned cases the parties were dealing with each other at a distance, which may have been significant. The position might elicit a different approach when the parties are dealing inter praesentes - in each others' presence.

In *Phillips* v *Brooks Ltd* (1919) the rogue had misrepresented his identity, and although the shopkeeper had checked that there was a person of that name at the address that was given, the shopkeeper's claim to the goods was defeated by an innocent third party having acquired title to the goods the rogue had obtained by his deception. A similar result ensued in *Lewis* v *Averay* (1972). In this case when the rogue, who had misrepresented his identity, proffered a cheque in payment of the car he had bought, the owner of the car requested proof of the claimed identity. Being satisfied by the document then produced the owner parted with possession of the car in return for a worthless cheque. Before the fraud was detected the rogue had sold the car to an innocent third party, whose rights prevailed.

A case which does not accord with the previous two cases is that of *Ingram* v *Little* (1961) which also involved the purchase of a car. When the rogue produced a cheque book in order to pay for the car, Miss Ingram had said, in effect, that a cheque was unacceptable and that 'the deal was off'. Thereupon the rogue said that he was a Mr P G M Hutchinson of a certain address. One of Miss Ingram's sisters checked the name and address at a post office and as this was deemed satisfactory, possession of the car was parted with for the worthless cheque. The Court of Appeal, by a majority, held that the contract with the rogue was void. Devlin LJ dissented on the ground that the identity of Hutchinson was immaterial to Miss Ingram, she was only concerned with his creditworthiness. His Lordship also said that where the parties are face to face there is the presumption that the one party intends to deal with the person in front of him. The majority decision in this case is difficult to reconcile with the previous two. A possible explanation is that after initially rejecting a cheque, Miss Ingram only intended to deal with Hutchinson, but this does not bear examination.

It seems therefore that mistake as to identity will only render a contract void where the identity is of crucial importance and where the intention is to deal only with a specific named person. This would explain the decisions which held the contracts void in *Hardman* v *Booth* (1863) and *Lake* v *Simmons* (1927). It is sometimes said that the distinction is between mistake as to identity and mistake as to attributes. but in *Lewis* v *Averay* Lord Denning rejected this as being a 'distinction without a difference'.

On the present facts it is submitted that *Phillips* v *Brooks Ltd* and *Lewis* v *Averay* must be followed, and accordingly R's mistake does not render the contract void. However, R has been the victim of a fraudulent misrepresentation, and it remains to consider his rights in this regard. The appropriate remedy would be rescission which would enable R to regain possession of the car. But S has sold the car to X. By virtue of s23 Sale of Goods Act 1979 where the seller of goods (S in this instance) has a voidable title to them, but his title has not been avoided at the time of the sale, the buyer (X in this instance) acquires a good title to the goods provided he buys them in good faith and without knowledge of the seller's defect of title. The fact that X bought the car for half the price that S paid might conceivably suggest lack of good faith or that his suspicions should have been aroused but there is no hard evidence to this effect. The remaining question is whether S's title has been avoided before the sale to X.

Notice of rescission should normally be communicated to the other contracting party, but S cannot be traced. R contacted the police and local garages before S sold the car to X. Does this constitute effective rescission and timeously avoid S's title? The facts here are on all fours with those in *Car and Universal Finance Co Ltd* v *Caldwell* (1965) where the Court of Appeal held that there had been effective avoidance of title. Applying this case would entitle R to regain possession of the car from X. (It is to be noted that the decision in the above case has been strongly criticised by the Law Reform Committee (Twelfth Report (*Transfer of Title to Chattels*), Cmnd 2958, para 16) as going far to destroy the value of s23 Sale of Goods Act 1979.)

SUGGESTED ANSWER TO QUESTION FOUR

General Comment

This is by no means a straightforward question. At first sight it seems that it could be answered by reference to the law relating to mistake. This would provide an incomplete answer, as it would ignore the rest of the information furnished. Discussion is also required of other matters, namely: certain of the rules relating to offer and acceptance; features of the law of sale of goods; and the classification of terms of a contract and the consequences thereof.

Key Points

- Was this an offer and acceptance mistake, which would render the contract void?
- On the assumption that there was no operative mistake, was there a valid contract, applying the rules as to offer and acceptance?
- Assuming that there was a valid contract, the effect of the car being taken and written off – the passing of risk
- The effect of the minor defects – the remedies B might have

Suggested Answer

A was referring to the Morris car, whereas B thought he was referring to the Austin. This suggests an application of the decision in *Scriven Bros & Co* v *Hindley & Co* (1913), where the parties were similarly at cross purposes. There the defendant buyers mistakenly bid at an auction for one commodity, believing it was the one being offered. In fact, what was being offered was another commodity of very little value. The plaintiff sellers' offer was ambiguous. A T Lawrence J said that the plaintiffs could only recover if the defendants were estopped from denying what was now admittedly the truth. He held that the defendants were not estopped, since their mistake had been caused by the plaintiffs' negligence.

This case may be distinguishable from the facts before me. There is no suggestion here of negligence on the part of A, and on an objective view A might have been entitled to believe that B was also referring to the Morris, and B might be estopped from denying this. I submit, on the basis of *Smith* v *Hughes* (1871), that the contract would only be held void for mistake if A knew that B believed that he (A) was contracting to sell the Austin. This does not appear to be the position, and I conclude that the contract would not be void for mistake.

That being so, it is necessary to examine the rules as to offer and acceptance to determine whether a contract was concluded.

It is clear that A has made an offer to sell the Morris. B's reply, objectively, relates to the same car. Was it an unqualified acceptance of the offer? B adds the words 'provided it is in good condition'. If this was to be construed as a counter-offer it would have destroyed A's offer: *Hyde* v *Wrench* (1840). But B's reply does not materially alter the terms of the offer, and is not, therefore, a counter-offer but can be characterised as a modifying acceptance. I would follow the approach propounded in *Anson's Law of Contract* ((27th ed), p40), as follows:

> 'If an offeror receives a reply to an offer which purports to be an acceptance but which contains additional or different terms which do not materially alter the terms of the offer and does not promptly object to the offeree about the discrepancy, the terms of the contract consist of the terms of the offer subject to the modifications contained in the acceptance.'

I am confirmed in the view that the offer has been accepted by B's undertaking to post a cheque, and subsequently doing so.

A valid contract has therefore been concluded. B is not therefore entitled to refuse the car; and A, having tendered delivery, is not obliged to return B's money.

The effect of the car being taken and written off by joyriders must now be addressed. This requires reference to the Sale of Goods Act (SGA) 1979 to determine who would bear the risk of this.

Under r1 of s18 SGA 1979 where there is a sale of specific goods the property in the goods passes to the buyer when the contract is made, it being immaterial whether the time of delivery was postponed. The contract was made when B accepted A's offer. Property in the Morris passed to B at that stage.

Risk passes with property: s20(1) SGA 1979 provides that when the property in the goods is transferred to the buyer the goods are at the buyer's risk whether delivery has been made or not.

Applying these provisions, risk had already passed to B when the car was taken by joyriders, and he must accordingly bear the loss.

The alternative scenario to consider is that instead of being taken and written off, the car had a large number of minor defects.

We are not informed that A was a seller in the course of a business so the implied term of satisfactory quality in s14(2) SGA 1979 does not apply.

However, it had been suggested, following *Anson* (above), that, A not having made any objection thereto, the terms of the contract include the term that the car 'is in good condition'. One cannot be certain, but having a large number of minor defects does compel the view that this constitutes a breach of that term. If that is so, B's remedies depend on the classification of that term as a condition, warranty or innominate term.

B's insistence on the additional phrase 'in good condition' and A's implied acquiesence to this additional term, does suggest it is a condition. If so defects in the car, however minor, would constitute a repudiatory breach and entitle B to reject the car. I am more inclined to the view, however, that it should be classified an an innominate term. I base this view particularly on the decision of the Court of Appeal in *Cehave NV* v *Bremer Handelsgesellschaft mbH, The Hansa Nord* (1976), where the phrase 'in good condition' was interpreted as an innominate term, and where Roskill LJ stated that the courts should not be too ready to interpret contractual clauses as conditions.

If it is an innominate term, whether it is treated as a breach of condition or only of warranty, depends on the nature, consequences and effect of the breach: see the speech of Lord Scarman in *Bunge Corporation* v *Tradax Export SA* (1980).

If the minor defects in the car were such as to treat them only as a warranty, B would only be entitled to damages or a set-off against the purchase price.

SUGGESTED ANSWER TO QUESTION FIVE

General Comment

Various issues of mistake are raised in this question, but it also requires some reference to misrepresentation and to a sale by description.

Key Points

- The sale of the teapot: misrepresentation – mistake, the nature of the mistake – sale by description
- The sale of the cup and saucer: unilateral mistake
- The sale of the tea service to O: mistake as to identity

Suggested Answer

The sale of the teapot

The labelling of the teapot as 'Gaudy Welsh' by M appears clearly to be a misrepresentation. This would entitle N to rescission of the contract – no bars to rescission are suggested. Alternatively (perhaps in addition) N would have a claim in damages. On the information provided one cannot conclude that the misrepresentation was fraudulent, but damages would appear to be available under s2(1) Misrepresentation Act 1967. As a dealer M is unlikely to be able to discharge the onus imposed on him by that section.

It seems clear, also, that M is in breach of s13(1) Sale of Goods Act 1979, which provides that:

> 'Where there is a contract for the sale of goods by description, there is an implied term [condition] that the goods will correspond with the description.'

However, what must be more fully explored is the question of mistake.

If M knows that N is buying a 'Gaudy Welsh' teapot, whereas he knows that he is selling a Staffordshire piece, then it is an offer and acceptance mistake, and the contract is void: *Smith* v *Hughes* (1871). What is also possible is that both parties share the same erroneous assumption that it is the former; in this event it is a common mistake and the effect of this on the contract must now be analysed.

The common mistake here is a mistake as to quality. The effect of operative mistake at common law is to render the contract void. In *Bell* v *Lever Brothers Ltd* (1932) Lord Atkin held:

> '... a mistake will not affect assent unless it is the mistake of both parties, and is as to the existence of some quality which makes the thing without the quality essentially different from the thing as it was believed to be.'

If the mistake in *Bell* did not pass that test it is difficult to see how it could ever be satisfied. And the actual decision has been interpreted as confining operative common mistake to very narrow limits at common law. In successive editions of *Cheshire, Fifoot and Furmston's Law of Contract* ((13th ed), p246) the learned authors argued that at common law there was no doctrine of common mistake as such, and that a contract would only be void if there was nothing to contract about. In *Magee* v *Pennine Insurance Co Ltd* (1969) Lord Denning MR said that: 'A common mistake, even on a most fundamental matter, does not make a contract void at law.'

This interpretation has been criticised by Steyn J in *Associated Japanese Bank (International) Ltd* v *Credit du Nord SA* (1988) which, his Lordship felt, was based on a misunderstanding of the speeches in Bell. Steyn J suggested that there was scope, albeit narrow, for finding a contract void at common law for common mistake as to quality, and enunciated a number of propositions to determine when such mistake would be operative.

Common mistakes as to quality, even fundamental ones, have been held not to affect the validity of the contract in a number of cases, for example: *Leaf* v *International Galleries* (1950); *Harrison & Jones Ltd* v *Bunten & Lancaster Ltd* (1953); *Oscar Chess Ltd* v *Williams* (1957). Indeed it is difficult to find a case which has found such operative mistake. A case which did so was *Nicholson & Venn* v *Smith-Marriott* (1947), but this decision has been criticised by Denning LJ in *Solle* v *Butcher* (1950). Steyn J would have been prepared to find the contract of guarantee void of mistake in *Associated Japanese Bank* (above), but based his decision on other grounds.

The balance of authorities suggest, therefore, that contract for the teapot would not be held void for mistake. Where a common mistake does not make a contract void at law, it makes it liable to be set aside in equity: *Solle* v *Butcher* (above); *Magee* v *Pennine Insurance Co Ltd* (above); *Grist* v *Bailey* (1976); *Laurence* v *Lexcourt Holdings Ltd* (1978). But the correctness of the decisions in the latter two cases has been doubted by Hoffmann LJ in *William Sindall plc* v *Cambridgeshire County Council* (1994) on the grounds that the judges who decided those cases did not advert to the question of the contractual risk. Hoffmann LJ quoted the statement of Steyn J in *Associated Japanese Bank* (above) to the effect that before one can turn to the rules of mistake, whether at common law or in equity, one must first determine whether the contract itself, expressly or impliedly, provides who bears the risk of the relevant mistake. It may well be that this contract imposes such risk on the buyer, N, the law being caveat emptor. That being so the equitable principle will also not avail N.

The contract for the cup and saucer
The mistake here is unilateral and is inoperative at common law: *Smith* v *Hughes* (above). Nor is the equitable remedy of rescission available for unilateral mistake: *Riverlate Properties Ltd* v *Paul* (1975).

The sale of the tea service to O
This involves a mistake as to identity. One could discuss a number of cases in this area, but, on the given facts, it is sufficient to say that the mistake does not render the contract void on the authority of *Phillips* v *Brooks* (1919) and *Lewis* v *Averay* (1972).

However, the contract would be voidable for misrepresentation if third party rights had not intervened. Under s23 Sale of Goods Act 1979, P would have acquired good title to the goods if he bought them in good faith and without notice of O's defect of title, before the sale to O had been avoided. The question is whether M's notification to the police is sufficient to constitute rescission.

Similar action was held to constitute effective rescission in *Car and Universal Finance Co Ltd* v *Caldwell* (1965). But this case has been severely criticised. The Law Reform Committee thought that the decision 'goes far to destroy the value of s23 of the Sale of Goods Act ... We think that unless and until notice of the rescission of the contract is communicated to the other contracting party an innocent purchaser from the latter should be able to acquire good title': Twelfth Report (*Transfer of Title to Chattels*), Cmnd 2958, para 16.

If the latter view prevails M would not be able to recover the goods from P.

SUGGESTED ANSWER TO QUESTION SIX

General Comment

A four-part problem question requiring examination of the various aspects of mistake. The first part requires an analysis of the law relating to common mistake, the second on mistake as to quality and the relevance of 'caveat emptor'. The third and fourth parts call for a discussion on the effects of common law and the passing of title respectively.

Key Points

a) The type of mistake; the effect of the mistake at common law and the possible equitable remedy
b) Common mistake as to quality; but should caveat emptor apply?
c) The effect at common law of H having purchased his own property
d) The issue here is whether H could have acquired title to goods stolen from the lawful owner

Suggested Answer

a) I am assuming here that the mistake can be characterised as common mistake; both parties assumed that the contract of employment was mutually binding, whereas it could have been terminated by H without notice and without payment of compensation. Thus far it resembles the facts in *Bell* v *Lever Brothers Ltd* (1932), where the House of Lords held, by a three to two majority, that the payment of compensation for premature termination of the service contracts could not be recovered. But there is a significant difference. In that case the House of Lords kept in mind the finding of the jury acquitting the defendants of fraudulent misrepresentation or concealment in procuring the agreements in question. Whilst actual misrepresentation is not suggested here, it does appear that G concealed his/her misconduct from H, which (s)he must have known would have entitled H to invoke summary dismissal. However, in *Bell* v *Lever Brothers Ltd* Lord Atkin did observe that an employee is under no duty to disclose his misconduct to an employer, in the absence of any direct question.

I must conclude, therefore, that, despite G's concealment of the misconduct, the principle established by the House of Lords must apply, and that the contract whereby H agreed to make the payment is not void at common law. The effect of the mistake in equity must now be considered.

The leading case in this regard is *Solle* v *Butcher* (1950). The Court of Appeal, in a majority decision, held that the common mistake there did not render the contract void at law, but that the equitable remedy of rescission was available to the aggrieved party. In the words of Denning LJ:

> 'A contract is ... liable to be set aside in equity if the parties were under a common misapprehension either as to the facts or as to their relative and respective rights, provided that the misapprehension was fundamental and that the party seeking to set it aside was not himself at fault.'

(Jenkin LJ dissented, holding that the mistake was one of law.) The principle in this case was applied, again by a majority decision of the Court of Appeal, in *Magee* v *Pennine Insurance Co Ltd* (1969). It was also applied in *Grist* v *Bailey* (1967) and in *Laurence* v *Lexcourt Holdings Ltd* (1978), although the correctness of these two decisions has been doubted by Hoffmann LJ in *William Sindall plc* v *Cambridgeshire County Council* (1994) (this is amplified below).

Despite the doubts cast on the equitable doctrine it does provide a measure of flexibility in dealing with the consequences of common mistake, and I submit that it would be applied in the present problem so as to afford H the right of rescission, which would enable him to recover the £80,000.

b) It is pertinent to begin an examination of the situation here with reference to the judgment of Steyn J in *Associated Japanese Bank (International) Ltd* v *Credit du Nord SA* (1989). His Lordship said:

> 'Logically, before one can turn to the rules of mistake, whether at common law or in equity, one must first determine whether the contract itself, by express or implied condition or otherwise, provides who bears the risk of the relevant

> mistake. It is at this hurdle that many pleas of mistake will either fail or prove to have been unnecessary. Only if the contract is silent on the point is there scope for invoking mistake.'

The High Court, in *Clarion Ltd* v *National Provident Institution* (2000), reaffirmed the principles enunciated in the *Associated Japanese Bank* case. In *William Sindall plc* v *Cambridgeshire County Council* (above), Hoffmann LJ said that when Steyn J spoke of contractual allocation of the risk of mistake, 'I think he includes rules of general law applicable to the contract and which, for example, provide that, in the absence of express warranty, the law is caveat emptor.' Hoffmann LJ also said: 'I should say that neither in *Grist* v *Bailey*, nor in *Laurence* v *Lexcourt Holdings Ltd*, did the judges who decided those cases at first instance advert to the question of contractual allocation of risk. I am not sure that the decisions would have been the same if they had.'

In the problem before me, as there has been no express warranty as to the authenticity of the teapot, I submit that the rule caveat emptor applies, and that H must bear the risk of the mistake.

c) The problem of H's purchase of the flat can be answered by reference to *Cooper* v *Phibbs* (1867); the facts are on all fours. Although in that case Lord Westbury applied the principle that the contract was liable to be set aside, it is clear from the observations of Lord Atkin in *Bell* v *Lever Brothers Ltd* that the contract was in fact void. The contract for the purchase of the flat is therefore void at common law for mistake; the two years' delay is irrelevant. H can recover the £100,000 on the basis of a total failure of consideration.

d) Candidates may have been deceived here into a discussion of mistake as to identity. The situation is that Lemon had no title whatsoever to the picture, and could not, therefore, confer title on H. Lord Kink is entitled to its return. H's only recourse is an action against Lemon for breach of the implied term in s12(1) Sale of Goods Act 1979, and recovery of the purchase price for a total failure of consideration. If he has suffered other losses in connection with the purchase, he could recover damages from Lemon for the fraud.

SUGGESTED ANSWER TO QUESTION SEVEN

General Comment

An essay question which calls for a discussion on the principles of common law and equity in relation to the doctrine of mistake. The various classes of mistake must be discussed, raising the intervention of equity wherever relevant.

Key Points

- Mistake at common law – the effect of operative mistake
- Mistake as to the identity of the subject matter
- Mistake as to the existence of the subject matter
- Mistake as to quality of the subject matter
- The intervention of equity

Suggested Answer

Mistake at common law

'If mistake operates at all it operates so as to negative or in some cases to nullify consent': per Lord Atkin in *Bell* v *Lever Brothers Ltd* (1932). I shall refer to mistake which negatives consent as 'unilateral mistake' and to mistake which nullifies consent as 'common mistake'. (Different terminology is sometimes employed, for example, in Cheshire, Fifoot and Furmston's *Law of Contract.*) Common mistake is a mistake shared by both parties to the contract.

Mistake as to the identity of the subject matter

Such mistake usually falls within the area of unilateral mistake. The mistake may operate so as to negative consent, in the sense that there is no coincidence between offer and acceptance, as where the parties are at cross-purposes: *Raffles* v *Wichelhaus* (1864); *Scriven Bros & Co* v *Hindley & Co* (1913). However, the mere fact that one party knows the other to be mistaken will not necessarily affect the validity of the contract: *Smith* v *Hughes* (1871). If, in that case, the buyer had mistakenly believed that the seller's offer was to sell old oats, and the seller knew that the buyer had misunderstood his offer, then there would have been an offer and acceptance mistake.

It may be that common mistake would operate to nullify consent, where both parties thought that they were negotiating about one thing when they were in fact negotiating about another. But there appears to be no English case on this point.

Mistake as to existence of the subject matter

Where both parties are mistaken as to the existence of the subject matter, the mistake may operate so as to nullify consent.

Section 6 Sale of Goods Act 1979 provides that:

> 'Where there is a contract for the sale of specific goods, and the goods without the knowledge of the seller have perished at the time when the contract is made, the contract is void.'

It appears that this section was intended to give statutory effect to the decision of the House of Lords in *Couturier* v *Hastie* (1856). But the legal basis for the decision in that case has given rise to some controversy: see the discussion by McKendrick (*Contract Law*, 2nd ed, pp224–225). It has been suggested that the case decides that mistake as to the existence of the subject matter always renders the contract void, but the word 'mistake' was not used in any of the judgments.

Couturier was distinguished by the High Court of Australia in *McRae* v *Commonwealth Disposals Commission* (1951), where it was held that, on the facts, there was an implied term of the contract that the subject matter existed. The court also held that a party could not rely on a mistaken belief which is entertained by him without any reasonable ground and which is deliberately induced by him in the mind of the other party.

Mistake as to quality of the subject matter

The question here is whether common mistake as to the quality of the subject matter can operate so as to nullify consent and thus render the contract void. The effect of common mistake in this context has been confined to very narrow limits since the decision of the House of Lords in *Bell* v *Lever Brothers Limited*. 'Mistake as to quality of the thing contracted for will not affect assent,' said Lord Atkin, 'unless it is the mistake of both parties, and is as to the existence of some quality which makes the thing without the quality essentially different from the thing as it was believed to be.' This stringent test was held to be satisfied on the facts before him by Steyn J in *Associated Japanese Bank (International) Ltd* v *Credit du Nord SA* (1988) where his Lordship found that 'For both parties the guarantee of obligations under a lease with non-existent machines was essentially different from a guarantee of a lease with four machines which both parties at the time of the contract believed to exist.'

In the case just cited Steyn J also observed that:

> 'Logically, before one can turn to the rules of mistake, whether at common law or in equity, one must first determine whether the contract itself, by express or implied condition precedent or otherwise, provides who bears the risk of the relevant mistake. It is at this hurdle that many pleas of mistake will either fail or prove to have been unnecessary. Only if the contract is silent on the point is there scope for invoking mistake.'

This approach was affirmed and adopted by Hoffmann LJ in *William Sindall plc* v *Cambridgeshire County Council* (1994).

Mistake in equity

The equitable remedy of rescission has proved available where a common mistake has not rendered the contract void at law. In *Magee* v *Pennine Insurance Co Ltd* (1969) Lord Denning MR said that: 'A common mistake, even on a most fundamental matter, does not make contract void at law, but it makes it voidable in equity.' Lord Denning was applying his earlier decision in *Solle* v *Butcher* (1950).

Solle v *Butcher* was followed by the High Court in *Grist* v *Bailey* (1967) and by the Court of Appeal in *Laurence* v *Lexcourt Holdings Ltd* (1978). The correctness of these two decisions has, however, been doubted by Hoffmann LJ in *William Sindall plc* v *Cambridgeshire County Council* (above). Applying the approach which has been referred to, his Lordship said that in neither of these two decisions 'did the judges who decided these cases at first instance advert to the question of contractual allocation of risk. I am not sure that the decisions would have been the same if they had.'

It remains to note that the equitable remedy of rescission is not available for unilateral mistake unless the one party had contributed to the other's mistake: *Riverlate Properties Ltd* v *Paul* (1975). Equitable intervention, in the case of unilateral mistake, can, however, take the form of refusing to order specific performance: *Malins* v *Freeman* (1837).

8

Duress and Undue Influence

Introduction

Proof of a contract having been procured by duress or undue influence will vitiate the contract. As duress has historically been confined to threatened or actual violence, it has in practice proved to be a rarer claim than that of undue influence. However, the extension of duress to include 'economic duress' has given it new life. Economic duress is generally to be found in business-to-business contracts, while undue influence will usually nowadays involve some domestic relationship. Questions in this area are perhaps more unusual than in some others. However, there is scope for both problem and essay-type questions. Recent cases in this area include *Dunbar Bank plc* v *Nadeem* (1998), *Alf Vaughan & Co Ltd* v *Royscot Trust plc* (1999), *Huyton SA* v *Peter Cremer GmbH & Co Inc* (1999) and *Royal Bank of Scotland* v *Etridge (No 2)* (2001).

Questions

INTERROGRAMS

1. What is meant by a 'special relationship' in the context of undue influence?
2. '... English law gives relief to one, who, without independent advice, enters into a contract ... when his bargaining power is grievously impaired ...' (Lord Denning in *Lloyds Bank* v *Bundy*). To what extent is this true?
3. To what extent has equity extended the scope of the common law doctrine of duress?

QUESTION ONE

J had lived with his girlfriend K for three years. They each contributed 50 per cent of the council tax and shared the other household expenses equally. J offered to buy for £10,000 K's shares in Big Bank plc, which she had inherited from her father. They were worth £100,000 and J knew this. K agreed because she was afraid that if she did not agree J would leave her. L, J's brother, threatened to tell J that he and K had had an affair before K had started to live with J. L forced K to sign a guarantee for a loan which L was taking from a bank as his business was in difficulty. The guarantee was secured by a charge on the flat in which K and J lived and which K owned.

Advise K. What would be your advice on the following alternative assumptions: (a) J had left K threatening to publish intimate photographs which he had taken when they were living together; or (b) L had become insolvent and the bank were seeking to enforce the guarantee; or (c) when K had agreed to the sale and guarantee she was only seventeen years old?

University of London LLB Examination
(for external students) Elements of the Law of Contract June 1995 Q5

QUESTION TWO

'I would suggest that … there runs a single thread … "inequality of bargaining power". By virtue of it, the English law gives relief to one who, without independent advice, enters into a contract upon terms which are very unfair or transfers property for a consideration which is grossly inadequate …': Lord Denning in *Lloyds Bank* v *Bundy* (1975).

Discuss this statement.

Written by the Author

QUESTION THREE

'The fact that one party is arguably (always) in a more superior bargaining position suggests that the concept of economic duress is built on shaky foundations.'

Discuss.

Written by the Editor

Answers

ANSWERS TO INTERROGAMS

1. Where a contract has been procured by the undue influence of one of the contracting parties over the other, the contract is voidable in equity at the option of the innocent party.

   Such influence is presumed where there is a special relationship between the parties. There are specific categories which have been recognised as 'special relationships': parent and child – *Wright* v *Vanderplank* (1855); solicitor and client – *Wright* v *Carter* (1903); doctor and patient – *Mitchell* v *Homfray* (1881); trustee and beneficiary – *Ellis* v *Barker* (1871); religious adviser and disciple – *Roche* v *Sherrington* (1982). Perhaps surprisingly, there is no presumption of a special relationship between husband and wife (*Midland Bank* v *Shephard* (1988)) unless there are particular circumstances of dependency and mutual trust (*Simpson* v *Simpson* (1988)). Nor is there such presumption of relationship between banker and customer (*Lloyds Bank* v *Bundy* (1975)) or between master and servant (*Mathew* v *Bobbins* (1980)). The categories of special relationship are not closed and it is open to the court to extend the presumption to other kinds of relationship if appropriate. The recent decision of the House of Lords in *Royal Bank of Scotland* v *Etridge (No 2)* (2001) reaffirms this.

   Where influence is presumed, the party seeking to rely on the doctrine has nothing further to prove and the burden falls on the other party to prove that there has been no undue influence in the circumstances (very often, but not exclusively, by proving that the person relying on the doctrine was independently advised). Where there is no special relationship, to rely on the doctrine the party must prove actual undue influence, which is clearly a greater burden.
2. The extract from Lord Denning's judgment in *Lloyds Bank* v *Bundy* from which this

statement is taken has given rise to academic speculation that there is a principle of inequality of bargaining power. In his judgment, Lord Denning appeared to consider that this principle, albeit a limited one, gave a broad relief to anyone who:

> '... without independent advice, enters into a contract on terms which are very unfair or transfers property for a consideration which is grossly inadequate, when his bargaining power is grievously impaired by reason of his own needs or desires, or by his own ignorance or infirmity, coupled with undue influences or pressures brought to bear on him by or for the benefit of another.'

This alternative reason for his judgment in the case was further reiterated in *Clifford Davis* v *WEA Records* (1975) and *Levison* v *Patent Steam Carpet Cleaning Co* (1978) and appeared to receive support from Lord Diplock in *Schroeder Music Publishing Co Ltd* v *Macaulay* (1974).

However, pleas to set aside an agreement purely on the basis of inequality of bargaining power have been rejected in *Burmah Oil* v *Bank of England* (1981) and *Alec Lobb (Garages) Ltd* v *Total Oil (Great Britain) Ltd* (1985). Indeed in that case Dillon LJ said that it was rare in any transaction for the bargaining power of the parties to be equal. In *National Westminster Bank plc* v *Morgan* (1985), Lord Scarman doubted whether '... there is any need in the modern law to erect a general principle of relief against inequality of bargaining power', a view which had been apparent previously in his Lordship's judgment in *Pao On* v *Lau Yiu Long* (1980). The reason is probably that, as Trietel observes, the doctrine of economic duress, upheld in that case, has reduced the need for such a principle in modern law.

3. The common law doctrine of duress required actual or threatened violence to the victim (*Barton* v *Armstrong* (1976). There was some doubt as to whether threats to seize goods could amount to duress (compare *Skeate* v *Beale* (1840) and *Maskell* v *Horner* (1915)). However, it seems that the common law relief is now definitely confined to threatened or actual physical violence: see Kerr J in *Occidental Worldwide Investment Corp* v *Skibs A/S Avanti, The Siboen and The Sibotre* (1976) and Mocatta J in *North Ocean Shipping Co* v *Hyundai, The Atlantic Baron* (1979). A party who proves duress can avoid the contract. There was an idea at one time that a contract procured by duress was void but this has now been rejected.

   Modern law has extended the doctrine to include 'economic duress'. This extension has its roots in the tort of intimidation. This tort was extended to include threat of breach of contract as well as threatened violence: *Rookes* v *Barnard* (1964) and *Morgan* v *Fry* (1968). The thinking of Lord Denning which lay behind this latter decision was also evident in his judgment in *D & C Builders Ltd* v *Rees* (1966), where he compared undue pressure to intimidation, while refusing to extend the doctrine of equitable estoppel to a defendant who had procured the promise to forbear by exerting economic pressure.

   However, economic pressure will not of itself constitute duress. In *The Siboen and The Sibotre*, while upholding the doctrine of 'economic duress', Kerr J expressed the view that the innocent party's will must be 'overborne by compulsion so as to deprive him of any animus contrahendi'.

   The relief is an equitable one as is clear from *The Atlantic Baron* where the threat involved was the threat to break a contract which would have had catastrophic dealings on a transaction dependent upon the completion of the contract. Mocatta J found that there had been economic duress but that the contract could not be set aside because the injured party had delayed in taking action.

In a leading case on economic duress in recent times, *Pao On* v *Lau Yiu Long* (1980), the Privy Council upheld Kerr J's view in *The Sibeon and The Sibotre* and laid down a four-part test for whether the doctrine will apply:

a) did the party seeking to rely on the doctrine protest?
b) did he have an adequate legal remedy?
c) was he independently legally advised?
d) did he take steps to avoid the contract?

Further indication of the Lords' views on economic duress came in *The Universe Sentinel* (1983), where the Court of Appeal had made a finding of economic duress. Upholding the Court's finding, the Lords departed from the earlier strict requirements. Lord Scarman spoke of the 'compulsion of the will' of the victim but described it as:

> '... the victim's intentional submission arising from the realisation that there is no other practical choice open to him ...'.

Moreover, while the pressure exerted must be 'illegitimate', ie improper in the legal sense (see *The Evia Luck* (1991)), it is not a requirement that the party exerting it must realise that his victim is acting under it.

SUGGESTED ANSWER TO QUESTION ONE

General Comment

A problem question raising questions relating to the doctrine of undue influence and its classifications. Issues of duress also need to be raised contextually. Third party rights and contractual liability also require examination.

Key Points

- A summary of the doctrine of undue influence - actual influence and presumed influence
- The sale of the shares: whether entered into under undue influence
- The signing of the guarantee: the nature of the influence
- The alternative assumptions: the threat to publish the photographs
- Undue influence and duress considered - the enforcement of the guarantee by the bank
- The position of a third party - the question of K's capacity to contract

Suggested Answer

A person who has been induced to enter into a contract by the undue influence of another (the wrongdoer) is entitled to have that contract set aside as against the wrongdoer. Undue influence is either actual or presumed. The classification of undue influence adopted by the Court of Appeal in *Bank of Credit and Commerce International SA* v *Aboody* (1989) and by the House of Lords in *Barclays Bank plc* v *O'Brien* (1994) was on the following lines.

1. *Class 1: actual undue influence*. This involves actual pressure, and it is for the claimant to prove that the wrongdoer exerted the undue influence on the complainant to enter into the particular transaction. The case of *Royal Bank of Scotland* v *Etridge (No 2)* (2001) provides a useful illustration of this fact.
2. *Class 2: presumed undue influence*. Where the complainant shows that there was a particular relationship of trust and confidence between the complainant and the wrongdoer, the presumption will arise that the wrongdoer abused that relationship in inducing the complainant to enter into the transaction. In this class it is not necessary for the complainant to prove undue influence in relation to the particular transaction. Once the confidential relationship is established the burden then passes to the wrongdoer to rebut the presumption, by proving that the complainant entered into the transaction voluntarily. An illustration is provided by *Dunbar Bank plc* v *Nadeem* (1998).
3. *Class 2A: special relationships*. Certain relationships, such as solicitor and client, doctor and patient, will give rise to the presumption of undue influence.
4. *Class 2B: de facto relationships*. The presumption of undue influence will arise even in the absence of a special relationship if the complainant shows that there was a relationship of trust and confidence between the complainant and the wrongdoer.

The transactions into which K entered must be examined in the light of the above principles.

The sale of the shares to J

The relationship between J and K is one falling within Class 2B. Where there is an emotional relationship between cohabitees there is, as Lord Browne-Wilkinson said in *Barclays Bank plc* v *O'Brien*, an underlying risk of one cohabitee exploiting the emotional involvement and trust of the other. It seems clear, because of K's fear that J would leave her, and her agreeing to sell shares worth £100,000 for £10,000, that a relationship of trust and confidence existed. In *Lloyds Bank Ltd* v *Bundy* (1975) Sir Eric Sachs said that the presumption of undue influence arises:

> '... where someone one relies on the guidance or advice of another, where the other is aware of that reliance and where the person on whom reliance is placed obtains, or may well obtain, a benefit from the transaction.'

This approach was approved by the House of Lords in *National Westminster Bank plc* v *Morgan* (1985). In the latter case it was also held that, where the presumption of undue influence arose, it was also necessary for the complainant to show that there was 'manifest disadvantage' to the complainant in the transaction. This again is clearly the position here.

The onus now falls on J to prove that K entered into the transaction voluntarily. The most usual way of doing this is to show that the complainant had independent advice. Whilst there is no invariable rule that independent advice is necessary, this may be the only means by which the presumption of undue influence can be rebutted: *Inche Noriah* v *Shaik Allie Bin Omar* (1929). *Barclays Bank plc* v *Thomson* (1997) further stated that manifest disadvantage must be proven in order for undue influence to be pleaded successfully.

It does not appear that K had independent advice, nor are any other circumstances suggested which would enable J to prove that K entered into the transaction voluntarily. Accordingly K would be entitled to set the transaction aside.

The signing of the guarantee on behalf of L

This situation falls within Class 1: actual undue influence. We are told that L forced K to sign the guarantee by his threat. Once actual influence has been established it is not necessary for K to show that the transaction was to her disadvantage: *CIBC Mortgages* v *Pitt* (1993).

K could also have this transaction set aside.

It remains to consider the alternative assumptions.

a) *J's threat to publish the photographs*

Presumably J uttered this threat in order to induce K to sell him the shares. Although this is not clearly stated, it is difficult to see how it would be otherwise be relevant.

As the relationship between J and K has terminated, in the circumstances described, the presumption of undue influence cannot arise: there is no longer a relationship of trust and confidence. It would appear, however, that there has been actual influence, with the consequences set out above. Moreover, the threat raises the possibility of invoking the doctrine of duress. Duress involves the application of illegitimate pressure on the victim which gives the victim no real choice but to submit: *Universe Tankships Inc of Monrovia* v *International Transport Workers' Federation, The Universe Sentinel* (1983). It is not clear that the threat to publish the photographs constitutes illegitimate pressure, but it is blackmail, and in *The Universe Sentinel* Lord Scarman stated that the doctrine of duress should extend to blackmail.

On this assumption, therefore, K would also be entitled to have the transaction set aside.

b) *The enforcement of the guarantee by the bank*

It has been submitted that the guarantee was executed as a result of the actual influence. The position of the bank depends on whether they had constructive notice of the actual influence. If the bank did, it would have had to take reasonable steps to satisfy itself that K had entered into the obligation freely and with knowledge of the true facts. Otherwise the bank will not be able to enforce the guarantee: *Barclays Bank plc* v *O'Brien* (above). If the bank could not be held to have had constructive notice of the actual influence, it would not be tainted by the wrong, and K would not be able to resist enforcement: *CIBC Mortgages* v *Pitt*.

c) *The situation if K was only 17 years old at the relevant times*

As K was a minor at the the time she entered into the sale and the guarantee the transactions would not be binding on her. If, however, the shares had been transferred to J, she could not recover them merely by reason of her minority: *Corpe* v *Overton* (1833).

SUGGESTED ANSWER TO QUESTION TWO

General Comment

An essay question on the law relating to duress and undue influence. The relevance of common law and statutory controls must be raised in the context of inequality of bargaining power. Lord Denning's statement must also be analysed within context.

Key Points

- Duress
- Undue influence
- Statutory controls
- Inequality of bargaining power
- Denning's argument
- Refutation of that argument

Suggested Answer

The twin doctrines of laissez faire and freedom of contract have meant that the courts have never been particularly interested in the fairness or otherwise of a bargain or the relative status of parties to the contract. However, the very fact that for a valid contract to exist, the parties must voluntarily consent to the agreement means that the courts have been forced to recognise the fact that this reality of consent will not be present if one party has been subjected to improper pressure by the other. Note that it is important that the pressure must be 'improper', normal commercial competition is not at all the same thing.

The law recognises various kinds of improper pressure, falling within the following categories: duress, undue influence, inequality of bargaining power and certain forms of pressure proscribed by statute.

Duress, a common law concept, originally existed only within narrowly defined limits (*Skeate* v *Beale* (1840)), though in modern times the doctrine has been extended and become more flexible. In particular the courts have developed a form of 'economic' duress in *Occidental Worldwide Investment Corp* v *Skibs A/S Avanti* (1976); Kerr J declared that commercial pressure alone was not enough to constitute economic duress. 'The court must be satisfied that the consent of one party was overborne by compulsion so as to deprive him of any animus contrahendi.' This contention was recently reiterated in *Alf Vaughan & Co* v *Royscot Trust plc* (1999) where the court held that unless the pressure exercised was unconscionable and unjustified, economic duress does not materialise. This was recently reviewed and affirmed by the House of Lords in *Royal Bank of Scotland* v *Etridge (No 2)* (2001).

Much will obviously depend on the facts of the particular case whether this is so. See

North Ocean Shipping v *Hyundai Construction* (1979), *Pao On* v *Lau Yiu Long* (1980) and *Universe Tankships Inc of Monrovia* v *International Transport Workers' Federation, The Universe Sentinel* (1983).

The narrowness of the original concept of duress led to the development of undue influence. The basis of the doctrine was best explained in *Allcard* v *Skinner* (1887) and the rules of undue influence are based on manifest disadvantage of one party conferring benefit on the other. Undue influence may take two forms, that where the law presumes because of the relationship of the parties that undue influence exists and that which must be proved expressly.

Certain statutes, eg Consumer Credit Act 1974 and Fair Trading Act 1973 seek to control transactions where one party may be at a notable disadvantage to the other.

In *Lloyds Bank Ltd* v *Bundy* (1975) Lord Denning, after examining duress, the various forms of improper pressure and inconscionable bargains, sought to derive a general principle from these categories. He felt they all rested in inequality of bargaining power. 'By virtue of it' he said, 'English law gives relief to one who, without independent advice, enters into a contract on terms which are very unfair or transfers property for a consideration which is grossly inadequate, when his bargaining power is grievously impaired by reason of his own needs or desires, or by his own ignorance or infirmity, coupled with undue influence or pressures brought to bear on him by or for the benefit of the other.' The principle, said Denning, did not depend on any proof of wrongdoing, there was no need to establish improper pressure.

In subsequent cases Lord Denning went on to reiterate his view that the concept of inequality of bargaining power is recognised by English law: see *Clifford Davis Management Ltd* v *WEA Records Ltd* (1975) and *Levison* v *Patent Steam Carpet Cleaning Co Ltd* (1978). The equitable rules of undue influence were recently evaluated by the Court of Appeal in *Banco Exterior Internacional SA* v *Thomas and Another* (1997) and *Barclays Bank plc* v *Thomson* (1997). In both these cases the Court stated that the presumption of undue influence may arise by way of constructive notice and the onus was on the lender (bank) to prove the absence of such a notice so as to effectively rebut the presumption.

But did others agree with him? Some support for Denning's argument is derived from the speech of Lord Diplock in *Schroeder Music Publishing Co Ltd* v *Macaulay* (1974), but it should be remembered that Diplock was dealing with the particularly narrow problem of standard form restraint of trade contracts.

Otherwise there has been little indication of judicial support. In *Bundy* itself the other members of the Court of Appeal based their decision on undue influence and did not find it necessary to comment on Denning's argument. A further illustration is provided by the recent case of *Dunbar Bank plc* v *Nadeem* (1998). See also *Royal Bank of Scotland* v *Etridge (No 2)* on the same point.

In *Pao On* v *Lau Yiu Long* Lord Scarman stated that if duress was not established, to treat the unfair use of a dominant bargaining position as a ground for invalidating a contract was 'unhelpful in the development of law' and a year later in *Burmah Oil* v *Bank of England* (1981) the court rejected the argument that inequality of bargaining power is of itself a ground of invalidity.

In *Alec Lobb (Garages) Ltd* v *Total Oil (GB) Ltd* (1985) the plaintiff sought to have the transaction set aside on the grounds, inter alia, that the bargain was harsh and unconscionable. It was argued that because of Total Oil's superior economic position and the financial pressures faced by the plaintiff, the parties were in a position of unequal bargaining power and the courts should apply criteria to assess whether the terms were fair and reasonable.

The Court of Appeal rejected this argument. Dillon LJ observed that it was seldom in any contract that the bargaining power of the two parties was absolutely equal. The courts, said Dillon LJ, 'would only interfere in exceptional cases where as a matter of common fairness it was not right that the strong should be allowed to push the weak to the wall'.

In *National Westminster Bank* v *Morgan* (1985) Lord Scarman pointing out the increasing growth of (particularly) statutory restrictions on freedom of contract declared: 'I question whether there is any need in the modern law to erect a general principle of relief against inequality of bargaining power.'

In conclusion, therefore, it may be said that Denning's proposal has found little support among the judiciary. The increasing importance attached to economic duress and the widening of the scope of this concept has largely, as Treitel points out, rendered Denning's 'golden thread' irrelevant. While it is true to say that most forms of duress and undue influence stem from the inequality of the parties, it is not true that the mere fact that the parties are not on an equal footing will give grounds for declaring the contract invalid.

SUGGESTED ANSWER TO QUESTION THREE

General Comment

This question requires an examination of the development by the courts of the concept of economic duress, and an evaluation of the limits and possible uncertainties of the concept.

Key Points

- The origins of the concept
- Interpretations and approaches by the courts
- The uncertainties
- The limits of the concept
- Possible justification

Suggested Answer

The concept of economic duress is of recent origin, receiving the first clear judicial recognition in *Occidental Worldwide Investment Corporation* v *Skibs A/S Avanti, The Sibeon and The Sibotre* (1976) where Kerr J rejected the earlier narrow confines of duress and held that, in certain circumstances, a contract entered into as a result of economic pressure could be liable to be set aside. Kerr J emphasised, however, that mere commercial pressure, exerted by one party, was not in itself sufficient to constitute duress. He said that the court must be satisfied that the consent of the other party was overborne by compulsion so as to deprive him of his animus contrahendi. The concept of economic duress received further recognition in *North Ocean Shipping Co* v *Hyundai Construction Co, The Atlantic Baron* (1979) where Mocatta J held that a threat to break a contract could amount to duress.

The existence of the doctrine of economic duress has been affirmed by the Court of Appeal in *B & S Contracts and Design Ltd* v *Victor Green Publications Ltd* (1984), by the House of Lords in *Universe Tankships Inc of Monrovia* v *International Transport Workers' Federation* (1983), and by the Judicial Committee of the Privy Council in *Pao On* v *Lau Yiu Long* (1980). In two more recent cases the doctrine has been regarded as firmly established. In *Vantage Navigation Corporation* v *Suhail and Saud Bahwan Building Materials LLC, The Alev* (1989) Hobhouse J stated that the doctrine is 'now well established', and in *Atlas Express Ltd* v *Kafco (Importers and Distributors) Ltd* (1989) Tucker J observed that it was 'a concept recognised by English law'.

There is, it is submitted, still some uncertainty surrounding the operation of the concept. In *The Sibeon* and *The Sibotre*, as has been noted above, duress was distinguished from mere commercial pressure: it was necessary to show that the will of the party concerned had been overborne by compulsion. In *Pao On* the Judicial Committee of the Privy Council endorsed this approach. Lord Scarman said that there must be the presence of some factor 'which could be regarded as coercion of his will so as to vitiate his consent'. The factors to consider were:

1. whether the person alleged to have been coerced did or did not protest;
2. whether he had an adequate legal remedy;
3. whether he was independently legally advised; and
4. whether he subsequently took steps to avoid the contract.

This approach has been subsequently modified. In the *Universe Tankships* case Lord Scarman said that compulsion had been described in the authorities as coercion or the vitiation of consent. But his Lordship went on to say that:

> 'The classic case of duress is, however, not the lack of will to submit but the victim's intentional submission arising from the realisation that there is no other practical choice open to him.'

Lord Scarman emphasised that the lack of choice would be proved in various ways – by protest, by the absence of independent advice, by the steps taken to avoid the contract – but none of these evidentiary matters went to the essence of duress. 'The victims' silence will not assist the bully, if the lack of any practicable choice but to submit is proved.'

It has been suggested that to regard these matters as merely 'evidentiary' creates considerable uncertainty in applying the doctrine: see Andrew Phang 'Whither Economic Duress' (1990) 53 MLR 216. Moreover, whilst the decisions focus on the illegitimacy of the pressure there is some doubt as to what constitutes illegitimate pressure. In *Universe Tankships* Lord Scarman suggested that 'illegitimate' pressure could include pressure that was not 'unlawful' but this suggestion was not elaborated on.

The courts have often stressed the distinction between duress and commercial pressure. In *Lloyds Bank Ltd* v *Bundy* (1975) Lord Denning MR sought to merge the concept of duress with the broader doctrine of 'inequality of bargaining power'. Subsequently, Lord Denning reiterated the view that English law recognised the doctrine in *Clifford Davis Management Ltd* v *WEA Records Ltd* (1975) and *Levison* v *Patent Steam Cleaning Co Ltd* (1978). Some recognition appeared to be afforded to the doctrine by the speech of Lord Diplock in *Schroeder Music Publishing Co Ltd* v *Macaulay* (1974), but this was in the particular context of a restraint of trade clause in a standard form contract.

But this broad doctrine was doubted by the Privy Council in *Pao On* and expressly disapproved by the House of Lords in *National Westminster Bank plc* v *Morgan* (1985). Lord Scarman observed that the legislature had undertaken the task of enacting restrictions on freedom of contract, and he doubted whether the courts should assume the burden of formulating further restrictions. In the Court of Appeal, in *Alec Lobb (Garages) Ltd* v *Total Oil (Great Britain) Ltd* (1985), Dillon LJ, in rejecting the argument based on unequal bargaining power, noted that it was seldom in any negotiation that the bargaining power of the parties was absolutely equal.

Recently there has been confirmation that the concept of economic duress is still developing: see *Alf Vaughan & Co* v *Royscot Trust plc* (1999). Whilst this may be so the success of such a case still remains doubtful.

9

Privity of Contract and Assignment of Contractual Rights

Introduction

This chapter is concerned principally with the doctrine of privity of contract. The doctrine states that only parties to a contract may have rights and obligations under it. However, to mitigate the harshness which this would sometimes mean to the plaintiff, both the courts and Parliament have devised exceptions to the doctrine. This then culminated in the passing of the Contracts (Rights of Third Parties) Act 1999, which positively grants right to 'eligible' third parties. Thus, there is a great deal of scope for both problem and discussion questions in this area.

While someone not a party to a contract can take neither the benefit nor the burden, there is nothing to stop a party assigning his rights to another. This must, however, be done in accordance with the common law and equitable rules which Parliament and the courts have devised.

Questions

INTERROGRAMS

1. While the courts will allow the benefit of a contract to be enforced by and for third parties, it will not allow enforcement of the burdens against third parties. Discuss.
2. Why, despite criticism, does the law still uphold the doctrine of privity of contract?
3. Explain the following legal phrases:

   a) chose in action;
   b) novation;
   c) negotiable instrument.

4. Discuss the role of equity in developing the law relating to contractual assignment.

QUESTION ONE

'The doctrine of privity has become largely irrelevant as a result of recent changes.'
Discuss.

University of London LLB Examination
(for external students) Elements of the Law of Contract June 2001 Q6

QUESTION TWO

'Privity of contract is dead.'

Discuss.

University of London LLB Examination
(for external students) Elements of the Law of Contract June 1999 Q8

QUESTION THREE

'Allowing third parties to enforce contractual rights creates more problems than it solves.'

Discuss.

University of London LLB Examination
(for external students) Elements of the Law of Contract June 1997 Q5

QUESTION FOUR

'The commercial reality is that contracts are made for the benefit of third parties and the law finds ways of enforcing them; for better or for worse, burdens do not pass.'

Discuss.

University of London LLB Examination
(for external students) Elements of the Law of Contract June 1994 Q6

Answers

ANSWERS TO INTERROGRAMS

1. With regard to the imposition of burdens on third parties the general principle is that a contract cannot do so. This aspect of the doctrine of privity of contract has not led to the controversy which has followed attempts to extend the doctrine in respect of conferring benefits on third parties. There can be little justification for a party having to submit to obligations in a contract to which he was not a party. The only exceptions to this principle are in the law of property. Covenants in leases are binding not only on the original parties, but also on their successors in title. Covenants restricting the use of land may be binding in equity on subsequent purchasers of the land with notice of the covenant: *Tulk* v *Moxhay* (1848). In *Taddy* v *Sterious* (1904) the court refused to extend this principle to goods. The attempted extension of the principle to contracts for the hire of ships by the Privy Council in *Lord Strathcona Steamship Co* v *Dominion Coal Co* (1926) has been disavowed: *Port Line Ltd* v *Ben Line Steamers Ltd* (1958); *Bendall* v *McWhirter* (1952).

   While this represents the state of the law at present, there are ways of imposing a burden on a third party such as the creation of a lien or the creation of an equitable interest or irrevocable licence. Additionally, where there has been interference with contractual rights a cause of action may arise in tort, but not in contract, against the third party guilty of the interference: *Lumley* v *Gye* (1853); *British Motor Trade Association* v *Salvadori* (1949).

2. The doctrine of privity of contract has two aspects: the first is that a person who was not party to a contract cannot acquire rights under it; the second is that a person not party to the contract cannot have obligations imposed on him by that contract. The doctrine has been much criticised, certainly in relation to the first aspect, and Lord Denning made frequent attempts to abandon it, but at the time of writing it remains part of our law. The second aspect of the doctrine can be justified, but it is the refusal of English law to recognise third party rights in the conferring of benefits that is more difficult to justify. Treitel suggests four possible reasons for the retention of the doctrine. The first is that a contract is a personal affair, affecting only the parties to it; the second is that it would not be just to allow a person to sue on a contract when he could not be sued on it; the third is that to allow third party rights would interfere with the rights of the contracting parties to vary or rescind the contract; and the fourth possible reason is that the third party is often a mere donee and that it would be contrary to principle to allow him a contractual right.

   A further feature of the privity of contract doctrine is that the promisee cannot sue for the third party's loss: see *Woodar Investment Development Ltd* v *Wimpey Construction (UK) Ltd* (1980) where the House of Lords disapproved the view of Lord Denning to the contrary in *Jackson* v *Horizon Holidays* (1975). In *Forster* v *Silvermere Golf and Equestrian Centre* (1981) Dillon J referred to this rule as 'a blot on our law and most unjust'.

   Abolition of the rule that a third party cannot enforce the benefit was recommended by the Law Revision Committee in 1937. And in *Woodar* v *Wimpey* (1980) Lord Scarman remarked that as the legislature had not acted to implement that recommendation the courts might have to. The Law Commission have recently published a consultation paper recommending that a third party should be able to enforce contractual promises subject to the promisor having the same defences and the same rights as to set-off and counter-claim as he would have against the promisee. The Commission recommends that parties to a contract should not be able thereby to impose duties on a third party.

   In view of the judicial criticisms and repeated calls for the modification of the doctrine of privity of contract it is difficult to see why English law retains the doctrine.

3. a) A chose in action is intangible property which includes not only contractual rights but all kinds of other rights which may only be enforced by legal action. Examples are insurance policies, copyright, patents and rights under trusts or wills. A chose in action may be legal or equitable depending on its nature. In *Torkington* v *Magee* (1902), Channell J defined them as follows:

   > 'Chose in action' is a known legal expression used to describe all personal rights of property which can only be claimed or enforced by action, and not by taking possession.'

   b) One way of transferring contractual benefits and burdens to a third party is by novation. All the parties to the contract and the third party who is to take over the contract must consent to novation. However, novation may be implied where the third party assumes the benefit and burden of the contract and the other party allows him to do so: *Howard* v *Patent Ivory Manufacturing Co* (1888).

c) Negotiable instruments are a type of chose in action which have specific characteristics. First, the holder of a negotiable instrument may sue in his or her own name. He may sue all previous parties to the instrument. Second, the instrument is transferred not by assignment but by indorsement or delivery (where payable to order) or mere delivery (where payable to bearer). Third, the transferee takes rights of ownership free of equities (so long as he is a holder in due course).

There are three main types of negotiable instrument in use today. By far the most important of these is the cheque (which is actually a bill of exchange but drawn on a banker and payable on demand – s73 Bills of Exchange Act 1882). There are also other types of bills of exchange, much used in international commercial transactions. The requirements for an instrument to be a bill of exchange are laid down in s3(1) Bills of Exchange Act (1882): it must be an unconditional order in writing addressed by one person to another, signed by the person giving it, and requiring the person to whom it is addressed to pay on demand a sum certain in money to or to the order of a specified person or to bearer.

4. Apart from certain specific exceptions such as negotiable instruments, the common law did not allow transfer of choses in action. Equity not only recognised such assignments but would recognise even the intention to carry out an assignment without any formal execution. The assignment gives the assignee the right to sue in his own name.

Assignments of certain equitable interests do however have to be in writing (s53(1)(c) Law of Property Act 1925).

It is not necessary to give notice to the debtor that the rights have been assigned, but it is desirable from the assignee's point of view, for the rule in *Dearle* v *Hall* (1828) provides that priority of claim is established by the order in which assignees give notice to the debtor.

There are certain principles which stem from an equitable assignment. Firstly, the assignee takes 'subject to the equities', ie any defence which the debtor might have used against the assignor will be available against the assignee. Secondly, the assignee will not be able to enforce the debt unless he has given consideration for the assignment ('Equity will not assist a volunteer'). Thirdly, the assignee must join the assignor in any action against the debtor.

There are some further general limits to assignment. Assignments which are against public policy or which may prejudice the debtor are not enforceable. Examples of the former include the assignment by a wife of her maintenance payments and the assignment of his salary by the holder of a public office. Examples of the latter include personal contracts where the identity of a party is important and contracts to give financial assistance to a party to commence an action.

SUGGESTED ANSWER TO QUESTION ONE

General Comment

What is required here is a discussion of the current status of the doctrine of privity of contract; an examination of the rules concerning the conferring of benefits; and the imposition of liabilities on third parties and the modifications to those rules effected by the Contracts (Rights of Third Parties) Act 1999.

Key Points

- Privity of contract: the two rules – the conferring of benefits and the imposition of liabilities
- The conferring of benefits – the common law rules and the modifications of those rules by the 1999 Act
- The imposition of liabilities – the current law

Suggested Answer

The doctrine of privity of contract involves the application of the two rules: one, that a person could not enforce a benefit conferred on him by a contract to which he was not a party; two, that a person cannot have a liability imposed on him by a contract to which he was not a party. I shall examine each of these rules in turn.

The conferring of a benefit

In *Dunlop Pneumatic Tyre Co Ltd* v *Selfridge & Co Ltd* (1915) Viscount Haldane LC held as a fundamental principle in the law of England 'that only a person who is a party to a contract can sue on it.' This meant that even where a contract expressly conferred a benefit on a third party, he could not enforce it.

The rule derives from the decision in *Tweddle* v *Atkinson* (1861) and was reaffirmed by the House of Lords in *Beswick* v *Beswick* (1968). In that case the promisor had contracted with his uncle to pay a pension to the uncle's widow on the former's death, and when he failed to do so the widow, not being a party to the contract, could not enforce the promise in her personal capacity.

Whilst the promisee might be able to enforce the promise, he could not, as a rule, claim for the third party's loss: *Woodar Investment Development Ltd* v *Wimpey Construction (UK) Ltd* (1980); *Forster* v *Silvermere Golf and Equestrian Centre* (1981). The exceptional situation is where it is found that it was within the contemplation of the contracting parties that any breach of it would cause loss to an identifiable third party.

The rule had long been criticised. Attempts to circumvent it by the trust concept were largely unsuccessful: see *Re Schebsman* (1944); *Vandepitte* v *Preferred Accident Insurance Corp of New York* (1933).

Attempts to confer the benefit of an exemption clause on third parties created difficulties. The third party could not rely on the exemption clause in a contract in *Scruttons Ltd* v *Midland Silicones Ltd* (1962). Allowing a third party to enforce an exemption clause was obtained in *The Eurymedon* (1975) and *The New York Star*

(1981) by the somewhat questionable approach of inferring a contract between the promisor and the third party.

The rule as to conferring a benefit on a third party has not been abrogated, but has been substantially modified by the Contracts (Rights of Third Parties) Act 1999. The Act allows a third party to enforce a contract in specified circumstances. (Note: This dispenses with the usual requirement that consideration must move from the promisee.)

Section1(1) of the 1999 Act sets out the circumstances in which a third party can enforce a term of the contract: (a) where the contract expressly provides that he may; and (b) where the term purports to confer a benefit on him. But s1(1)(b) does not apply if it appears that the parties did not intend the term to be enforceable by the third party: s1(2).

Section 1(3) provides the important requirement that the third party must be expressly identified in the contract by name, class or description. But the third party need not be in existence when the contract is made. This allows the contracting parties to confer enforceable rights on, for example, an unborn child, a future spouse or a company that has not yet been incorporated.

It is open to the contracting parties to limit or place conditions on the third party's rights of enforcement (s1(4)); but subject to that the third party will have available to him the remedies for breach of contract that would have been available if he had been a contracting party: s1(5).

The question of third party enforcement of exemption clauses is dealt with in s1(6) which makes it clear that the Act enables a third party to take advantage of an exemption clause in a contract.

It may be possible for the contracting parties to rescind or vary the contract subject to the provisions of s2.

This does not purport to be an exhaustive exposition of the Act, merely of its salient provisions. But it is clear from the above discussion that there will be situations where the Act does not apply.

When the Act does not apply certain difficulties may remain. Thus, in *Panatown Ltd* v *Alfred McAlpine Construction Ltd* (2000) the claimant contracted with the defendant to do building work on land owned by a third party and required the defendant to execute a deed giving the latter a remedy for any failure to exercise reasonable care and skill. Alleging breach of contract, the claimant, who had not suffered any loss, sought damages for the loss suffered by the third party. The House of Lords held by a majority that the claim could not succeed. The exception to the rule regarding recovery for a third party's loss (mentioned above) did not apply where it was intended that the third party should have a direct claim against the defendant.

Imposing a liability

The common law rule in this regard is unaffected by the Act. It remains the position that a person cannot have a liability imposed on him by a contract to which he was not a party. The one real exception to this is in the law of property where restrictive covenants relating to the use of land may bind successors in title to the land: *Tulk* v *Moxhay* (1848).

Whilst a person cannot have contractual liability imposed on him by a contract to which he was a stranger, he may incur liability in tort if he induces a breach of that contract or interferes with the contractual rights of the contracting parties: *Lumley* v *Gye* (1853); *British Motor Trade Association* v *Salvadori* (1949); *Law Debenture Trust Corporation* v *Ural Caspian Oil Corporation Ltd* (1993).

It is thus incorrect to state that the doctrine of privity 'has become largely irrelevant'. The common law rules will still obtain with regard the the conferring of benefits where the 1999 Act does not apply and remain in force with regard to the imposition of liabilities.

SUGGESTED ANSWER TO QUESTION TWO

General Comment

The particular emphasis required in this question is on the provisions of the Contracts (Rights of Third Parties) Act 1999. The other aspect to be considered is the imposing of liabilities on third parties.

Key Points

- Conferring benefits on third parties: the previous common law rules
- The provisions of the Act: the right of a third party to enforce contractual terms
- Imposing liability on a third party

Suggested Answer

The two matters to be considered in a discussion of privity of contract are, first, contracts which confer benefits on third parties and, second, contracts which impose liabilities on third parties.

Conferring benefits on third parties

The common law principle was stated thus by Viscount Haldane LC in *Dunlop Pneumatic Tyre Co Ltd* v *Selfridge & Co Ltd* (1915):

> 'My Lords, in the law of England certain principles are fundamental. One is that only a person who is a party to a contract can sue on it. Our law knows nothing of a jus quaesitum tertio arising by way of contract.'

The rule established in the middle of the nineteenth century by *Tweddle* v *Atkinson* (1861) was that where the terms of a contract conferred a benefit on a third party, those terms could not be enforced by that third party, a ruling endorsed by the House of Lords a century later in *Beswick* v *Beswick* (1968).

This rules endured despite the many criticisms of it, and attempts to evade it by the use of the trust concept were largely unsuccessful.

The common law in this regard has now been substantially altered by the Contracts (Rights of Third Parties) Act 1999, the main provisions of which must now be examined. (What follows does not purport to be an exhaustive review of the entire Act.)

The main thrust of the Act is in s1. This effectively abrogates the rule in *Tweddle* v *Atkinson* (above).

Section 1(1) sets out the circumstances in which a third party may enforce the terms of a contract. First, where the contract itself expressly so provides and, second, where the contract purports to confer a benefit on the third party, unless it appears on the true construction of the contract that the contracting parties did not intend the term to be enforceable by the third party: s1(2).

Section 1(3) states the requirements necessary for these circumstances to apply. The third party must be expressly identified by name, class or description. But such third parties need not be in existence when the contract is made. This allows contracting parties to confer enforceable rights on, for example, an unborn child or a future spouse or a company that is yet to be incorporated.

Section 1(4) provides that the contracting parties may impose limits or conditions on enforcement by the third party.

Section 1(5) establishes that the third party who is entitled to enforce the contract shall have the same remedies available to him as if he were a contracting party.

Section 1(6) clarifies the position with regard to the right of third parties to take advantage of an exclusion or limitation clause in a contract. Previously, at common law, the third party could not avail himself of the benefit of such a clause unless in somewhat special circumstances: compare *Scruttons Ltd* v *Midland Silicones Ltd* (1962) with *New Zealand Shipping Co Ltd* v *AM Satterthwaite & Co Ltd* (1975). This subsection makes it clear that the Act applies so as to enable a third party to take advantage of an exclusion or limitation clause. It allows, for example, a term of a contract which excludes or limits the promisee's liability to the promisor for the tort of negligence, and states expressly that the term is for the benefit of the promisee's 'employees agents etc', to be enforceable by those third parties.

Section 2 regulates the variation and rescission of a contract. In broad terms the contracting parties may not by agreement rescind the contract, or vary it so as to extinguish or alter the third party's rights, without his consent. This is in the absence of an express term in the contract that can be rescinded or varied without the third party's consent.

Section 3 provides that, in a claim by the third party, the promisor can rely on any defence or set-off arising out of the contract and relevant to the term being enforced, which would have been available to him had the claim been made by the promisee.

At common law the privity rule did not debar the promisee from enforcing that contract, and this is preserved by s4. At common law, however, the promisee cannot sue for the third party's loss: *Woodar Investment Development Ltd* v *Wimpey Construction (UK) Ltd* (1980). This had not been altered, but it is perhaps unnecessary to do so, in view of the right now afforded to the third party.

Imposing liabilities on third parties

It would obviously be wholly unreasonable for contracting parties to be able to impose a burden on someone who was not party to their contract. This was and remains the law. The one exception to this is in contracts concerning land. In *Tulk* v *Moxhay* (1848) the plaintiff sold land subject to a restrictive covenant. After several conveyances the land was eventually conveyed to the defendant, who had notice of the covenant. By virtue of having such notice the defendant was bound by a contract to which he was not a party.

In *Lord Strathcona Steamship Co* v *Dominion Coal Co Ltd* (1926) the Privy Council sought to extend the rule in *Tulk* v *Moxhay* to apply to an obligation in favour of the plaintiffs relating to a ship. The plaintiffs were granted an injunction restraining the defendants from using the ship in any way inconsistent with this obligation. The defendants, although not a party to the contract creating the obligation, had notice of it. This proved a controversial decision and in *Bendall* v *McWhirter* (1952) and *Port Line Ltd* v *Ben Line Steamers Ltd* (1958) the courts refused to follow it. However, in *Law Debenture Trust Corporation* v *Ural Caspian Oil Corporation Ltd* (1993) Hoffmann J said that he considered the decision to be good law.

There is a method of circumventing the privity rule with regard to imposing liability on a third party. That is by application of the tort of inference with contractual rights. This derives from the case of *Lumley* v *Gye* (1853), which held that a wrong had been committed by the defendant's inference with the plaintiff's rights under a contract. Although not a party to that contract, the defendant knew of the plaintiff's rights, and the interference was deliberate. The result in the *Strathcona* case can be justified by reference to this tort.

A useful method of evading the privity rule is to find a collateral contract between the promisor and the third party: *Shanklin Pier Ltd* v *Detel Products Ltd* (1951); *Charnock* v *Liverpool Corporation* (1968).

The recent Act has considerably extended the scope for the enforcement of benefits by a third party but the doctrine of privity of contract is far from dead.

SUGGESTED ANSWER TO QUESTION THREE

General Comment

A direct question raising issues in relation to the doctrine of privity of contract, its justifications and the recent advent of the Contracts (Rights of Third Parties) Act 1999.

Key Points

- The present law with regard to the enforcement of third party rights
- The rationale for the present law: the problems that might ensue in allowing third party enforcement
- The Contracts (Rights of Third Parties) Act 1999

Suggested Answer

The present law, in the words of Lord Haldane in *Dunlop Pneumatic Tyre Co Ltd* v *Selfridge & Co Ltd* (1915) is:

> '... in the law of England certain principles are fundamental. One is that only a person who is a party to a contract can sue on it. Our law knows nothing of a jus quaesitum tertio arising by way of contract.'

The doctrine was established in *Tweddle* v *Atkinson* (1861), and has been affirmed by the House of Lords in *Scruttons Ltd* v *Midland Silicones Ltd* (1962) and in the leading modern case of *Beswick* v *Beswick* (1968).

The rationale for the present doctrine appears to be as follows: (i) only the parties to a contract should have rights arising out of it; (ii) it would not be just to allow a third party the right to sue on a contract on which he could not be sued; (iii) if the third party could enforce the contract that would debar the contracting parties from varying or rescinding it; and (iv) consideration would often not have moved from the third party.

The consequence of the privity rule is not only that the third party cannot enforce the rights conferred upon him by the contract. In the event of breach by the promisor, whilst the promisee might be able to enforce the contract by way of an order for specific performance (as in *Beswick* v *Beswick*), he cannot sue for damages for the third party's loss: *Woodar Investment Development Ltd* v *Wimpey Construction (UK) Ltd* (1980); *Forster* v *Silvermere Golf and Equestrian Centre Ltd* (1981). Nor can a third party rely on the benefit of an exclusion clause in a contract to which he was not party (see *Scruttons Ltd* v *Midland Silicones Ltd*), save in the particular circumstances of *The Eurymedon* (1975) and *The New York Star* (1980).

The privity rule has been heavily criticised in a number of judicial decisions. The rationale for the doctrine has been mentioned. The obstacles in the path of reform have been said to include: the problem that consideration may not have moved from the third party; the difficulties in defining exactly what classes of persons can acquire rights under the contract; and in defining precisely how those rights would be affected by defences available to the contracting parties themselves.

Parliament has recently passed the Contracts (Rights of Third Parties) Act 1999. It came into effect on 11 November 1999.

The new Act sets out a two-limbed test for the circumstances in which a third party may enforce the contract: (i) where the contract expressly so provides; and (ii) where the contract purports to confer a benefit on the third party, unless it appears on a true construction of the contract that the contracting parties did not intend him to have the right to enforce it. The third party must be expressly identified in the contract by name, class or description, but need not be in existence when the contract is made - for example, the third party may be a future spouse, an unborn child or a company not yet incorporated.

The new Act also provides that all the remedies available to a plaintiff for breach of contract may be awarded to a third party, and the normal rules applicable to those remedies would apply.

The Act would further entitle a third party to the benefit of an exclusion or limitation clause.

Where a third party has the right of enforceability, the Act sets out the extent to which the contracting parties can vary or cancel the contract without the third party's consent. The contracting parties may not vary or cancel the contract after the third party has communicated his assent to the contract to the promisor; or after the third party has relied on the contract, where the promisor is aware of the reliance or could reasonably be expected to have foreseen it. However, these rules would be displaced by an express term in the contract providing that the contract can be cancelled or varied without the third party's consent, or specifying different circumstances in which such consent is required.

The Act also provides that the promisor would have available to him any defence or set-off which would have been available to him if the action had been brought by the promisee.

The new Act would effectively mitigate the harshness of the old rule. Be that as it may, parties may nonetheless choose to exclude its application in their contract, by way of an express term.

SUGGESTED ANSWER TO QUESTION FOUR

General Comment

Another essay-type question which calls for a discussion of the doctrine of privity of contract. Central to the question is the issue of enforcement by third parties and whether the 1999 Act creates problems as opposed to resolving them.

Key Points

- Statement of the doctrine
- Enforcement by the third party
- Remedies of the promisee
- Benefit of exclusion clauses
- Evasion of and exceptions to the doctrine
- The application of the Contracts (Rights of Third Parties) Act 1999
- Imposing burdens on third parties

Suggested Answer

The principle of law in relation to third party rights under a contract was expressed by Viscount Haldane LC in *Dunlop Pneumatic Tyre Co Ltd* v *Selfridge & Co Ltd* (1915) as follows:

> '... in the law of England certain principles are fundamental. One is that only a person who is a party to a contract can sue on it. Our law knows nothing of a jus quaesitum tertio arising by way of contract.'

This principle derives from the decision in *Tweddle* v *Atkinson* (1861) and was re-affirmed by the House of Lords in *Beswick* v *Beswick* (1968), where their Lordships rejected the argument that the common law had been radically altered by s56(1) Law of Property Act 1925 – an argument which had found favour in the Court of Appeal.

Whilst it is the general rule that the third party cannot enforce the promise in the contract, a remedy may be available to the promisee: in *Beswick* v *Beswick* the promisee was able to obtain an order for specific performance.

This is an uncertain remedy, specific performance being an equitable, discretionary remedy, may not always be available.

A remedy in damages may also not be available to the promisee. The promisee would be entitled to sue for his own loss, but in many circumstances he would not have suffered any loss. It seems clear that the promisee cannot sue for the third party's loss. In

Jackson v *Horizon Holidays Ltd* (1975) Lord Denning MR had held that he could do so, but this view was rejected by the House of Lords in *Woodar Investment Development Ltd* v *Wimpey Construction (UK) Ltd* (1980). The rule that the promisee can recover only for his own loss and not that of the third party was regarded by Dillon J in *Forster* v *Silvermere Golf and Equestrian Centre* (1981) as 'a blot on our law and most unjust'.

Where A promises B, for consideration, not to sue C, although this would not provide a defence to C, it may be possible for B to prevent A from doing so, where B has a sufficient interest in the enforcement of the promise: *Gore* v *Van Der Lann* (1967); *Snelling* v *Snelling Ltd* (1973).

A third party cannot generally rely on the benefit of an exclusion clause in a contract: *Scruttons Ltd* v *Midland Silicones Ltd* (1962). However, in that case Lord Reid set out certain conditions which might enable him to do so. These were (i) that the third party was intended to be benefited by the provisions of the exclusion clause; (ii) that the promisee made it clear that in addition to acting on his own behalf, he was also acting as agent for the third party; (iii) that he had authority to do so; and (iv) that any difficulty about consideration moving from the third party was overcome. These conditions were held to be satisfied in *New Zealand Shipping Co Ltd* v *A M Satterthwaite & Co Ltd, The Eurymedon* (1975) and *Port Jackson Stevedoring Pty Ltd* v *Salmond & Spraggon Pty Ltd, The New York Star* (1980).

In *Norwich City Council* v *Harvey* (1989) the contract between the plaintiff and the contractors provided that the risk of loss or damage by fire should be borne by the plaintiff. The sub-contractors, who were not privy to that contract, set fire to the building. Though they would have been in breach of duty to the plaintiff, the provisions of the main contract, in the circumstances of the case, negatived that duty. Thus the third party could invoke those provisions as a defence to the claim against him.

The trust concept might provide a possibility for the third party to enforce the benefit. If it can be shown that in a contract between A and B, conferring a benefit on C, B was acting as trustee for C, then C can directly enforce A's obligation in equity. However, the trust concept can rarely be successfully invoked: *Vandepitte* v *Preferred Accident Insurance Corp of New York* (1933). *In Re Schebsman* (1944) Lord Greene MR said that, 'it is not legitimate to import into a contract the idea of a trust when the parties have given no indication that such was their intention.'

Whilst, therefore, the law can find ways of enforcing contracts for the benefit of third parties, the doctrine of privity of contract limits the circumstances in which this can be achieved at common law. There are a number of statutory exceptions to the doctrine: s11 Married Woman's Property Act 1882; s14(2) Marine Insurance Act 1906; ss47(1), 56(1) Law of Property Act 1925; s148(7) Road Traffic Act 1988.

With regard to the imposition of burdens on third parties the general principle is that a contract cannot do so. This aspect of the doctrine of privity of contract is less open to controversy; there can be little justification for a party having to submit to obligations in a contract to which he was not a party. The only exceptions to this principle are in the law of property. Covenants in leases are binding not only on the original parties, but also on their successors in title. Covenants restricting the use of land may be binding in equity on subsequent purchasers of the land with notice of the covenant: *Tulk* v *Moxhay*

(1848). In *Taddy & Co Ltd* v *Sterious & Co Ltd* (1904) the court refused to extend this principle to goods. The attempted extension of the principle to contracts for the hire of ships by the Privy Council in *Lord Strathcona Steamship Co* v *Dominion Coal Co* (1926) has been disavowed: *Port Line Ltd* v *Ben Line Steamers Ltd* (1958); *Bendall* v *McWhirter* (1952).

Where there has been interference with contractual rights a cause of action may arise in tort, but not in contract, against the third party guilty of the interference: *Lumley* v *Gye* (1853).

Whilst this may have been the position until 1999, the recent passing of the Contracts (Rights of Third Parties) Act 1999, which came into effect on 11 November 1999, now provides that third parties can enforce contracts. Particular attention must be paid to ss1(1)(a), (b) and 1(2) which outline the way in which third parties may seek enforcement. This is notwithstanding the fact that the main contracting parties are still in control.

10

Illegality

Introduction

The court will not enforce a contract which is void for illegality. If the contract is not void, however, some rights and obligations may be enforceable. Contracts may be illegal as formed or illegal in performance, and the candidate must be able to explain the different effects of each. Both may appear in the same question. The candidate must also be aware of the situations in which the court will refuse to enforce a contract on grounds of public policy. Principal among these are contracts in restraint of trade. Restraint clauses have long been held to be void if too wide to protect the interests of the party who inserted the clauses. Although a restraint clause may appear in any kind of contract, there are two particular kinds of contract which have attracted a large body of case law: contracts of employment and contracts for the sale of a business. A successful candidate will be required to show familiarity with the cases in question, as well as more recent cases involving 'solus agreements', tying the tenant of a petrol station to a particular petrol company. There have been several recent decisions on this area: *Awwad* v *Geraghty & Co* (2000), *Birkett* v *Acorn Business Machines Ltd* (1999), *Carnduff* v *Rock* (2001), *Mohamed* v *Alaga & Co (A Firm)* (2000), *Factortame Ltd* v *Secretary of State for the Environment, Transport and the Regions (No 2)* (2002) and *Callery* v *Gray (Nos 1 and 2)* (2002). Note also the relevance of the Financial Services and Markets Act 2000 (Gaming Contracts) Order 2001.

Questions

INTERROGRAMS

1. There are several kinds of contract which the courts refuse to enforce on the grounds of public policy. A contract in restraint of trade is one example. Explain and illustrate some of the others.
2. Explain, illustrating with examples from case law, how the doctrine of restraint of trade has been applied to many diverse factual situations.
3. 'Neither party to an illegal contract can enforce it.' Discuss

QUESTION ONE

Peter was a licensed dealer in pet food under the (fictitional) Licensing of Pet Food Act 2001. Section 1 of the Act requires any person selling pet food to be licensed and if 'anyone shall trade in pet food without the appropriate licence he shall be guilty of a criminal offence.' Section 2 requires sales of pet food to be accompanied by a 'statutory invoice' which must contain details of the food supplied and a statement of the quantity supplied.

a) Peter supplied Queenie with pet food costing £500 but failed to provide a statutory invoice at the time of delivery because it had fallen out of the box in which it had been placed by Peter's employee. Queenie refused to pay for the pet food.
b) Peter supplied Robert with pet food but failed to provide a statutory invoice after Robert had said, 'Between friends no formalities are required.' Robert refused to pay for the pet food and claimed damages from Peter because, he claimed, the pet food was of poor quality.
c) Peter was paid £600 by Stephan for pet food to be delivered to Stephan's restaurant. Peter suspected that Stephan might be using the food for human consumption (which was prohibited by statute). It was subsequently, discovered that Stephan was using the pet food for this purpose. Stephan sought the repayment of the £600.
d) Peter agreed to supply pet food costing £2,000 to Thomas which Thomas paid for in advance. It was then discovered that, unknown to Peter, his licence had expired. Peter refused to deliver the pet food to Thomas or to return the £2,000 which Thomas had paid in advance.

Advise the parties.

University of London LLB Examination
(for external students) Elements of the Law of Contract June 2001 Q5

QUESTION TWO

K was a licensed dealer in gaudy china under the (fictitious) Antiques Dealers Act 2000. Section 1 of the Act prohibits dispositions of gaudy china by dealers without a licence. According to s2 of the Act all dispositions have to be accompanied by a statutory notice describing the goods, stating the quantity and indicating the price.

K sold and delivered two gaudy cups and saucers to L. They were described as Aberdare pattern but the statutory notice failed to state the agreed price of £200.

K sold and delivered a gaudy bowl to M for £400. However, K did not deliver a statutory notice after M had said that he did not need one.

K sold and delivered two gaudy jugs to N for £600. K supplied a statutory notice two days after delivery. Subsequently, N discovered that one of the jugs had been repaired and wanted to return the two jugs to K.

K sold and delivered two gaudy teapots to P for £800 with a statutory notice but unknown to K his licence under the Act had expired.

Advise K. K has not been paid for any of the china expect by N who has paid £600 in advance.

University of London LLB Examination
(for external students) Elements of the Law of Contract June 2000 Q6

QUESTION THREE

C was a registered supplier of Welsh ink. A statute provides that, because it is poisonous, the ink can be supplied only by registered suppliers and only to licensed recipients. Each delivery has to be accompanied by a statutory invoice describing the contents.

C supplied 20 gallons of ink to D, a licensed recipient, but C failed to deliver a statutory invoice because D had said he did not require one.

C sold and delivered 10 gallons of ink with a statutory invoice to E who was not a licensed recipient.

C supplied 10 gallons of ink to F who was a licensed recipient. F knew that C had failed to provide an invoice when the ink was delivered.

C sold and delivered 15 gallons of ink to G, a licensed recipient, when, unknown to C, his registration had expired.

None of the recipients paid for the ink.

Advise C.

University of London LLB Examination
(for external students) Elements of the Law of Contract June 1999 Q2

QUESTION FOUR

F was a prostitute who had just moved to London where she was not known. She leased a flat in a fashionable part of town from E, agreeing to pay £1,000 a week rent. E did not know that F was a prostitute: he guessed that she must either be a very highly paid executive or a prostitute, but he was not sure which. F arranged for G to refurbish the flat for £28,000: this included £12,000 for a luxurious bed. F bought food and wine from H which cost £4,500. F bought a large car with a specially constructed rear seat from J. J did not know that F was a prostitute, though the request for a large back seat was unusual. F has paid for none of these items. K paid £12,000 in advance for 48 'love sessions' at £250 each. After four sessions F refused either to perform with K or return his money.

Advise F. What difference, if any, would it make to your advice if F was only 17 years old?

University of London LLB Examination
(for external students) Elements of the Law of Contract June 1998 Q4

QUESTION FIVE

'The reality of illegality is that both parties to the contract are unable to enforce it.'

Discuss.

Written by the Editor

Answers

ANSWERS TO INTERROGRAMS

1. The categories of case which the courts refuse to enforce on grounds of public policy are as follows:

   Contracts which pervert the course of justice
   Agreements to conceal or compound a crime are unenforceable. Compounding a

criminal offence is defined by s5 Criminal Law Act 1967. While concealing evidence would fall within this definition, it appears that the court is not prepared to extend this to an agreement not to give evidence in a civil hearing, see *Fulham Football Club Ltd* v *Cabra Estates plc* (1992) which concerned an agreement by plaintiffs with a development company that they would not give evidence to support the local authority's application for planning permission rather than the development company's.

Agreements not to appear in court and give evidence in criminal proceedings are unenforceable as is an agreement to indemnify someone who has stood surety for bail.

In the area of bankruptcy and liquidation, statute makes voidable agreements to transfer property which would amount to a fraudulent conveyance or the fraudulent preference of a creditor over others.

Champterty and maintenance

Both of these grounds concern civil rather than criminal litigation. Maintenance is interference in litigation by a person who has no concern or interest in it. Champerty is where one party agrees to finance another's action in return for a share in the winnings. Both were formerly torts and crimes but under ss13 and 14 Criminal Law Act 1967 they are no longer. However, contracts made for these purposes are still unenforceable. Examples of cases are *Martell* v *Consett Iron Co Ltd* (1955) where an association for the protection of rivers from pollution supports an action by one of its members and *Picton-Jones & Co* v *Arcadia Developments* (1989) where surveyors agreed to act for defendants on terms that fees would only be payable if the action were successful.

Interference with government or foreign relations

The common law offence of accepting a bribe or showing favour as a public officer has now been replaced by s117 Local Government Act 1972, but any contract by a public officer to do so is unenforceable. Equally unenforceable is a contract to procure an honour or public office in return for payment: *Parkinson* v *Royal College of Ambulance* (1925).

There are a number of examples of cases where a contract to mislead a public authority by concealing or misrepresenting facts has been held void. One is *Alexander* v *Rayson* (1936) which concerned a contract to deceive the rating authority as to the rates payable in respect of a service flat.

The principle that contracts to trade with the enemy are unenforceable has, of course, only been relevant when the country has been at war. A contract to interfere with foreign relations can, however, be relevant at any time. Where a contract aids a party to circumvent the law in their own country, it will be illegal and unenforceable, as illustrated by *Regazzoni* v *KC Sethia* (1958), which concerned an agreement to export Indian goods to South Africa via Italy to avoid sanctions. A recent example is *Howard* v *Shirlstar Container Transport Ltd* (1990), where the defendants agreed to pay the plaintiff a sum of money to fly an aircraft belonging to them out of Nigeria without obtaining the necessary clearance. The court, however, allowed the plaintiff to claim the money because, although the contract was illegal, the purpose had been to save his own and his crew's lives.

Family contracts
Marriage brokerage contracts are void (*Hermann* v *Charlesworth* (1905)) and also contracts to restrain or prevent a marriage (*Lowe* v *Peers* (1768)). A contract by parties to divorce proceedings is void if made with a corrupt intention. For example, in *Brodie* v *Brodie* (1917), a contract between a couple who had felt obliged to marry because the woman was pregnant, that they would not live together after the marriage, was held to be void.

Contracts to promote sexual immorality
These are contracts which promote extra-marital sexual intercourse. A contract between lovers is not now generally illegal even if the purpose is to provide a mistress with a home: see, for example, *Tanner* v *Tanner* (1975). However, contracts concerning prostitution are invalid (*Pearce* v *Brooks* (1866)), although it is not illegal of itself to contract with a prostitute: *Appleton* v *Campbell* (1826).

Contracts interfering with personal liberty
This last category is concerned with contracts which restrict an individual's liberty without due cause. An example is *Howard* v *Millar's Timber and Trading Co* (1917), where the contract to lend money imposed restrictions on the disposal of the plaintiff's house, his leaving his job, borrowing more money or leaving home. Due cause was found in *Denny* v *Denny* (1919), where a father imposed restrictions in return for paying his son's debts. It was held that this was for the son's moral benefit.

2. In *Petrofina (Great Britain) Ltd* v *Martin* (1966) Diplock J (as he then was) defined a contract in restraint of trade as being one in which a party (the covenantor) agrees with the other (the covenantee) to restrict his liberty in future to trade with others in such manner as he chooses. The restraint of trade doctrine can operate in an infinite variety of situations. This answer will consider some of the more notable ones and the application principles in each case.

   However, before looking at particular examples of the application of the doctrine, some general principles which apply in all cases can be briefly stated. In *Nordenfelt* v *Maxim Nordenfelt Guns & Ammunition Co Ltd* (1894), the starting point for any analysis of the modern law of restraint of trade, the House of Lords held that all contracts in restraint of trade are prima facie unenforceable, that there is no difference between a partial and a total restraint, and that it is a question of law whether in any given case the circumstances justify the restraint which is sought to be imposed, judged at the time the contract was concluded. Further, their Lordships held that for a restraint to be justified it had to be both reasonable as between the parties (as to which the burden of proof is on the covenantee) and also reasonable in the interests of the public (where the burden of proof is on the covenantor).

   To these principles may be added certain propositions derived from a late House of Lords decision, *Esso Petroleum Co Ltd* v *Harper's Garage (Stourport) Ltd* (1968), where their Lordships stressed that the categories of contracts to which the doctrine applies are not closed and that it can apply as well to the use of land as to the activities of an individual. Now some examples of contracts in restraint of trade can be considered. The most common example is that of a covenant contained in a contract of employment whereby an employer seeks to restrict his employee's activities after termination of the employment.

Employer–employee covenants are of broadly three types:

a) Covenants restraining the use of confidential information. Even in the absence of an express obligation, an employee will usually be under an implied duty not to disclose or make use of confidential information: *Faccenda Chicken* v *Fowler* (1986). However, an express covenant has the advantage of drawing the employee's attention to this duty, and providing the information can properly be regarded as confidential and being the property of the employer (*Printers & Finishers* v *Holloway* (1965)), the covenant will usually be enforced.
b) Non-solicitation covenants. These too are normally regarded as unobjectionable by the courts providing (a) the employee has had contact with and acquired influences over customers and (b) it is limited to soliciting persons who were customers of the employer whilst the employee worked for him: *Konski* v *Peet* (1915). Although such covenants are often defined as to area and direction, consideration of time and space are not usually considered crucial: *Plowman* v *Ash* (1964).
c) Covenants against doing business. These are the most drastic and wide ranging types of covenant because they effectively prevent the employee from earning his living in the same field as his employer. Because of this sterilising effect, the courts scrutinise them with particular care. Matters to which the courts especially have regard are the areas to which the covenant extends, its duration, the activity restrained and the seniority or otherwise of the position held by the employee. Essentially the courts have to embark on a balancing exercise, considering on the one hand the necessity of preventing the employer from obtaining an unfair advantage over his employee, and on the other the desirability of allowing every man to earn his living as he chooses.

Consequently each case turns on its particular facts and reported decisions can only be a guide to future cases. Thus in *Mason* v *Provident Clothing & Supply Co Ltd* (1913) an area within 25 miles of Islington was regarded as being too wide, whereas in *Forster & Sons Ltd* v *Suggett* (1918) a nationwide, and in *Nordenfelt* a worldwide, restraint was upheld. Similarly in *Fitch* v *Dewes* (1921) a lifelong restraint was considered reasonable, yet in *M & S Drapers* v *Reynolds* (1957) a five-year restraint was unenforceable. In each of these cases the court struck the balance between the parties' and the public interest in a different way.

Finally on employer–employee covenants, it should be noted that in certain cases the doctrine of severance has been applied such that it may be possible to delete the offending, excessive part and leave behind a reasonable and enforceable covenant: *Goldsoll* v *Goldman* (1915). However, severance must not remove the bulk of the contractual consideration supplied by one party (*Alec Lobb* v *Total Oil* (1985)), nor can the court rewrite the covenant: *Attwood* v *Lamont* (1920).

Not dissimilar principles to those discussed above apply to covenants in contracts for the sale of a business (*Vancouver Malt* v *Vancouver Breweries* (1934)) or in partnership agreements: *Bridge* v *Deacons* (1984). Here, though, the courts take a less strict line, since generally in such cases the parties will have been in more equal bargaining positions than in employer-employee cases. A relatively recent example of a contract to which the doctrine applies is that of solus petrol agreements. A succession of cases from the mid-1960s show that the doctrine may apply to an exclusive dealing agreement between a petrol station and an oil company. The courts have enumerated the following distinction. The doctrine will apply to a solus tie whereby a person in occupation of land restricts his freedom to trade; it will not apply where the solus tie is contained in a conveyance or lease whereby a person acquires the right to occupy land, albeit subject to that restriction: *Esso Petroleum Co Ltd* v *Harper's Garage (Stourport) Ltd* (1968).

Although the validity of this distinction has been questioned by some commentators, it has been adopted and applied in later cases, eg *Cleveland Petroleum Co Ltd* v *Dartstone Ltd* (1969) and *Texaco* v *Mulberry Filling Station* (1972). The courts have, however, been astute to prevent oil companies taking advantage of this distinction by devising elaborate schematic transactions such as a lease and lease-back (*Amoco* v *Rocca Bros* (1975)) or a lease and lease-back to a company specifically incorporated for this purpose *(Alec Lobb).*

Lastly, simply to show the wide variety of situations to which the doctrine has been applied, one might refer to *Eastham* v *Newcastle United Football Club* (1964) (Football Association's player transfer system held unenforceable), *Greig* v *Insole* (1978) (ban on cricketers who joined Mr Packer's 'circus' likewise), and *Schroeder Music Publishing Co Ltd* v *Macaulay* (1974) (grossly disadvantageous contract between a music publisher and a songwriter struck down). Thus although the doctrine applies to certain commonly encountered types of contract, it can apply to unusual and one-off instances as well.

3. In discussing the enforceability of illegal contracts it is necessary to consider the respective positions of the guilty and the innocent parties.

The guilty party

The general rule is that the guilty party, that is one who knew of the illegality, cannot enforce an illegal contract: *Pearce* v *Brooks* (1866).

Whilst the guilty party cannot enforce an illegal contract, he is not debarred from bringing an action on a wrong independent of the illegal contract. Thus in *Edler* v *Auerbach* (1950) the landlord succeeded in a claim in tort in respect of a bath wrongfully removed by the tenant of premises let under an illegal lease.

Where the illegality lies in the method of performance, the guilty party may be able to enforce it. The shipowner in *St John Shipping Corporation* v *Joseph Rank Ltd* (1957) successfully claimed his freight charges although he had overloaded his ship, contrary to statute. In *Howard* v *Shirlstar Container Transport Ltd* (1990) the defendants engaged the plaintiff to fly aircraft, which they owned, out of Nigeria for a fee. The plaintiff in doing so committed breaches of Nigerian air traffic control regulations. It was held that this did not debar him from claiming his fee. The basis of that decision was that 'it would not amount to an affront to the public conscience to afford the plaintiff the relief he sought'. This 'public conscience' test was, however, rejected by the House of Lords in *Tinsley* v *Milligan* (1994). The House of Lords held that the purpose of the legislation in *Howard* as in *St John Shipping* was not to invalidate contracts but only to prohibit conduct. The contract would not be enforceable where the intention that one party should do an illegal act existed at the time of contracting: *Ashmore, Benson, Pease & Co Ltd* v *A V Dawson Ltd* (1973).

The innocent party

A party to an illegal contract may be innocent, because he is mistaken either as to the law or as to the facts. The general rule is that mistake of law does not give the innocent party the right to enforce the contract: *Nash* v *Stevenson Transport Ltd* (1936). Where a party is mistaken as to the facts he may be able to enforce it. There are cases where a claim by an innocent party has been upheld, and cases where the claim has been rejected. In *Archbolds (Freightage) Ltd* v *S Spanglett Ltd* (1961) the defendants contracted to carry the plaintiffs' whisky in a van which was not licensed to carry goods belonging to third parties, thus committing a statutory offence. The whisky was stolen, and the plaintiffs, who did not know that the van was not properly licensed, were able to recover damages for breach of contract. A leading case where the claim of the innocent party was rejected is that of *Re Mahmoud and Ispahani* (1921). A contract was made to sell linseed oil. At that time it was an offence, by legislation, to buy or sell linseed oil without a licence. The seller had a licence to sell and was induced to enter into the contract by the buyer's fraudulent misrepresentation that he also had a licence. The buyer later refused to accept the oil and it was held that the seller could not claim damages for non-acceptance.

The tests upon which to decide whether an illegal contract should or should not be enforceable are not entirely clear. One suggestion is that the innocent party can sue if the contract is illegal as performed, but not where it is illegal in its formation. This appears to be the approach in Cheshire, Fifoot and Furmston's *Law of Contract*, but Treitel observes that this does not fit all the cases.

With regard to statutory prohibitions, the principles on which it should be decided whether an innocent party's claim should be accepted or rejected were set out by Kerr LJ in *Phoenix General Insurance Co of Greece SA* v *Administration Asiguraliror de Stat* (1988). His Lordship held that where a statute prohibits both parties from concluding or performing a contract when both or either of them have no authority to do so, the contract is impliedly prohibited. But where a statute merely prohibits one party from entering into a contract and/or imposes a penalty on him if he does so, it does not follow that the contract itself is impliedly prohibited. Whether or not the statute has this effect depends on considerations of public policy.

Even if the innocent party is not able to enforce the contract he may have alternative remedies. He may have an action on a collateral contract or a claim based on misrepresentation. In *Strongman (1945) Ltd* v *Sincock* (1955) the defendant employed a firm of builders to effect work on his house. He promised to obtain the necessary licences, without which it was illegal to do the work. He only got licences for part of the work. The builders could not sue on the building contract, which was illegal, but recovered damages for breach of the collateral undertaking to obtain the necessary licences.

In *Shelley* v *Paddock* (1980) the plaintiff was induced by the fraudulent misrepresentation of the defendant to enter into a contract to buy a house in Spain. This involved a violation of exchange control regulations. As the plaintiff's breach of the law was innocent, she was entitled to damages for the fraud.

SUGGESTED ANSWER TO QUESTION ONE

General Comment

This area of the law, illegal contracts, has been a favoured topic for the examiners over the past few years. It requires exploration of whether the contract is illegal as formed, or merely illegal in its performance. In this context the effects of the illegal contract must be examined to determine whether it is enforceable by either party.

Key Points

- The purpose of the Act – whether it totally prohibits the conclusion or performance of a contract, or merely penalises behaviour
- The consequent position of the guilty and innocent parties – whether either can enforce the contract
- The application of the principles derived to each of the situations presented
- The possibility of restitutionary claims

Suggested Answer

The general rule is as follows.

Where the statute (or regulation) totally prohibits a contract neither party can enforce it: *Re Mahmoud and Ispahani* (1921). Where the statute merely prescribes a method of performance of the contract, coupled with a sanction for non-compliance, the innocent party may be able to enforce it, provided it is not against public policy to allow this: *Archbolds (Freightage) Ltd* v *S Spanglett Ltd* (1961). On the latter interpretation of the statute, the guilty party may also be able to enforce the contract, provided again that this would not be against public policy: *St John's Shipping Corporation* v *Joseph Rank Ltd* (1957). This general statement of the law is supported by the judgment of Kerr LJ in *Phoenix General Insurance Co Greece SA* v *Administration Asigurarilor de Stat* (1987).

It is now necessary to apply these principles to each of the contracts into which Peter entered.

a) *The contract with Queenie*
   Peter's failure to deliver the statutory invoice appears to have been inadvertent: he did not intend to perform the contract in an illegal manner. Despite this I incline to the view that Peter could not enforce the contract. In *Anderson Ltd* v *Daniel* (1924) where the seller delivered goods without the required invoice stating the percentage of certain chemicals therein, he was denied enforcement: he had failed to perform

the contract in the only way it was permitted. In *Marles* v *Philip Trant & Sons Ltd* (1954) Denning LJ approved this decision, and referring to the antecedent transaction in the case before him he said 'The seed merchants [the original sellers] performed [their contract] in an illegal way in that they omitted to furnish the prescribed particulars. That renders the contract unenforceable by them.' (It did not render a subsequent transaction illegal.)

It is possible that Peter could have a restitutionary claim, not for the purchase price but on a quantum valebat basis. In *Mohamed* v *Alaga & Co (A Firm)* (1999) the Court of Appeal allowed a restitutionary claim for reasonable remuneration for services performed under an illegal contract on a quantum meruit basis. But whether that decision could be applied to this situation is uncertain. The restitutionary principle will not be invoked where it would be against public policy to do so: *Awwad* v *Geraghty & Co* (2000). It is conceivable that it would be against public policy to apply the principle in the case of foodstuff.

b) *The contract with Robert*

Here both parties intended to perform the contract in an illegal manner. In *St John's Shipping Corporation* v *Joseph Rank Ltd* (above) Devlin J held:

> '... a contract which is entered into with the object of committing an illegal act is unenforceable. The application of this principle depends upon the proof of intent, at the time the contract was made, to break the law; if the intent is mutual the contract is not enforceable at all ...'

The intent to break the law in this instance was clearly mutual. This debars Peter from claiming the purchase price and Robert from seeking a remedy in damages. A further barrier to Robert's claim would be the decision in *Ashmore, Benson Pease & Co Ltd* v *A V Dawson Ltd* (1973) (participation in the illegality).

c) *The contract with Stephan*

Stephan is purchasing the pet food for an illegal purpose. Peter is apparently aware of this. This knowledge would debar enforcement on his part; he would have participated in the illegality: *Ashmore Benson* (above).

Because of the illegal purpose the contract would also be unenforceable by Stephan. It is not clear from the question whether Stephan has in general used pet food for human consumption or if he has so used this particular consignment. If he has not yet used this particular consignment for that purpose he may be able to recover the £600 provided that he repudiates the illegal purpose before it has been implemented.

d) *The contract with Thomas*

As Peter has traded without the requisite licence the contract is illegal as formed and neither party can enforce it. If this is unknown to Thomas, he might, as an innocent party, be able to recover the £2,000 on a restitutionary basis.

SUGGESTED ANSWER TO QUESTION TWO

General Comment

This area, illegal contracts, has been the frequent subject of a question in recent years. The issue posed is the effect of illegality, the extent to which a guilty and an innocent party can enforce an illegal contract.

Key Points

- In each of K's contracts the purpose of the Act in question will have to be examined as to whether the contract is illegal as formed, or merely illegal in its performance
- Does the Act prohibit the contract entirely, or only impose an obligation on one of the parties to it?
- In this context the requirements of a licence and the furnishing of a statutory notice will have to be considered

Suggested Answer

In *Phoenix General Insurance Co Greece SA* v *Administration Asigurarilor de Stat* (1987) Kerr LJ summarised the position with regard to the statutory control of contracts as follows:

> '(i) Where a statute prohibits both parties from concluding or performing a contract when both or either of them have no authority to do so, the contract is impliedly prohibited: see *Re Mahmoud and Ispahani* (1921): ...
> (ii) But where a statute merely prevents one party from entering into a contract without authority and/or imposes a penalty on him if he does so (ie a unilateral prohibition) it does not follow that the contract itself is impliedly prohibited so as to render it illegal and void.'

This statement of the law will now be applied to each of K's contracts.

The contract with L
The Act has imposed a unilateral obligation on K, with which he has not fully complied. Provided that K did not intend to perform the contract in an illegal manner at the time it was concluded (and this is not suggested) it would appear that he is entitled to enforce it: *St John's Shipping Corporation* v *Joseph Rank Ltd* (1957). In *Shaw* v *Groom* (1970) a lessor had failed to furnish his tenant with a rent-book as required by the statute but was nevertheless entitled to sue for the rent, because the purpose of the statute was to punish his failure to issue a rent-book, not to invalidate the tenancy agreement. I would be satisfied that K could enforce payment of the purchase price, but the doubt stems from the earlier decision in *Anderson Ltd* v *Daniel* (1924) where a seller was denied enforcement because of his failure to issue a statutory notice: he had failed to perform the contract in the only way that it was permitted.

The contract with M
Here it would appear that both parties intended to perform the contract in an illegal manner. In *St John's Shipping Corporation* v *Joseph Rank Ltd* (above) Devlin J said

> '... a contract which is entered into with the object of committing an illegal act is unenforceable. The application of this principle depends upon the proof of intent, at the time the contract was made, to break the law; if the intent is mutual the contract is not enforceable at all, and if is unilateral it is unenforceable at the suit of the party who is proved to have it.'

As there does seem to have been this intent at the time the contract was made, K will not be able to enforce the contract, and will be not be entitled to sue for the purchase price.

The contract with N

Here N appears to be an innocent party. There is authority to the effect that such party may be debarred from recovery if he could be found to have 'participated' in the illegal act: *Ashmore, Benson Pease & Co Ltd* v *A V Dawson Ltd* (1973). In the absence of evidence to this effect I shall assume that this case does not apply.

It is suggested that there has been a breach of contract by K. Either the goods did not correspond with the description (s13 Sale of Goods Act 1979) or were not of satisfactory quality: s14(2) of that Act.

N is therefore an innocent party who has suffered loss as a result of the breach. It has already been submitted that the purpose of the Act, with regard to the furnishing of the statutory notice, was not to prohibit the disposition of the goods in question, but to control the sellers of such goods. N is therefore able to enforce the contract: *Archbolds (Freightage) Ltd* v *S Spanglett Ltd* (1961). As the breach was one of a condition (or conditions) N would be entitled to reject the two jugs, and recover his advance payment.

The contract with P

With regard to the requirement of a licence, it is clear that the Act prohibits the disposition of the goods without such licence. K is therefore not able to enforce this particular contract. The fact that he is unaware of its expiry is irrelevant.

I have concluded that K can probably enforce the contract against L, has no defence to the claim by N, and cannot enforce the contracts against M and P. It remains to consider whether K can recover the goods from these two parties as goods transferred under illegal contracts. Property has passed to them: *Singh* v *Ali* (1960). The rule in pari delicto potior est conditio defendentis would debar him from doing so. He cannot establish a right without relying on the illegality.

SUGGESTED ANSWER TO QUESTION THREE

General Comment

This question is confined to one issue: the enforceability of illegal contracts.

Key Points

- A general statement of the law relating to the enforcement of illegal contracts – the respective positions of the guilty and innocent parties – and the restitution of money paid or property transferred under an illegal contract

- Discussion of the rights of C against each of the other contracting parties

Suggested Answer

The general rule is that a guilty party (that is, one who knows of the illegality) will not be able to enforce a contract formed for an illegal purpose. He may be able to enforce it, however, if there is a mere illegality in the performance of an otherwise legal contract. The innocent party may be able to enforce it, depending on the nature of the prohibition.

With regard to the recovery of money paid or property transferred under an illegal contract, the general rule is that recovery is not possible - in pari delicto potior est conditio defendentis. But there are exceptions to the in pari delicto rule.

The application of these rules will be amplified in discussion of each of the contracts into which C entered.

The contract with D

A contract that is illegal as formed will not be enforceable by the guilty party: *Pearce* v *Brooks* (1866). But such party may be able to enforce it if the illegality is in the performance of the contract. Whilst there is a total prohibition on a contract where the supplier is not registered or the recipient is not licensed, the requirement of the delivery of a statutory invoice relates to the performance of the contract. In *St John Shipping Corporation* v *Joseph Rank Ltd* (1957) in a contract for the carriage of goods by sea, the ship was overloaded in contravention of a particular statute. The plaintiff was held entitled to enforce payment of the freight charges. To determine whether this decision applies here it is necessary to examine the judgment in that case. Devlin J said:

> '... a contract which is entered into with the object of committing an illegal act is unenforceable. The application of this principle depends upon proof of intent, at the time the contract was made, to break the law; if the intent is mutual the contract is not enforceable at all, and, if unilateral, it is unenforceable at the suit of the party who is proved to have it. This principle is not involved here. Whether or not the overloading was deliberate when it was done, there is no proof that it was contemplated when the contract of carriage was made.'

It seems that the question here is of the intent of the parties at the time the contract was made. On the facts presented, the position is not entirely clear as to whether the parties (or C) entered into the contract with the intention of performing it in an illegal manner.

The test of enforceability is whether the statute intended to prohibit the contract, or merely to penalise conduct. Thus in *Shaw* v *Groom* (1970) a landlord committed an offence by failing to give his tenant a rent book. The landlord was held entitled to sue for the rent because the purpose behind the legislation was to penalise his failure to issue a rent book, not to invalidate the tenancy agreement. In the problem before me the purpose behind the statute appears to have been to penalise the conduct of the supplier, and the fact that D, the recipient, participated in the illegal performance should not entitle him to evade payment.

I would be more confident of advising C that he could enforce payment against D, were it not for the decision in *Anderson Ltd* v *Daniel* (1924). The facts there were very similar to the ones before me. There the sellers of artificial fertilisers were required by statute to furnish the buyer with an invoice stating the percentage of certain chemical substances contained in the goods. The sellers' failure to furnish the required invoice meant that they lost their action for the price of the goods. They had failed to perform the contract in the only way in which the statute allowed it to be performed.

As it is difficult to distinguish this case from the present facts I must advise C that his prospects in an action against D for the purchase price are, at best, doubtful.

The contract with E

If C knew that E was not a licensed recipient, he clearly could not enforce the contract. Let us assume that C did not know this and was, therefore, an innocent party.

The relevant case here is that of *Re Mahmoud and Ispahani* (1921). There by legislation licences were necessary for either the sale or purchase of linseed oil. The plaintiff sold linseed oil to the defendant. The plaintiff had a licence and was informed by the defendant that he too had a licence. He had not. When the defendant refused to accept delivery the plaintiff sued for damages for non-acceptance, but failed to recover because the contract was illegal.

The principle derived from this case was stated by Kerr LJ in *Phoenix General Insurance Co of Greece SA* v *Administration Asiguraliror de Stat* (1988) as follows:

> 'Where a statute prohibits both parties from concluding or performing a contract when both or either of them have no authority to do so the contract is impliedly prohibited ...'

It is abundantly clear here that there is a total prohibition on the contract with E and C has no remedy arising from the sale.

The contract with F

The position here is not distinguishable from that of the contract with D.

The contract with G

Here, as with the sale to E, C has no remedy, as such a contract is totally prohibited. The fact that he was unaware that his registration had expired is immaterial.

It remains to consider whether C could recover the goods from any of the other contracting parties by relying on one of the exceptions to the in pari delicto rule. It does not appear so. The only relevant exception is the one which would allow recovery where no reliance is placed on the illegal contract, as in *Bowmakers Ltd* v *Barnet Instruments Ltd* (1945). But there property in the goods had remained with the plaintiff. Here property in the goods has passed to each of the recipients: *Singh* v *Ali* (1960). The recipients' defence that the property had passed to them could only be countered by raising the illegality. This would be fatal to any claim by C: *Taylor* v *Chester* (1869).

SUGGESTED ANSWER TO QUESTION FOUR

General Comment

This question is mainly on the area of illegal contracts, in particular the enforcement of such contracts. The reference to the situation if F was only 17 years old requires some discussion of contracts entered into by minors.

Key Points

- Enforcement of an illegal contract by the guilty party and the innocent party - the application of the rules to E, G, H and J
- Recovery of property passed or money paid under an illegal contract - the application of the in pari delecto rule to G and J and as between F and K
- Consideration of the effect of the above contracts if F was a minor: whether any of the contracts are for the supply of necessaries - whether G and J can obtain restitution under s3(1) Minors' Contracts Act 1987

Suggested Answer

The general rule is that a guilty party cannot enforce an illegal contract, the innocent party may be able to do so. With regard to the recovery of money paid or property passed under an illegal contract the general rule is that recovery is not possible - in pari delicto potior est conditio defendentis: to this rule there are a number of exceptions.

I shall consider these rules in relation to each of the parties involved.

The contract with E

A contract with a prostitute would be illegal as one promoting sexual immorality and therefore contrary to public policy. Thus, in *Pearce* v *Brooks* (1866) a contract to hire out a brougham to a prostitute for the use in her profession was held to be illegal, and the owner was not entitled to enforce. Here, however, the court stressed that the owner of the brougham knew of the use to which it was to be put. This case might be distinguishable from the lease with E. He might have suspected that F was a prostitute, but it is questionable whether mere suspicion, as distinct from certain knowledge, is sufficient to deny him a remedy. Nor is it entirely clear that he knew, or should have known, the use to which the flat would be put. A contract to let a room to a prostitute who practised her profession elsewhere was held to be valid 'because persons of that description must have a place to lay their heads': *Appleton* v *Campbell* (1826). It is also possible that the courts in this more permissive age might adopt a less censorious attitude to sexual immorality than they did in Victorian times. In *Armhouse Lee Ltd* v *Chappell* (1996) the Court of Appeal held that promotional material for telephone sex lines was not so immoral that the courts would decline to enforce the payments for the advertisements.

I conclude therefore, although not without some doubt, that E would be able to enforce the lease.

The contract with G

Here it appears that G is entirely innocent of any question of illegality. There is no suggestion that he was, or should have been, aware of the purpose to which F might put the flat. '£12,000 for a luxurious bed' does not necessarily have a sinister connotation. That being so, G is entitled to enforce the contract: *Archbolds (Freightage) Ltd* v *S Spanglett Ltd* (1961). Even if G is deemed to have constructive notice that F was a prostitute and was using the flat for that purpose, he would be entitled to recover possession of the bed under the exception to the pari delicto rule whereby recovery will be allowed where no reliance is placed on the illegal contract: *Bowmakers Ltd* v *Barnet Instruments Ltd* (1945).

The contract with H

H, again it appears an innocent party, can enforce the contract.

The contract with J

The suggestion here is that, although J did not know that F was a prostitute, the request for a specially constructed large back seat was so unusual as to put him on inquiry. If it appears that his suspicions were aroused, but that he deliberately chose to ignore them, he may well have forfeited the right to be deemed an innocent party. In this even he could not enforce the contract: *Pearce* v *Brooks* (above). Whether or not he is deemed innocent of the illegality, recovery of the car would be permitted for the reasons set out in relation to the contract with G.

The contract with K

A further exception to the in pari delicto rule is that a plaintiff is entitled to recover a payment made under an illegal contract if he repudiates the illegal purpose in time. The payer has a locus poenitentiae and may withdraw from the illegal contract and recover the payment he has made. Can K avail himself of this? There are two important qualifications to this entitlement. First, the repudiation must take place before the illegal purpose has been effected, as in *Taylor* v *Bowers* (1876), where recovery was allowed, but recovery will not be allowed when the repudiation takes place after performance of the illegal purpose has actually begun: *Kearley* v *Thomson* (1890). There is an element of doubt here. Genuine repentance is probably not required and whilst complete performance of the illegal purpose is a bar to recovery, apparently partial performance is not: *Tribe* v *Tribe* (1995). How partial the performance can be is uncertain.

Whilst there may be this suggestion of doubt as to whether the partial performance is a bar to recovery, the second qualification is fatal to K's claim: the repudiation must be voluntary; it must not be forced on the party claiming recovery by the other party's breach of contract: *Bigos* v *Bousted* (1951). This is precisely the situation here.

The situation if F was a minor

If F was only 17 years old she would have been a minor in law. A minor is only bound by contracts for necessary goods, defined in s3(3) Sale of Goods Act 1979 as 'goods suitable to the condition in life of the minor … and to his actual requirements at the time of the sale and delivery.' There seems little doubt that the luxurious bed purchased from G, and the car purchased from J could not be regarded as necessaries. Payment for these items could not, therefore, be exacted from her. However, under s3(1) Minors' Contracts Act 1987 the court may require her to restore them to the respective parties.

With regard to the lease entered into with E, this falls within the category of contracts voidable at the instance of the minor. F could set aside this contract, provided she did so before attaining majority or within a reasonable time thereafter. By doing so she would avoid any further liability, but could not recover any payments made before that: *Steinberg* v *Scala (Leeds) Ltd* (1923).

SUGGESTED ANSWER TO QUESTION FIVE

General Comment

This question is a much welcomed one as far as students are concerned as there is no confusion as to what is required in the answer.

Key Points

- A brief discussion of the doctrine
- Analysis of its applicability as well as the issue of enforceability by both parties, ie the innocent and guilty party

Suggested Answer

In discussing the enforceability of illegal contracts, it is necessary to consider the respective positions of the guilty and the innocent parties. However, before doing that, it is worth stating that when a contract is illegal it will be unenforceable and neither party can plead innocence or ignorance as an excuse.

As far as a guilty party is concerned, the general rule is that the party who knew of the illegality cannot enforce an illegal contract - as laid down in *Pearce* v *Brooks* (1866).

Whilst the guilty party cannot enforce an illegal contract, he is not debarred from bringing an action on a wrong, independent of the illegal contract. Thus, in *Edler* v *Auerbach* (1950) the landlord succeeded in a claim in tort in respect of a bath wrongfully removed by the tenant of the premises let under an illegal lease.

Where the illegality lies in the method of performance, the guilty party may be able to enforce it. For example, in *St John Shipping Corporation* v *Joseph Rank Ltd* (1957) the shipowner successfully claimed his freight charges even though he had overloaded his ship contrary to shipping regulations. In *Howard* v *Shirlstar Container Transport Ltd* (1990) the defendants engaged the plaintiff to fly an aircraft, which they owned, out of Nigeria for a fee. In so doing, the plaintiff committed breaches of Nigerian air traffic control regulations. It was held that this did not debar him from claiming his fee. The basis of that decision was that 'it would not amount to an affront to the public conscience to afford the plaintiff the relief he sought'. This 'public conscience' test was, however, rejected by the House of Lords in *Tinsley* v *Milligan* (1994). The House of Lords held that the purpose of the legislation in *Howard* as in *St John Shipping* was not to invalidate contracts but only to prohibit conduct.

The contract would not be enforceable where the intention that one party should do an illegal act existed at the time of contracting - as in *Ashmore, Benson, Pease & Co Ltd* v *A V Dawson Ltd* (1973).

In relation to the position of the innocent party, a party to an illegal contract may be innocent because he is mistaken either as to law or as to the facts. The general rule is that mistake of law does not give the innocent party the right to enforce the contract, as in *Nash* v *Stevenson Transport Ltd* (1936). Where a party is mistaken as to the facts, he may be able to enforce it. There are cases where a claim by an innocent party has been upheld, and cases where the claim has been rejected.

In *Archbolds Ltd* v *S Spanglett Ltd* (1961) the defendants contracted to carry the plaintiffs' whisky in a van which was not licensed to carry goods belonging to third parties, thus committing a statutory offence. The whisky was stolen, and the plaintiffs, who did not know that the van was not properly licensed, were able to recover damages for breach of contract.

A leading case where the claim of the innocent party was rejected is that of *Re Mahmoud and Ispahani* (1921). Here a contract was made to sell linseed oil. At that time it was an offence to buy or sell linseed oil without a licence. The seller had a licence to sell and was induced to enter into the contract by the buyer's fraudulent misrepresentation that he also had a licence. The buyer later refused to accept the oil and it was held that the seller could not claim damages for non-acceptance.

The tests upon which to decide whether an illegal contract should or should not be enforceable are not entirely clear. One suggestion is that the innocent party can sue if the contract is illegal as performed, but not where it is illegal in its formation. This seems to be the approach of some academics such as Cheshire and Fifoot (*Elements of the Law of Contract,* 12th edn, p375), but Treitel (*Law of Contract* (9th edn, p444)) on the other hand suggests that this does not fit all the cases.

With regard to statutory prohibitions, the principles on which it should be decided whether an innocent party's claim should be accepted or rejected were set out by Kerr LJ in *Phoenix General Insurance Co Greece SA* v *Administration Asiguraliror de Stat* (1988). His Lordship held that where a statute prohibits both parties from concluding or performing a contract when both or either of them have no authority to do so, the contract is impliedly prohibited. But where a statute merely prohibits one party from entering into a contract and/or imposes a penalty on him if he does so, it does not follow that the contract itself is impliedly prohibited. Whether or not statute has this effect depends on considerations of public policy.

Even if the innocent party is not able to enforce the contract, he may have alternative remedies. He may have an action on a collateral contract or a claim based on misrepresentation.

In *Strongman (1945) Ltd* v *Sincock* (1955) the defendant employed a firm of builders to carry out work on his house. He promised to obtain the necessary licences, without which it was illegal to do the work. He only got licences for part of the work. The builders could not sue on the building contract, which was illegal, but recovered damages for breach of the collateral undertaking to obtain the necessary licences.

In *Shelley* v *Paddock* (1980) the plaintiff was induced by the fraudulent misrepresentation of the defendant to enter into a contract to buy a house in Spain. This involved a violation of exchange control regulations. As the plaintiff's breach of the contract was innocent, she was entitled to damages for the fraud.

Two recent cases, namely *Birkett* v *Acorn Business Machines Ltd* (1999) and *Mohamed* v *Alaga & Co (A Firm)* (1999), provide useful illustrations of the approach employed by the courts in declaring whether a contract is void on the grounds of public policy. This is very much dependant on the role and knowledge of the parties to the contract.

Finally, it can be safely assumed that the courts have no problem declaring a contract illegal on the grounds of it being contrary to public policy: see *Carnduff* v *Rock* (2001).

11

Frustration, Discharge and Breach

Introduction

This chapter is concerned with the performance of contractual obligations or, perhaps more accurately, non-performance giving rise to an action for breach of contract or a claim that the contract has become frustrated due to supervening events and no further performance is due.

Frustration is one of the most popular topics in examinations and may be the basis of either problem or discussion questions. However, the topic is complex. The courts have over the decades shifted their view of the theoretical basis on which the doctrine is founded and the cases are sometimes subject to fine distinctions. However simple a question may seem on the face of it, the unprepared candidate faces considerable danger when entering these waters.

The questions below give a good indication of the complexities involved and how these may be dealt with in a competent answer. Questions on repudiatory breaches of contract and the likely outcome of an action for breach have been included. This topic is, however, closely allied with the importance which the court attaches to the contractual term broken.

Questions

INTERROGRAMS

1. Explain the 'radical change in obligations test'.
2. What effect did the Law Reform (Frustrated Contracts) Act 1943 have on the common law relating to frustration?

QUESTION ONE

Fanny, aged 17 years, agreed with Gertrude and Hildergard to form a pop group called 'The Glands'. They each agreed to pay £2,000 into a fund to buy a set of musical instruments and to split any profits equally between them. They bought the instruments, rehearsed and advertised their availability to perform at country house concerts.

a) Ian engaged The Glands to perform at a concert in his stately home but because of a nearby outbreak of foot and mouth disease the concert was called off by Ian a day before the concert was scheduled to take place. Ian required the £5,000 which he had paid in advanced to be returned. This the group refused to do.
b) Ken engaged The Glands to perform at his country house and agreed to pay the group £6,000. Their performance at the concert was so bad that many of the paying customers who were forced to listen to them began to slow hand clap before

becoming restive and, in some cases, disruptive. Ken ordered the group off the stage to protect his property. He refused to pay The Glands anything relying on what he described as the poor quality of their performance.

c) Janice engaged The Glands to perform for £4,000 at her stately home and sold £25,000 worth of tickets. On the morning of the concert Hildergard gave premature birth to twins and, therefore, was unable to perform at the concert. Fanny and Gertrude refused to perform unless Janice paid an extra £5,000 for them to 'go on'. Because of the danger of damage to her property from angry fans Janice agreed to pay the additional sum. After the concert she paid Gertrude £4,000 and refused to pay the additional £5,000.

Advise Ian, Ken and Janice of their contractual liability.

University of London LLB Examination
(for external students) Elements of the Law of Contract June 2001 Q4

QUESTION TWO

Z, the manager of The Rocking Burps, a pop group, agreed with X for a fee of £15,000 that the group would perform two weeks later at a concert organised by X. The lead singer of the group, Windy, took drugs on the day before the concert and as a result was unable to perform properly as he was in a dazed state. Although he started to perform he was booed off the stage. As a result X, who had paid £16,000 to hire the venue, had to return £28,000 to dissatisfied fans.

Advise X. What difference, if any, would it make to your advice if Windy's beer had been laced with the drug by some unknown third party?

University of London LLB Examination
(for external students) Elements of the Law of Contract June 1988 Q8

QUESTION THREE

K advertised in a local newspaper that he had a Sumpter 1997 car for sale for £7,200. The vehicle was described as in excellent condition. J went to the address which K had given. After a test drive J agreed to buy the car. Two days later, when J's wife was driving the car, a wheel came off; the car crashed through the window of a police station and J and his wife were injured. The agreement between K and J contained the following clauses:

22. It is agreed that K has not made any statement which has induced the contract.
23. The parties agree that there is no undertaking of quality or fitness for purpose.
24. There is a limit of £500 for damages for breach of contract by K.
25. There is no liability for consequential loss.

Advise J. What difference, if any, would it make to your advice if K had sold the car in the course of his business?

University of London LLB Examination
(for external students) Elements of the Law of Contract June 1999 Q4

QUESTION FOUR

'It remains unsatisfactory that the law is unclear about when an innocent party can bring a contract to an end for breach, especially as damages are often uncertain or difficult to quantify.'

Discuss.

University of London LLB Examination
(for external students) Elements of the Law of Contract June 2000 Q8

QUESTION FIVE

Bryan rents Cecil's cottage for £50 per week. Lately, he got behind and owes Cecil £250. He saw Cecil last week to offer him a part payment of £100 and a promise of the rest this week. Cecil, however, believed he had just won a fortune on the lottery and said to Bryan, 'Forget it, mate. I'm in the money now!' Cecil then discovered he had lost his lottery ticket and now wants to claim the outstanding rent. Bryan has, however, spent the money. Advise Bryan.

How would your answer differ if Bryan had offered Cecil a gold watch worth £100 in settlement of the debt and Cecil had accepted it?

Written by the Editor

QUESTION SIX

'As to when the doctrine of frustration can be properly employed to help a party out of a difficulty which he could have foreseen is unpredictable, given the inconsistency of the approach of the courts.'

Discuss.

Written by the Editor

Answers

ANSWERS TO INTERROGRAMS

1. The given quotation requires an analysis of the test employed to determine whether or not a contract has been frustrated. Prior to 1863 contractual obligations were regarded as absolute, irrespective of the change in circumstances: *Paradine* v *Jane* (1647). At that date the doctrine of frustration was introduced into English law by the decision in *Taylor* v *Caldwell* (1863), where it was held that a contract for the use of a music hall was frustrated when the building was destroyed by fire. This was said to rest on there being an implied term of the contract that the building should continue to exist, and on its destruction the parties were discharged of further obligations.

   The courts have subsequently discarded the implied term approach in favour of the radical change in obligations tests, first propounded in the speech of Lord Radcliffe in *Davis Contractors Ltd* v *Fareham Urban District Council* (1956). His Lordship said that

> '... frustration occurs whenever the law recognises that without default of either party a contractual obligation has become incapable of being performed because the circumstances in which performance is called for would render it a thing radically different from that which was undertaken by the contract. Non haec in foedera veni. It was not this that I promised to do.'

The principle enunciated by Viscount Radcliffe has been approved by two further decisions of the House of Lords: *National Carriers Panalpina (Northern) Ltd* (1981) and *The Nema* (1982).

Two further points emerge from Viscount Radcliffe's speech. The first is that it is not hardship or inconvenience or material loss itself which calls the principle of frustration into play. The second is that although his Lordship referred to a contractual obligation being 'incapable of being performed' he did not mean that frustration occurs only when the contract is physically impossible of performance. Elsewhere in his speech he refers to such a change in the significance of the obligation that the thing undertaken would, if performed, be a different thing from that contracted for.

Davis v *Fareham* is itself an illustration of the first point. Delay caused by bad weather and the shortage of labour rendered the contract unprofitable for the appellants, but this did not constitute a frustrating event. Further illustration is afforded by *The Eugenia* (1964) where the closure of the Suez Canal caused delay and considerable additional expense. Lord Denning emphasised the point, saying: 'The fact that it has become more onerous or more expensive for one party than he thought is not sufficient to bring about a frustration. It must be more than merely more onerous or more expensive. It must be positively unjust to hold the parties bound.'

The second point, that it is not only physical impossibility that causes frustration, is illustrated by cases such as *Jackson* v *Union Marine Insurance Co* (1873) and *Krell* v *Henry* (1903). In both these cases physical performance was still possible but the supervening events had rendered the nature of the contractual obligations fundamentally different.

The question is, therefore, not simply whether there has been a radical change in the circumstances, but whether there has been a radical change in the obligation. Was 'performance ... fundamentally different in a commercial sense?': *Tsakiroglou & Co Ltd* v *Noblee Thorl GmbH* (1962).

2. The effect of frustration is to excuse the parties from further performance but this common law principle has been partially modified by the Law Reform (Frustrated Contracts) Act 1943.

Under sl(2) of the Act all sums paid or payable in pursuance of a frustrated contract shall be recoverable or cease to be payable. This is subject to the proviso that if the payee has incurred expense in or for the purpose of the performance of the contract, the payee may retain all or part of such sums as the court considers just, up to the amount of the expenses incurred. However, if a party had not stipulated for pre-payment he will not be able to recover.

Section 1(3) provides that where a party to the contract has, by reason of anything done by another party in or for the purpose of the performance of the contract, obtained a valuable benefit before discharge, the other party may recover from him such sum not exceeding the value of the benefit as the court considers just, having regard to all the circumstances of the case. There is some academic controversy about how the meaning of 'valuable benefit' should be construed.

The relationship between the subsections was considered by Robert Goff J in *BP Exploration* v *Hunt (No 2)* (1982) and the following principles emerge from his judgment:

a) The Act was designed to prevent unjust enrichment.
b) Under s1(3) the court is concerned with doing justice between the parties.
c) The court should endeavour to achieve consistency between the sections because they both stem from principle (a).
d) The purpose of the Act is not to do such things as apportion loss, put the parties into the position they would have been in had the contract been performed, or restore the parties to the position they were in before the contract was made.
e) The valuable benefit should be the end product of services rendered not just the service itself.
f) The benefit is to be valued at the date of frustration.
g) Money paid is recoverable but if the benefit is not money it is the reasonable value of the plaintiff's performance, ie reasonable remuneration for services or a reasonable price for goods.

Finally, it should be noted that the Act does not apply to four types of contract: voyage charterparties; contracts for carriage of goods by sea; insurance contracts and contracts for the sale of specific goods which perish.

SUGGESTED ANSWER TO QUESTION ONE

General Comment

The main topic to be discussed here is the doctrine of frustration. Attention will also have to be paid to the possible breach of contract in one of the situations, and to the question of duress in another.

Key Points

- The situation postulated in (a): when frustration of a contract occurs, and the limitations of the doctrine - the effect of the doctrine at common law - the application of the Law Reform (Frustrated Contracts) Act 1943
- The situation in (b): whether there has been frustration or a breach of contract
- The situation in (c): whether the contract has been frustrated; the issue of duress

Suggested Answer

Situation (a)

In *Davis Contractors Ltd* v *Fareham Urban District Council* (1956) Lord Radcliffe held that:

> '... frustration occurs whenever the law recognises that without default of either party a contractual obligation has become incapable of being performed because the circumstances in which performance is called for would render it a thing radically different from that which was undertaken by the contract.'

The effect of frustration is to discharge the parties from further obligations: *Taylor* v *Caldwell* (1863).

But there are limits to the operation of the doctrine. The mere fact that the contract takes longer to perform than was envisaged, or proves more expensive, or more difficult, is not in itself sufficient to constitute frustration: see *Davis Contractors* (above); *British Movietone News Ltd* v *London & District Cinemas Ltd* (1952); *The Eugenia* (1964); *The Nema* (1982).

Ian cancels the contract because of the outbreak of foot and mouth disease. It is not possible on this limited information to determine with certainty whether this outbreak constitutes a frustrating event, but for the sake of further exposition I shall assume that it does.

The parties are, therefore, discharged from further obligations. The Glands have incurred certain expenses and Ian has made an advance payment. In order to see how the rights of the parties would be adjusted with regard to the expenses and the advance payment we must turn to the Law Reform (Frustrated Contracts) Act 1943.

Section 1(2) provides that advance payments are recoverable, subject to the proviso that if the party to whom it was made had incurred expenses in the performance of the contract the court has a discretion to allow him to retain, from the advance payment, an amount not exceeding such expenses. In *Gamerco SA* v *ICM/Fair Warning (Agency) Ltd* (1995) Garland J held that the court has a broad discretion in this regard; it may allow the retention of all, or some, or none of those expenses. The expenses incurred by The Glands have not been quantified, and it appears that they might have been incurred before the conclusion of this particular contract; nor do we know what loss Ian has sustained by the cancellation of the concert. It may well be that the court would allow Ian to recover the advance payment, without deduction, as it did in the case just cited. (No valuable benefit has been conferred, so s1(3) does not apply.)

Situation (b)

The doctrine of frustration does not appear to apply in this situation, unless one could regard the behaviour of the audience as a frustrating event. But this was occasioned by the 'so bad' performance of The Glands. The frustration might be said to be self-induced; negligence can constitute self-inducement: *J Lauritzen AS* v *Wijsmuller BV, The Super Servant Two* (1990). Lord Radcliffe in *Davis Contractors* (above) emphasised that the circumstances must have arisen 'without default of either party'.

The Glands appear to have been in breach of the implied term that they would perform their services with reasonable care and skill: s13 Supply of Goods and Services Act 1982. The consequences of the breach would seem to have justified Ken in terminating the contract. If they did not, he would have been in breach.

Situation (c)

I do not think that the frustration (if there was one) could be regarded as self-induced.

Self-inducement must consist of a deliberate act, as in *Maritime National Fish Ltd* v *Ocean Trawlers Ltd* (1935); or negligence (above).

The question is, however, whether Hildegard's inability to perform can constitute frustration. Incapacity of one of the parties can be a frustrating event: *Condor* v *The Barron Knights Ltd* (1966). But there only one performer was involved. The concert could have been performed by the two other members of the group, albeit in a different manner from the one intended.

The refusal by Fanny and Gertrude to perform unless Janice paid the additional sum amounts to a threat to break a contract. This constitutes duress. This can be defined as illegitimate pressure, which gives the victim no choice but to submit: *Universe Tankships Inc of Monrovia* v *International Transport Workers' Federation* (1983). This appears to be applicable here. This form of economic duress has been recognised in a number of cases: for example, *B & S Contracts and Design Ltd* v *Victor Green Publications Ltd* (1984); *Atlas Express Ltd* v *Kafco Ltd* (1989). Janice would, therefore, be justified in refusing to pay the additional £5,000.

In any event no fresh consideration has been furnished for the promise to pay this additional amount: *Stilk* v *Myrick* (1809). *Williams* v *Roffey Bros & Nicholls (Contractors) Ltd* (1990) would not apply because of the presence of duress.

(It is somewhat difficult to comprehend what purpose is served by introducing the fact that Fanny is a minor in law. Suffice it to say that the contracts with Ian, Ken and Janice, being to her benefit as a whole, would be binding on her. Her agreement with the other two members of The Glands constitutes a partnership and would be voidable at her instance.)

SUGGESTED ANSWER TO QUESTION TWO

General Comment

The area for discussion here is the doctrine of frustration. It will appear from the suggested solution that certain assumptions will have to be made in order to discuss the issues fully.

Key Points

- When can a contract be said to be frustrated?
- The effect of frustration
- Whether Windy's taking of drugs constituted self-induced frustration: the consequences if it did - anticipatory breach
- The situation where the drug taking was caused by a third party - the common law - the Law Reform (Frustrated Contracts) Act 1943

Suggested Answer

The test employed to determine whether a contract has been frustrated was set out by Lord Radcliffe in *Davis Contractors Ltd* v *Fareham Urban District Council* (1956) as follows:

> '... frustration occurs whenever the law recognises that without default of either party a contractual obligation has become incapable of being performed because the circumstances in which performance is called for would render it a thing radically different from that which was undertaken by the contract. Non haec in foedera veni. It was not this that I promised to do.'

This formulation, the radical change in obligations test, was also adopted by the House of Lords in *National Carriers Ltd* v *Panalpine (Northern) Ltd* (1981) and in *Pioneer Shipping Ltd* v *BTP Tioxide Ltd, The Nema* (1982).

The effect of frustration is to discharge the parties from further obligations under the contract: *Taylor* v *Caldwell* (1863).

Illness or incapacity of one of the parties can constitute a frustrating event: *Condor* v *The Barron Knights Ltd* (1966). The difficulty here is that it is Z, not Windy, who is the contracting party. However, I am assuming that Z, as manager, is agent for the group. I also have to make the assumption that the incapacity of the lead singer could frustrate the contract, although other members of the group would have been able to perform.

There are, however, limits to the operation of the doctrine. The relevant one here is that the frustration must not be self-induced: *Maritime National Fish Ltd* v *Ocean Trawlers Ltd* (1935); *J Lauritzen A/S* v *Wijsmuller BV, The Super Servant Two* (1990). It does seem that the taking of drugs by Windy would be regarded as self-induced frustration.

If that is so, Z, and the group for which he acted, have committed an anticipatory breach of contract. In theory X had the option of affirming the contract, or breaking the breach: clearly he has elected to accept the breach, and is entitled to damages. These would include the payment of £16,000 for the hiring of the venue, and the £28,000 returned to the fans.

The situation would be different if the drug had been administered to Windy by an unknown third party. Windy appears to have been an innocent victim, and no fault can be attributed to Z or the group.

On this scenario, and on the assumptions I have made with regard to Z having acted as agent for the group, and the effect of Windy's incapacity on performance by the group, the contract appears to have been frustrated. This, then would discharge the contract at common law, and the obligations of the parties would terminate at that point. Z would not have incurred liability for the damages sustained by X. Nor, of course, would X be required to make any, or any further, payment to Z.

It remains to consider the effect of the Law Reform (Frustrated Contracts) Act 1943.

We are told that there had been an agreed fee of £15,000, but not whether this or any part of it had been paid, or was payable, before the frustrating event. If the entire sum was only payable after the concert, then clearly that liability has been discharged. On the assumption that this sum, or part of it, was paid or was payable before the contract was discharged by frustration, we must consider s1(2) of the Act. This provides that sums paid before the discharge are recoverable and sums payable cease to be payable.

There is a proviso to this section however: where the party receiving the payment has incurred expenses in the performance of the contract, the court may, at its discretion, allow him to retain from the amount paid, or recover from the amount payable, a sum not exceeding his expenses. The court can also take into account the expenses incurred by the payer. In *Gamerco SA* v *ICM/Fair Warning (Agency) Ltd* (1995) Garland J held that the court had a broad discretion in this regard. There the promoters of a concert had made an advance payment to the performers, and the concert was then frustrated. As the loss sustained by the promoters greatly exceeded the prepayment the court made no deduction under the proviso.

In view of the considerable loss sustained by X, a total of £44,000, it might well be that the court would allow him to recover any prepayment in full. In any event we have not been informed as to any expenses incurred by Z.

As no 'valuable benefit' had been conferred on either party at the time of discharge the provision of s1(3) do not apply.

SUGGESTED ANSWER TO QUESTION THREE

General Comment

This involves discussion of both misrepresentation and breach of contract, and the effect thereon of the exclusion clauses, in the situations where K is a private seller and where he sells in the course of a business. The position of J's wife, as a third party, has also to be considered.

Key Points

- Misrepresentation, the nature thereof
- The effect of the exclusion clauses, whether they enable K to avoid liability for misrepresentation
- The remedies available to J if they do not
- Breach of contract, nature thereof and the effect of the clauses
- The position where K sold in the course of business
- The rights of J's wife

Suggested Answer

The misrepresentation here is in the (clearly false) statement that the car was 'in excellent condition'. This is more than a mere sales talk, nor can it be characterised as merely a statement of opinion. K was the owner of the car, and it does not appear to be an opinion he could reasonably have held: *Smith* v *Land & House Property Corporation* (1884). Nor could he have made any investigation on the basis of which the statement was made: *Brown* v *Raphael* (1958).

The statement was addressed to J (as well as other potential buyers). Although J bought the car after a test drive, which may have contributed to persuading him to buy it, the statement must have been, even if not the sole factor, a substantial factor in inducing him to enter into the contract. This is sufficient to constitute an actionable misrepresentation: *Edgington* v *Fitzmaurice* (1885).

There was, however, an attempt to exclude liability for mispresentation. The exclusion clauses were clearly incorporated and, in the context of misrepresentation, the relevant provisions are clauses 22 and 25. Whilst they cover the particular wrong, it has to be considered whether they will be rendered invalid by the applicable statutory controls.

Section 3 Misrepresentation Act (MA) 1967 provides that if a contractual term excludes or restricts any liability for misrepresentation or any remedy available by reason of such a misrepresentation, that term shall have no effect unless is satisfies the requirement of reasonableness under s11(1) Unfair Contract Terms Act (UCTA) 1977. Clauses 22 and 25 of the contract fall within this section. The onus is on K to prove that it does satisfy the requirement.

Under s11(1) this requirement is 'that the term shall have been a fair and reasonable one to be included having regard to the circumstances which were, or ought reasonably to have been, known to or in the contemplation of the parties when the contract was made.'

On the information given to me, I submit that, in view of the serious defect in the car, of which K should have known, or which investigation would have revealed, clauses 22 and 25 will fail to satisfy the reasonableness requirement. In consequence K cannot escape liability for misrepresentation.

The remedies available to J are rescission and damages. With regard to rescission there does not appear to be any bar to the exercise of that right; delay can be a bar, but in my view the lapse of two days would not be regarded as significant. There is nothing to suggest that J should have discovered the fault within that period.

Whilst there is no evidence indicating fraud on K's part, J would also be entitled to damages under s2(1) MA 1967. It has already been submitted that the description of the car as being 'in excellent condition' was not an opinion that could reasonably have been held; therefore K could not discharge the onus imposed on him by that section. J has a claim against K for his personal injuries.

Clauses 23 and 24 relate to breach of contract. This must now be addressed.

Where K is a private seller the implied terms in s14 Sale of Goods Act (SGA) 1979 do not apply. Clause 23 precludes any express term as to quality or fitness for purpose. There is no basis for finding that the limitation of damages in clause 24 would not apply.

If K sold the car in the course of his business the implied terms as to satisfactory quality in s14(2) and fitness for purpose in s14(3) would apply. There is clearly a breach of these terms. J dealt as a consumer, as defined by s12(1) UCTA 1977. Accordingly clauses 23 and 24 would be struck down by s6(2) of that Act. They would also not be binding on J by virtue of the Unfair Terms in Consumer Contracts Regulations 1999. J would accordingly have a contractual claim against K. As the implied terms are conditions J could reject the car, and could also claim in respect of his personal injuries. A claim for damages in respect of the liability he may have incurred for damage to the police station, would not, I submit, be too remote.

It may be that K was also guilty of negligence in selling a car with so serious a defect of which he should have been aware. If he were selling in the course of his business, this may well have been a breach of the implied duty to take reasonable care, or exercise reasonable skill in the performance of the contract: s1(1)(a) UCTA 1977. There is not sufficient information to determine that negligence was a feature, but if it were the clauses in question cannot be construed as excluding liability for negligence: *Smith* v *South Wales Switchgear Co Ltd* (1978). In any event clauses excluding liability for negligence would be void in respect of J's personal injuries under s2(1) UCTA 1977, and subject to the reasonableness requirement under s2(2) in respect of the other loss or damage. They would also be subject to the Regulations.

As J's wife is a third party she would have no contractual claim against K. Nor could J sue in respect of her loss.

SUGGESTED ANSWER TO QUESTION FOUR

General Comment

This question requires discussion of two areas of the law: when a contract can be terminated for breach and the quantification of damages. Although obviously related, they are separate areas, each of which would merit a question on its own. This makes it somewhat difficult to decide how much of the answer should be devoted to each area.

Key Points

- Remedies for breach of contract: the right to terminate and the entitlement to damages
- Breaches which entitle the innocent party to terminate the contract
- Conditions, warranties and innominate terms
- Damages and remoteness of damage

Suggested Answer

A party to a contract is required to perform all the obligations which rest upon him. Breach of any obligation entitles the innocent party to a claim in damages. But some obligations are regarded as going to the root of the contract, and breach of such obligation entitles the innocent party, in addition to a claim for damages, to treat the breach as a repudiation of the contract, and to be able to bring the contract to an end.

Whether the breach entitles the innocent party to terminate the contract depends on the nature of the term that has been breached. Traditionally terms were divided into conditions and warranties. A condition being a term which went to the root of the contract, the breach of which entitled the innocent party to terminate. A warranty is usefully defined in s61 Sale of Goods Act 1979 as being 'collateral to the main purpose of [the] contract, the breach of which gives rise to a claim for damages, but not to a right to reject the goods and treat the contract as repudiated.'

There is a third category - innominate terms - of which further discussion will follow.

It is not always easy to distinguish between a condition and a warranty; the distinction is often a fine one. Thus, in *Poussard* v *Spiers & Pond* (1876) the failure of a performer to attend for the opening performance was treated as a breach of condition, whereas the failure of a performer to attend on due date for rehearsals was treated as a breach of warranty *Bettini* v *Gye* (1876). But, of course, the former breach might have had more serious consequences.

Certain criteria can be employed to determine whether a term is a condition. A term will be a condition in the following circumstances:

1. Where statute provides that it is a condition: see, for example, ss12–15 Sale of Goods Act 1979; ss8–11 Supply of Goods (Implied Terms) Act 1973; ss2–5 and 7–10 Supply of Goods and Services Act 1982.
2. Where binding authority requires a court to hold that it is a condition. Thus, in commercial contracts time is usually regarded as a condition: *The Mihalis Angelos* (1971); *Bunge Corporation* v *Tradax Export SA* (1981). Where time is a condition any breach thereof is deemed to be repudiatory: *Union Eagle Ltd* v *Golden Achievement Ltd* (1997).
3. Where the parties have agreed that it is a condition. But determining the intention of the parties is not without difficulty: see *L Schuler AG* v *Wickman Machine Tool Sales Ltd* (1974) and compare *Lombard North Central plc* v *Butterworth* (1987).

As noted above, where a term is a condition any breach of it will be deemed to be repudiatory; no regard will be had to the seriousness or consequences of the breach. But the courts have recognised that certain terms cannot readily be categorised as conditions or warranties. In *Hongkong Fir Shipping Co Ltd* v *Kawasaki Kisen Kaisha Ltd* (1962) Diplock LJ said:

> 'Of such (terms) all that can be predicted is that some breaches will and others will not give rise to an event which will deprive the party not in default of substantially the whole benefit which it was intended that he should have obtained from the contract.'

These terms are called 'innominate terms', the third category referred to previously. This adds to the complexity of the classification. In *Bunge Corporation* v *Tradax* (above) Lord Scarman said that:

> 'Unless the contract makes it clear (either expressly or impliedly) that a particular stipulation is a condition or only a warranty, it is an innominate term the remedy for a breach of which depends on the nature, consequences and effect of the breach.'

This does add to the difficulty of determining when an innocent party can bring a contract to an end for breach.

Some attention must, however, be given to difficulties that may arise in the quantification of damages.

It has been said that the purpose of an award of damages for breach of contract is to put the injured party in the position he would have been in if his rights had been observed: *Robinson* v *Harman* (1848); *Victoria Laundry (Windsor) Ltd* v *Newman Industries Ltd* (1949). But Lord Hoffmann observed in *South Australia Asset Management Corp* v *York Montague Ltd* (1996) that this is not always the correct point from which to start. At times giving effect to this purpose would be wholly disproportionate to the loss that had been sustained: see *Ruxley Electronics and Construction Ltd* v *Forsyth* (1995).

There are further difficulties. In Victoria Laundry Asquith LJ said that the loss which could be recovered was that which was 'reasonably foreseeable'. In *The Heron II* (1969) the House of Lords preferred the test to be 'in the reasonable contemplation of the parties' as denoting a higher degree of probability. Thus the loss suffered by the miller in having to close his mill in *Hadley* v *Baxendale* (1854) was reasonably foreseeable, but not within the reasonable contemplation of the parties.

SUGGESTED ANSWER TO QUESTION FIVE

General Comment

This question concerns the waiver of rights under a contract. If any party makes a clear and unequivocal waiver of his rights, then he cannot later pursue them. The question is whether Cecil has in fact waived his rights.

Key Points

- Bryan has broken the contract which would enable Cecil to rescind
- Cecil may have waived his rights if there has been a clear and unequivocal representation to that effect: *David Blackstone Ltd* v *Burnetts (West End) Ltd* – *Peyman* v *Lanjani*
- The right to rescind is not normally lost by mere failure to exercise it unless the delay is unreasonable: *Tyrer & Co* v *Hessler & Co* – *The Laconia*
- There is no consideration for Cecil's forbearance
- If Cecil accepted part payment in full settlement, equitable estoppel will prevent him suing for the balance: *Central London Property Trust Ltd* v *High Trees House Ltd*
- This will not be the case if there was economic pressure on him to accept it: *D & C Builders Ltd* v *Rees* – *Foakes* v *Beer*
- Cecil may or may not be able to sue for future payments: *Central London Property Trust Ltd* v *High Trees House Ltd* – *Brikom Investments Ltd* v *Carr*
- A requested gift may be good satisfaction: *Pinnel's Case*

Suggested Answer

This question concerns the waiver of contractual rights. Bryan initially broke the contract by failing to pay the rent which may have enabled Cecil (subject to any statutory rights Bryan may have) to rescind the contract and bring the tenancy to an end However, Cecil does not appear to have exercised those rights and by failing to do so, may have waived them and affirmed the contract: *David Blackstone Ltd* v *Burnetts (West End) Ltd* (1973). However, waiver requires a 'clear and unequivocal representation': *Peyman* v *Lanjani* (1985). The right to rescind is not normally lost by mere failure to exercise it, however (*Tyrer & Co* v *Hessler & Co* (1902)) unless the delay is unreasonable: *The Laconia* (1977). In any event, even if he has elected to waive his right to rescind, Cecil has not abandoned his claim for the rent.

Later Bryan offers Cecil a part payment. It is not clear from the question whether Cecil accepted that part payment or whether his injunction to 'forget it, mate' applies to the whole of the back rent. Nor is it clear that those words, which may be used in a colloquial sense to mean 'don't worry about it', can be taken literally. Cecil may simply have meant that he was giving Bryan further time to pay. In any event, there appears to be no consideration for Cecil's forbearance.

If Cecil intended to abandon the whole debt, then he must show a clear and unequivocal intention to do so. Furthermore, that representation must have been acted upon by Bryan. Bryan has in fact changed his position by spending the money.

If Cecil accepted the part payment in full settlement of the outstanding debt, the doctrine of equitable estoppel will prevent him from suing for the balance: *Central London Property Trust Ltd* v *High Trees House Ltd* (1947). This is an equitable remedy only and, had Cecil been under economic pressure to accept the part payment, the doctrine would not have applied (*D & C Builders Ltd* v *Rees* (1966)) and the usual common law rule in *Pinnel's Case* (1602) (affirmed in *Foakes* v *Beer* (1884)) will apply. However, the reverse seems to have been the case. Promissory estoppel probably acts merely as a suspension of the creditor's rights so he would be able to enforce future payments. However, see *Brikom Investments Ltd* v *Carr* (1979) where the creditor's rights were wholly extinguished.

If Cecil's intention was merely to give Bryan time to pay the full debt, then the forbearance is as to time and may amount to a variation of the contract rather than an abandonment of his rights.

If Cecil had requested the gold watch in payment, he will be unable to claim the balance:

> 'The gift of a horse, hawk or robe, etc, in satisfaction is good, for it shall be intended that a horse, hawk or robe, etc, might be more beneficial than the money': *Pinnel's Case.*

If the watch was offered and accepted without Cecil having requested it, it is submitted that the doctrine of equitable estoppel would apply. The court would not in any event be prepared to act as valuer of the watch.

SUGGESTED ANSWER TO QUESTION SIX

General Comment

Whilst students may readily embark on a 'write all I know' about frustration approach, the focus of the question is quite clear – foreseen and foreseeable events. Thus, specific attention to this area is necessary. Self-induced frustration should be distinguished.

Key Points

- The nature and necessity of the doctrine
- The initial tests propounded by the courts
- The modern approach
- An analysis of *The Eugenia* and the dicta of Lord Denning

Suggested Answer

The doctrine of frustration has had an uneven development with regard to the question of foreseen and foreseeable events. At one time supervening or unforeseen events were not regarded as an excuse for non-performance, because the parties could provide for such accidents in their contracts: *Paradine* v *Jane* (1647). This approach was relaxed in

Taylor v *Caldwell* (1863) and in following cases such as *Jackson* v *Union Marine Insurance Co Ltd* (1873) and *Krell* v *Henry* (1903), which made it considerably easier to invoke the doctrine of frustration. These cases were based on the implied term theory now largely abandoned in favour of the 'radical change in the obligations' test enunciated by Lord Radcliffe in *Davies Contractors Ltd* v *Fareham Urban District Council* (1956), a test adopted by the House of Lords in *National Carriers Ltd* v *Panalpina (Northern) Ltd* (1981) and *Pioneer Shipping Ltd* v *BTP Tioxide Ltd, The Nema* (1982). In these three decisions the House of Lords reverted to a more restrictive approach, expressed by Lord Roskill in *The Nema* when his Lordship said that the doctrine of frustration was not to be invoked lightly to relieve contracting parties of the normal consequences of imprudent commercial bargains.

In the modern law, then, a frustrating event is a supervening, unforeseen event, which the courts will only recognise in exceptional circumstances as significantly changing the nature of the obligations. It should follow that an event which was foreseen or foreseeable should not permit the doctrine to be invoked. In *Walton Harvey Ltd* v *Walker & Homfrays Ltd* (1931) the defendants granted the plaintiffs the right to display an advertising sign on the defendants' hotel for seven years. Within this period the hotel was compulsorily acquired and demolished by the local authority. The contract was not frustrated because the defendants knew of the risk of compulsory acquisition. There are dicta in support of the view that an event which is foreseen or foreseeable cannot frustrate a contract (eg in *Krell* v *Henry* and in *Davis Contractors*) and in principle this seems correct. But this principle has not been consistently applied.

In *Ertel Bieber & Co* v *Rio Tinto Co Ltd* (1918) a contract was held to be frustrated by a wartime prohibition against trading with the enemy, even though the war was a foreseeable event. In *WJ Tatem Ltd* v *Gamboa* (1939) a ship which had been chartered by the defendant as agent for the republicans during the Spanish civil war detained by the nationalists. Whilst such an event was foreseeable, the contract was held to be frustrated; the basis of the decision appears to be that it was not foreseeable that the ship would be detained for the period involved. But Goddard J also expressed the view, obiter, that the contract would have been frustrated even if the detention period had been foreseen. He said:

> 'If the true foundation of the doctrine [of frustration] is that once the subject matter of the contract is destroyed or the existence of a state of facts has come to an end, the contract is at an end, that result follows whether or not the event causing it was contemplated by the parties.'

In *Ocean Tramp Tankers Corporation* v *V O Sovfracht, The Eugenia* (1964) Lord Denning MR stated also obiter that:

> 'It has frequently been said that the doctrine of frustration only applies when the new situation is "unforeseen" or "unexpected" or "uncontemplated", as if that were an essential feature. But it is not so. The only thing that is essential is that the parties should have made no provision for it in the contract.'

The exact status of these dicta is not clear. The usual inference is that the parties contracted with reference to a particular event and so took the risk of it occurring, thus precluding the operation of the doctrine of frustration. Treitel (*The Law of Contract* (8th edn, p800)) argues that this inference can only be drawn if the event was actually foreseen or if the degree of foreseeability was a very high one. 'To support the inference of risk-assumption, the event must be one which any person of ordinary intelligence would regard as likely to occur.'

It should also be noted that this inference can be excluded by the evidence of a contrary intention. In *Bank Line Ltd* v *Arthur Capel Ltd* (1919) the parties appeared to have foreseen the risk but had possibly not thought about its effect. If this were so, the contract could be held to be frustrated. The normal inference was displaced by the special terms of the contract.

12

Remedies and Quasi-Contract

Introduction

This chapter concerns itself solely with remedies available to a plaintiff in contract. The principal remedy sought is damages, that is to say, pecuniary compensation for loss or damage. Damages are the only available remedy at common law. They are available as of right and a plaintiff who has proved his case is entitled to an award of damages, even if these are only nominal. The measure of damages is subject to the principle first laid down in *Hadley* v *Baxendale* (1854), which has consistently been affirmed but has been restated and refined in a large number of cases since: see *Farley* v *Skinner* (2001), *Omar* v *El-Wakil* (2001) and *Bank of Credit and Commerce International SA* v *Ali (No 2)* (2002). These cases are covered in the solutions below and the student should be able to discuss them in a competent manner.

While the common law provides only one remedy, equity provides a number. These remedies, chief among which are rescission, specific performance and injunctions, are designed to mitigate the hardship which an award of damages only might cause the successful plaintiff. An award of damages is not entirely ruled out by an equitable remedy and the plaintiff may sometimes have both. Recently, in *Panatown Ltd* v *Alfred McAlpine Construction Ltd* (2000), the House of Lords dealt with the issue of damages in a recovery action on behalf of a third party.

Equitable remedies are only available at the court's discretion and are subject to general equitable principles. In addition, each remedy has its own distinct rules as to when the remedy will or will not be awarded. There have been occasions where questions have also been set incorporating quasi-contractual isues. The recent case of *National Westminster Bank plc* v *Somer International (UK) Ltd* (2002) illustrates its contextual relevance to remedies.

While a whole chapter has been devoted to the topic of remedies, it should never be forgotten that consideration of the appropriate remedy forms part of the answer to any contractual problem question. Students will therefore find this topic referred to elsewhere throughout the book and study of the principles contained in this section is vital to success in relation to other topics.

Questions

INTERROGRAMS

1. 'The aim of the court in assessing damages is that the party to be compensated is, so far as money can do it, to be placed in the same position as if the contract had been performed.' Discuss this statement.
2. Explain what is meant by quantum meruit.
3. When will the court refuse to grant specific performance of a contract?

QUESTION ONE

'The present legal rules allowing an innocent party to bring a contract to an end for breach are unclear and in need for reform. Fortunately, the rules concerning measure of damages for breach are unclear.'

Discuss.

University of London LLB Examination
(for external students) Elements of the Law of Contract June 2001 Q2

QUESTION TWO

'The principle that the damage must not be too remote is difficult to apply and often causes hardship to the plaintiff.'

Discuss.

University of London LLB Examination
(for external students) Elements of the Law of Contract June 1999 Q7

QUESTION THREE

'Damages for breach of contract can only be awarded in respect of loss of a financial kind.'

Discuss.

University of London LLB Examination
(for external students) Elements of the Law of Contract June 1998 Q3

QUESTION FOUR

'Equity has provided a plethora of reliefs and remedies where the common law has provided only one.'

Discuss.

Written by the Editor

Answers

ANSWERS TO INTERROGRAMS

1. The principle followed by the courts in assessing damages for breach of contract is that the purpose of the award is to compensate the plaintiff for the loss of bargain he has suffered as a consequence of the breach. The plaintiff must prove his loss and if he cannot do so he will be awarded only nominal damages. An alternative measure of damages to loss of bargain is to compensate the plaintiff for the wasted expenditure he has incurred as a result of the defendant's breach, see *Anglian Television Ltd* v *Reed* (1972). The plaintiff has the right to choose to claim either for loss of bargain or for wasted expenditure (*CCC Films (London) Ltd* v *Impact Quadrant Films Ltd* (1984)), subject to the overriding requirement that the plaintiff is not to be put in a

better position than he would have been if the contract had been fully performed: *C & P Haulage* v *Middleton* (1983).

The award of damages for loss of bargain is subject to the limitation that the damages must not be too remote. The purpose of putting the plaintiff in the position he would have been in if the contract had been performed would, if logically pursued, give the plaintiff a complete indemnity for all loss resulting from a breach however unpredictable or improbable. It is recognised that this would be too harsh. Accordingly rules have been developed to limit the liability of the defendant to loss which the law regards as sufficiently proximate.

The modern law stems from the judgement of Alderson B in *Hadley* v *Baxendale* (1854) where the rule was said to consist of two limbs. To be recoverable the damages should be such as may fairly and reasonably be considered either arising naturally, ie according to the usual course of things, from such breach of contract itself, or such as may reasonably be supposed to have been in the contemplation of both parties, at the time they made the contract, as the probable result of the breach of it.

The rule in *Hadley* v *Baxendale* was reformulated by Asquith J in *Victoria Laundry (Windsor) Ltd* v *Newman Industries Ltd* (1949) in the following propositions:

a) The aggrieved party is only entitled to recover loss which was at the time of the contract reasonably foreseeable as liable to result from the breach.
b) What was reasonably foreseeable depends on the knowledge then possessed by the parties.
c) Knowledge is of two types, imputed and actual. Imputed knowledge is the knowledge that everyone, as a reasonable person, is taken to have of the ordinary course of things. Actual knowledge is knowledge which the contract-breaker actually possesses, of special circumstances outside the ordinary course of things, which make additional loss liable to result.
d) The contract-breaker need not have actually asked himself what loss was liable to result, it is sufficient that as a reasonable man he would have done so.
e) The plaintiff need not prove that it would be foreseen that the loss would necessarily result from the breach; it was sufficient that it was a 'serious possibility' or a 'real danger'. This could be expressed as 'liable to result' or 'on the cards'.

These propositions were considered by the House of Lords in *The Heron II* (1969). Whilst they were generally approved, their Lordships held that the test was not one of 'reasonable foreseeability' but one of 'reasonable contemplation', a term denoting a higher degree of probability. Their Lordships also disapproved of the colloquialism 'on the cards', and used a variety of expressions to indicate the degree of probability, including 'not unlikely', 'liable to result', 'a real danger' and 'a serious possibility'. No single formulation was adopted.

In *H Parsons (Livestock) Ltd* v *Uttley Ingham & Co Ltd* (1978) Lord Denning said that different tests applied to physical (damage to person or property) and economic (deprivation of profit) loss. In the former it was sufficient if the loss was a slight possibility, in the latter it had to be shown that the loss was a serious possibility. Scarman J (with whom Orr J agreed) rejected Lord Denning's distinction and adopted the 'serious possibility' test.

Two further points must be noted. Firstly, difficulty of assessment is no bar to an award of damages: *Chaplin* v *Hicks* (1911). Secondly, damages may be awarded for distress, vexation and disappointment occasioned by a breach of contract, provided they are not too remote: see, for example, *Jarvis* v *Swans Tours Ltd* (1973), *Jackson* v *Horizon Holidays Ltd* (1975).

2. An order of specific performance decrees that the defendant be obliged to perform his part of the contract. An award of specific performance is subject to a number of provisos:

   a) It will not be awarded where damages would be an adequate remedy. In *Flint* v *Brandon* (1803) it was said that:

      > 'This court does not profess to decree a specific performance of contracts of every description. It is only where the legal remedy is inadequate or defective that it becomes necessary for courts of equity to interfere.'

      For example, a plaintiff may have contracted to buy a unique item which is not readily available in the market. The court may order specific performance rather than damages and the defendant is obliged to transfer property in that item to him. There are many cases where the courts have been prepared to order specific performance where the property in question is a house.

   b) Where the contract is for personal services, specific performance is not available: *Ryan* v *Mutual Tontine Association* (1893).
   c) Specific performance is not available where performance would require constant supervision: *Ryan* v *Mutual Tontine Association* (1893).
   d) It will not be awarded against one party where it could not be awarded against the other eg where the other's contract was one for personal services or where the other is a minor.
   e) The court is unwilling to grant specific performance to a party who has breached an essential condition as to time, even if the delay is slight: *Union Eagle Ltd* v *Golden Achievement Ltd* (1997).

3. Where the injured party has partly performed the contract, he may recover reasonable remuneration for work done or services provided on a quantum meruit basis: eg *De Bernardy* v *Harding* (1853). This may also be possible if the contract does not make full provision for payment: *Sir Lindsay Parkinson & Co Ltd* v *Commissioners of Works* (1949).

   Another possible basis for a claim is where the party has rendered services under a contract which he believes to be valid but which is in fact void: *Craven-Ellis* v *Canons Ltd* (1936).

   The amount which the court will award – if no contractual provision has been made – is determined by reasonableness in relation to the goods delivered or services rendered. This is now provided for in the Sale of Goods Act 1979 and the Supply of Goods and Services Act 1982 respectively.

SUGGESTED ANSWER TO QUESTION ONE

General Comment

This question is very similar to the one set in the examination for the year 2000, but a different emphasis seems to be required. The focus should be on the difficulties in treating a breach of contract as repudiatory, especially with regard to innominate terms. This should be contrasted with the suggested clarity concerning the measure of damages.

Key Points

- The relative importance of terms: conditions, warranties and innominate terms
- The criteria for establishing that a term is a condition
- The category of innominate terms and the difficulties this creates
- The rules concerning the measure of damages

Suggested Answer

An innocent party is only entitled to bring a contract to an end for breach if that breach is of a condition or is treated as such. For a breach of warranty the innocent party's remedy is only for damages. A term is a condition if statute so provides, or there is binding authority requiring such interpretation, or if such was the parties' intention.

Certain terms are classified as conditions by statute: inter alia, by ss12–15 Sale of Goods Act 1979. The strict application of the statute has been the subject of criticism following the case of *Arcos Ltd* v *E A Ronaasen & Son* (1933) where the breach was of s13 Sale of Goods Act 1979 (sale by description) but the breach was slight, and was seized on by the buyer in order to take advantage of a falling market. (This would now fall within s15A of the Act, whereby a slight breach could be treated as only a breach of warranty.) In *Cehave NV* v *Bremer Handelsgesellschaft mbH, The Hansa Nord* (1976) the breach was of the term 'shipped in good condition', but the Court of Appeal refused to treat this as a breach of the 'merchantable quality' condition in the Sale of Goods Act 1979 (as the section then read) as its consequences did not justify termination of the contract.

Binding authority requires certain terms to be treated as conditions, for example stipulations as to time in commercial contracts: *The Mihalis Angelos* (1971); *Bunge Corporation* v *Tradax Export SA* (1981).

Where the classification of the term as a condition reflects the intention of the parties, the courts will so treat it – subject to a situation such as that in *L Schuler AG* v *Wickman Machine Tools Sales Ltd* (1974). The consequences of so doing can be harsh, even unjust: see *Lombard North Central plc* v *Butterworth* (1987).

The major difficulties that arise, however, stem from the category of the innominate term.

The origin of the development of the innominate term is in the judgment of Diplock

LJ in *Hongkong Fir Shipping Co Ltd* v *Kawasaki Kisen Kaisha Ltd* (1962) where he said:

> 'There are many ... contractual undertakings ... which cannot be categorised as being "conditions" or "warranties" ... Of such undertakings all that can be predicted is that some breaches will and others will not give rise to an event which will deprive the party not in default of substantially the whole benefit which it was intended that he should obtain.'

In *Bunge Corporation* v *Tradax* (above) Lord Scarman said;

> 'Unless the contract makes it clear ... that a particular stipulation is a condition or only a warranty, it is an innominate term the remedy for a breach of which depends on the nature, consequences and effect of the breach.'

This leads to uncertainty; the consequences of the breach have to be awaited before the relevant term can be classified, which means that the parties cannot be sure of their obligations at the time they concluded the contract. This has also created problems for the Courts. For example, in *The Naxos* (1990) the majority of the House of Lords held that the obligation of the seller to have the cargo ready for delivery at a particular time was a condition, whereas the majority of the Court of Appeal and the judge at first instance held that it was not.

In the context of anticipatory breach it has occurred that a breach, on the face of it comparatively trivial, was treated as repudiatory because of the consequences that ensued: *Federal Commerce & Navigation Co Ltd* v *Molena Alpha Inc* (1979).

Whilst there is the need for certainty, too much emphasis on it can lead to injustice as in the case of *Arcos* v *Ronaasen* (above). The courts have on occasions been reluctant to treat a breach as a breach of condition, particularly where an award of damages would prove an adequate remedy. It remains to consider the rules concerning the measure of damages.

The purpose of an award of damages is to put the innocent party in the position he would have been in if the contract had been performed: *Robinson* v *Harman* (1848); *Victoria Laundry (Windsor) Ltd* v *Newman Industries Ltd* (1949). But, as Asquith LJ observed in the latter case:

> 'This purpose, if relentlessly pursued, would provide him with a complete indemnity for all loss de facto resulting from a particular breach, however improbable, however unpredictable. This, in contract at least, is recognised as too harsh a rule.'

The important limitation on the implementation of this purpose is that the damages must not be too remote. The rule is that the damages:

> '... should be such as may be fairly and reasonably be considered either arising naturally, that is, according to the usual course of things, from the breach of contract itself, or such as may be reasonably be supposed to have been in the contemplation of both parties, at the time they made the contract, as the probable result of the breach of it': *Hadley* v *Baxendale* (1854) per Alderson B.

Some ambiguity has resulted from this rule. In *Victoria Laundry* Asquith LJ defined the test as 'reasonable foreseeability', but the House of Lords in *The Heron II* (1969) preferred the test to be formulated as 'within the reasonable contemplation of the parties', which denoted a higher degree of probability.

It should be noted that if the party in default should have foreseen (or contemplated) the type of damage that would probably have resulted from the breach, it will not avail him that the extent of such damage could not have been within reasonable contemplation: *H Parsons (Livestock) Ltd* v *Uttley Ingham & Co Ltd* (1978).

SUGGESTED ANSWER TO QUESTION TWO

General Comment

Little general comment is required on this question. It requires discussion and analysis of the limitation on an award of damages by the application of the rule as to remoteness.

Key Points

- The rule in *Hadley* v *Baxendale*
- The two limbs of the rule
- The question of 'reasonably foreseeable' and 'in the reasonable contemplation of the parties'

Suggested Answer

The principles as to the limitation on an award of damages were laid down in *Hadley* v *Baxendale* (1854), where Alderson B held that:

> 'Where two parties have made a contract which one of them has broken, the damages which the other party ought to receive in respect of such breach of contract should be such as may fairly and reasonably be considered as either arising naturally, that is, according to the usual course of things, from such breach of contract itself, or such as may reasonably be supposed to have been in the contemplation of both parties, at the time they made the contract, as the probable result of the breach of it.'

These principles were amplified by Asquith LJ in *Victoria Laundry (Windsor) Ltd* v *Newman Industries Ltd* (1949). He limited the damages recoverable to what was reasonably foreseeable and this depended on the state of knowledge of the parties. Everyone is deemed to know the 'ordinary course of things'. But there may be special circumstances, outside the 'ordinary course of things' of such a kind that a breach would be liable to cause more loss. Of these special circumstances actual knowledge is required in order to fix the party in breach with liability.

A defendant is liable, even without special knowledge, if the loss occurs 'naturally', 'in the ordinary course of things'. A person who agrees to supply a profit-earning commodity is liable for the loss of profits resulting from the delay: *Fletcher* v *Taylor* (1885). A seller of poisonous cattle food is liable for the loss of the cattle to which it is fed: *Ashington Piggeries Ltd* v *Christopher Hill Ltd* (1972). A seller of defective seed to a farmer is liable for the loss of the expected crop: *George Mitchell (Chesterhall) Ltd* v *Finney Lock Seeds Ltd* (1983).

In order for loss to arise 'naturally' there must have been a 'serious possibility', or a 'real danger', or a 'very substantial probability' that the loss would occur: *Koufos* v *C Czarnikow Ltd, The Heron II* (1969). This is consistent with the decision in *Hadley* v *Baxendale* where the plaintiff could not recover for the loss caused by the closure of his mill, caused by the later delivery of the mill shaft; the closure of the mill was not the 'natural' result of the delayed delivery because the plaintiff might have been expected to have a spare shaft. In *Victoria Laundry* the defendants were not liable for the loss of an unusual and especially lucrative contract of which they were unaware. A supplier of electricity to a building contractor cannot be expected to foresee the full consequences of a power failure on a complex construction contract on which the contractor is engaged: *Balfour Beatty* v *Scottish Power plc* (1994).

In *The Heron II* (above) the House of Lords held that the test was not 'reasonable foreseeability', that was the test in tort, but what was in the 'reasonable contemplation of the parties'. That denoted a higher degree of probability. Their Lordships' justification of the different tests in tort and contract was that in contract it was open to the plaintiff to apprise the defendant of special circumstances which would increase the magnitude of the loss; but in tort the plaintiff would not have had this opportunity.

This view was challenged by Lord Denning MR in *H Parsons (Livestock) Ltd* v *Uttley, Ingham & Co Ltd* (1978). He drew the distinction between the loss of profit cases and physical damage cases, and suggested that the test of 'reasonable contemplation' should be kept to the former category. In the second class of case, physical damage, the defaulting party should be liable for any loss which he ought reasonably to have foreseen at the time of the breach as a possible consequence, even if it was only a slight possibility.

But Lord Denning's view was a minority one. Scarman LJ held that the cases did not support a distinction between loss of profit and physical damage cases. But he also said:

> 'I agree with him in thinking it absurd that the test for remoteness of damage should, in principle, differ according to the legal classification of the cause of action, though one must recognise that parties to a contract have the right to agree to a measure of damages which may be greater or less than the law would offer in the absence of agreement.'

The distinction between the test of remoteness in contract and the test in tort remains. In *Henderson* v *Merrett Syndicates Ltd* (1995) Lord Goff said that 'the rules as to remoteness of damage … are less restrictive in tort than they are in contract'.

If the defendant ought reasonably to have contemplated the kind of damage that would result from the breach, it is no answer for him to say that he could not have contemplated the extent of that damage. Thus, in *Parsons* v *Uttley Ingham* (above) the defendants supplied a container for animal food which was defective, as a result food stored in it became mouldy, and the animals who consumed it suffered a rare intestinal infection and some died. The defendants were held liable for the loss of the animals: they could have contemplated that, as a consequence of the defect, food would become mouldy and that animals who ate it would become ill, even though they might not have foreseen the extent of that illness. In *Wroth* v *Tyler* (1974) the defendant, in breach of contract, failed to deliver a house to the plaintiff, who was compelled to buy a similar house on the market. There had been during the relevant period a very sharp and unexpected rise in house prices. A measure of damages was awarded based on the difference between the contract price and the subsequent market price. A risk in prices was within the reasonable contemplation of the parties, even though the extent of it was not.

It is impossible to deny that the rules as to remoteness are difficult to apply. To revert to the decisions in, for example, *Hadley* v *Baxendale* and *Victoria Laundry* (above) it does seem harsh that the plaintiffs in those cases were denied the fruits of their contracts.

SUGGESTED ANSWER TO QUESTION THREE

General Comment

What this question clearly requires is a discussion of the cases in which damages have been awarded for non-financial loss resulting from a breach of contract.

Key Points

- The general rule, in this context, as to the limitation on damages for breach of contract
- The exceptions to the general rule, the class of cases in which damages for non-financial loss may be awarded

Suggested Answer

In *Watts* v *Morrow* (1991) Bingham LJ summarised the general rule, and the exceptions to that rule, as follows:

> 'A contract-breaker is not in general liable for any distress, frustration, anxiety, displeasure, vexation, tension or aggravation which his breach of contract may cause to the innocent party. ... But the rule is not absolute. Where the very object of a contract is to provide pleasure, relaxation, peace of mind or freedom from molestation, damages will be awarded if the fruit of the contract is not provided or if the contrary result is procured instead.'

A leading case which exemplifies the general rule is the decision of the House of Lords in *Addis* v *Gramophone Co Ltd* (1909), where an employee was wrongfully dismissed in a manner that was 'harsh and humiliating'. He recovered for the loss of salary and commission, but not for the injury to his feelings caused by the manner of his dismissal, or for loss of reputation. This was an employment case, but it has been accepted as authority for the wider principle that damages for injured feelings or loss of reputation cannot, in general, be recovered in an action for breach of contract. This principle has been more recently affirmed by the Court of Appeal in *Malik* v *BCCI* (1995), in which it was also held, however, that damages may be recovered where the loss of reputation caused by the breach of contract causes financial loss.

But, as Bingham LJ observed, the rule is not an absolute one. We must now consider the cases in which damages for non-financial loss have been awarded.

Damages can be awarded for physical inconvenience. In *Bailey* v *Bullock* (1950) a solicitor negligently failed to take proceedings for the recovery of his client's house. The solicitor was held liable for the inconvenience – but not for the distress – caused to his client by having to live for two years with his wife's parents.

Damages or distress have been awarded in two cases where tour operators had failed to provide the holidays for which the plaintiffs had contracted. The plaintiffs recovered damages for the disappointment occasioned by these breaches: *Jarvis* v *Swan Tours Ltd* (1973); *Jackson* v *Horizon Holidays Ltd* (1975). In *Jarvis* Lord Denning criticised the decision in *Bailey* v *Bullock* (above) which had limited the award to actual inconvenience. His Lordship said that:

> 'I think that these limitations are out of date. In a proper case damages for mental distress can be recovered in contract, just as damages for shock can be recovered in tort. One such case is a contract for a holiday, or any other contract to provide entertainment and enjoyment.'

In *Watts* v *Morrow* (above) the Court of Appeal awarded damages to a husband and wife for the physical inconvenience and directly related mental distress of living in a house undergoing extensive repairs. The repairs were necessitated by defects that had been negligently omitted from the defendant's survey report upon which the plaintiffs had relied in buying the house.

In *Heywood* v *Wellers (A Firm)* (1976) the plaintiff was awarded damages for the mental distress caused by the failure of the defendant solicitors to obtain a molestation order on her behalf.

In *Ruxley Electronics and Construction Ltd* v *Forsyth* (1995) the House of Lords approved the award of damages for loss of a pleasurable amenity. Lord Lloyd observed that if this 'involves a further inroad on the rule in *Addis* v *Gramophone Co Ltd* then so be it.'

But it does appear that damages for mental distress in contract are limited to certain classes of case. In *Bliss* v *South East Thames Regional Health Authority* (1987) Dillon LJ suggested the classification as:

> '… where the contract which has been broken was itself a contract to provide peace of mind or freedom from distress …'

Commenting on this classification in *Hayes* v *James & Charles Dodd (A Firm)* (1990) Staughton LJ said:

> 'It may be that the class is somewhat wider than that. But it should not, in my judgment, include any case where the object of the contract was not comfort or pleasure or the relief of discomfort, but simply carrying on a commercial activity with a view to profit.'

SUGGESTED ANSWER TO QUESTION FOUR

General Comment

The requirement for a good mark in this question is the ability to summarise the main remedies available in equity and their effectiveness as an alternative to damages. It is not necessary to discuss the rules applicable to an award for damages since the focus is on the equitable remedies. The pitfall with this type of question is a tendency to 'ramble' and write everything one knows about the topic without really answering the question. Students should remember that, in an examination, the inclusion of a good deal of irrelevant material wastes time and gains no marks. The ability to produce a well-structured summary of the law under examination conditions usually denotes an outstanding candidate.

Key Points

- Monetary compensation for loss or damage ('damages') is available as of right for the plaintiff who has won his case but the measure of damages may not be sufficient to compensate him in the circumstances
- Equitable remedies are more flexible but are only discretionary
- The plaintiff who seeks equity must come with 'clean hands' and without unreasonable delay
- Specific performance - where the plaintiff has good reason to want the contract performed rather than monetary compensation - is not always available
- Injunctions (prohibitory, mandatory and interlocutory) may force the defendant to do something or prevent him from doing something
- Rescission - puts the parties back in the position that they would have been in had the contract not been made - is subject to a number of 'bars' (restitution impossible; affirmation; third party rights; unreasonable delay)
- Restitution - the return of money paid - there must have been a 'total failure of consideration'
- Rectification - amending a contract to reflect what the parties actually agreed
- Equitable estoppel - preventing a party from enforcing his legal rights where he has forgone them
- Non est factum - signature of a deed while mistaken as to the nature of the transaction - the rules for granting this relief are very restrictive.

Suggested Answer

The common law remedy is damages which means monetary compensation for the loss or damage suffered by the plaintiff. However, there are many situations where the common law remedy will be harsh or inadequate. In a number of these instances, equity will provide relief of its own. As equity and the common law have been administered by the courts since the Judicature Acts 1873-75, equitable remedies are available to the plaintiff in appropriate situations. The important thing to remember that damages are available as of right. The plaintiff who has proved his case is always entitled to damages, even if these should be nominal only. Equitable remedies are available only in the court's discretion.

Equitable remedies may be categorised as follows:

Specific performance

An order of specific performance decrees that the defendant be obliged to perform his part of the contract. The order is available where damages would be an inadequate remedy. For example, a plaintiff may have contracted to buy a unique item which is not readily available in the market. The court may order specific performance rather than damages and the defendant is obliged to transfer property in that item to him. The courts are usually prepared to order specific performance where the property in question is a house.

The court will not order specific performance of a contract for personal services for that would interfere with personal liberty. Nor will an order be made in respect of a contract which requires constant supervision.

Injunctions

There are three types of injunction which the court may order: prohibitory, which prevents the defendant from doing something; mandatory, which compels the defendant to perform his contractual obligations; and interlocutory, which maintains the balance between the parties until full trial of the action.

A mandatory injunction is very similar to an order of specific performance but the court will not grant a mandatory injunction if it would be tantamount to an order for specific performance in a situation where specific performance would not be ordered (see above).

The court will not grant an injunction of unlimited duration where it might be used oppressively. In *Phonographic Performance Ltd* v *Maitra* (1997), which concerned a licence to play certain records, when the plaintiffs sought an unlimited injunction against the defendants it was held to be unnecessary. The plaintiffs had been accustomed to using injunctions to force payment for past unlicensed playing of records and the court found that this was oppressive.

Rescission

Rescission is the commonest equitable remedy. The injured party is entitled to avoid the contract and any further liability under it, and the court will attempt to put the parties back into the position they would have been in had the contract not been made. Rescission will generally be granted where a party has broken a condition of the contract. It will also be available in cases of misrepresentation and common mistake.

There are a number of restrictions on the grant of rescission:

a) Restitution in integrum must be possible – ie it must be possible to put the parties back into the position that they were before the contract was made.
b) The injured party must not have affirmed (evidenced an intention to continue with) the contract.
c) Third parties should not have gained rights to any property which is the subject matter of the contract.
d) The injured party should not have delayed unreasonably in enforcing his rights.

These restrictions are known as 'bars to rescission'.

While a right to rescind may be expressly provided for in the contract, it has been held that this right is not exhaustive. In *Stocznia Gdanska SA* v *Latvian Shipping Co* (1998) which concerned a contract to design and build two ships, the court held that there was a presumption that the party did not intend to abandon any remedies unless there were clear words in the contract to say so.

Restitution

Where a party has wholly or partly performed his side of the bargain, the court may award restitution, ie the return of money paid or recompense for benefits he has provided under the contract.

The rule with the former is that money paid can only be recovered if there has been a 'total failure of consideration'. There is no right if there has been only a partial failure, although this may give rise to a claim for rescission. There may be a total failure of consideration if the benefit received by the plaintiff is different in kind from that bargained for: *Rowland* v *Divall* (1923). For a modern discussion: see *Lipkin Gorman* v *Karpnale Ltd* (1991). Where the injured party has partly performed the contract, he may have a claim for his payment in respect of the services rendered. The amount which the court will award - if no contractual provision has been made - is determined by reasonableness in relation to the goods delivered or services rendered. This is now provided for in the Sale of Goods Act 1979 and the Supply of Goods and Services Act 1982 respectively. Equally, he may recover if the contract does not make full provision for payment: *Sir Lindsay Parkinson & Co Ltd* v *Commissioners of Works* (1949). Another possible basis for a claim is where the party has rendered services under a contract which he believes to be valid but which is in fact void: *Craven-Ellis* v *Canons Ltd* (1936).

Rectification

Where the contract does not reflect the exact terms agreed by the parties, rectification will be available. That is to say the court will order that the written contract be amended in accordance with the true agreement made by the parties. This may happen in the case of mistake.

While remedies are awarded to the plaintiff, reliefs are afforded to a defendant against whom equity decrees that it would be inequitable to allow an action. The two principal reliefs in contract are equitable or promissory estoppel and non est factum.

Equitable (or promissory) estoppel

This operates where a creditor has accepted part payment of a debt and then attempts to sue the debtor for the balance. The court will prevent the creditor from enforcing the action. It is generally thought that this relief acts as a suspension of the creditor's rights and does not extinguish them totally. Relief will not be granted where the debtor has used the creditor's economic position to force the creditor to accept a lesser payment: *D & C Builders* v *Rees.*

Non est factum

Equity will give relief to someone who has signed a deed while mistaken as to the nature of the transaction.

All remedies and reliefs are subject to equitable principles. It has already been mentioned that they are not available as of right and are discretionary only. The principle mentioned under the heading of rescission above, that the plaintiff should not unreasonably delay enforcing his claim (the doctrine of laches), applies to all equitable remedies. Further, equity demands that the plaintiff must come to equity 'with clean hands' and that 'he who seeks equity must do equity', so that anyone seeking an equitable remedy or relief must have behaved equitably himself – the basis of the *D & C Builders* decision (above).

Equity, therefore has remained flexible and responsive to the needs of those who come before the courts and, while in most cases damages will provide sufficient remedy, more appropriate remedies are available where they are needed.

13

Agency and Sale of Goods

Introduction

One of the major exceptions to the doctrine of privity is agency, which grew up whilst the doctrine was being formulated and has a long and venerable history of its own. An agent can make a contract which binds his principal (the person who appointed him) rather than himself. Agents must however act within the scope of their authority and the question of whether or not an agent has authority in a particular situation forms the basis of many problem questions. The contract of agency itself - that between the principal and agent - gives rise to specific rights and obligations, some of which are implied in law. The Commercial Agents (Council Directive) (Amendment) Regulations 1993 cover commercial agreements in line with European law. Questions on this area usually involve no more than a good knowledge and ability to describe the consequences of such a contract, although the implied duties may sometimes give rise to a problem question.

The implied terms under the sale of goods legislation are an important topic for the student to grasp, but the norm in degree examinations is to combine the topic with another such as exemption clauses. Note also the relevance of the Unfair Terms in Consumer Contracts (UTCC) Regulations 1999 which influence the validity of unfair exclusion clauses in consumer contracts. The questions below demonstrate such an intermingling of topics.

Questions

INTERROGRAMS

1. It is settled that for the principal to be bound his agent must act within the limits of the agent's authority. What kinds of authority can an agent have?
2. What is meant by the 'exceptions to the nemo dat rule'?
3. What remedies are available to the unpaid seller of goods?
4. What is the 'doctrine of the undisclosed principal'?

QUESTION ONE

Lovejoy, an antiques dealer, has recently been abroad for an extended visit. Before leaving, he asked Eric to 'mind the business for me and keep things ticking over'.

At Lovejoy's express request, Eric attended an auction to bid on Lovejoy's behalf for a George I silver epergne. Lovejoy's precise instructions to Eric were: 'Go up to £3,000 if you have to.' In the event, Eric secured the epergne for £5,000.

Lovejoy also asked Eric to buy a painting for him from another dealer, Gimbert. Lovejoy told Eric: 'Get the painting whatever it costs but don't tell Gimbert you are buying for me or he won't sell.' Eric told Gimbert he was buying the painting for a relative of his and Gimbert agreed to sell it to him for £8,000.

From abroad, Lovejoy wrote to Tinker, a fellow dealer saying: 'Eric will be minding the shop while I am away. Give him any help he asks for.' Eric went into Tinker's shop and selected a number of items, saying to Tinker: 'As you know, I'm running Lovejoy's business while he's away. He will pay you for these when he gets back.'

Lovejoy has now returned and discovered that the epergne is worth only £500 and he does not want to buy it. He also considers that the items Eric purported to buy on his behalf from Tinker are worthless and that he should not be liable to pay for them as Eric had no instructions to buy from Tinker. Meanwhile, Gimbert has discovered that the painting was intended for Lovejoy and refuses to part with it, even on payment of £8,000 cash.

Advise Lovejoy of his contractual rights and liabilities.

Written by the Editor

QUESTION TWO

G went to H's shipyard explaining that he needed a boat to realise his life's ambition to travel round the world. G was sold 'Jenny', a 42 foot boat for £40,000. It was a type suitable for world touring. G spent the remainder of his life savings to stock the boat with considerable quantities of provisions. G engaged J to survey the boat and he gave it a clean bill of health. Three months later G set out on his circumnavigation of the world. Three days into the Atlantic Ocean the boat developed a severe leak and G had to put about. The boat was found to be unsound and in need of considerable expenditure to make her seaworthy.

Advise G. What difference, if any, would it make to your advice if the contract between J and G had limited J's liability to the contract fee of £300?

University of London LLB Examination
(for external students) Elements of the Law of Contract June 2000 Q4

QUESTION THREE

H saw a 1936 Flying Standard car for sale on a Lom's Garage forecourt for £4,000. He stopped and examined it thoroughly before taking it out for a test drive. The sales manager stated that the car, 'was restored but not in concourse condition. You will have to buy it as found'. H agreed to take the car and drove it from the garage having arranged to buy it from Fortin Finance Co Ltd to whom Lom's Garage was going to sell it. H was to make monthly instalments of £200 per month for two years. Three months after he agreed to buy the car the brakes failed and H ran into a car driven by J. Both were seriously injured.

The agreement between H and Fortin Finance Co Ltd stated:

'44. It is understood that any statements made by the supplier have no contractual effect between us and the purchaser from us.

45. Fortin Finance Co Ltd accepts no responsibility for the condition of the vehicle and

shall not be liable for any consequential losses resulting from the condition, use or safety of the vehicle.
46. H agrees to indemnify Fortin Finance Co Ltd for any damages which are or may become payable under this contract in the event of any judgment that they are in breach of contract or any other legal duty.'

Advise H.

University of London LLB Examination (for external students) Elements of the Law of Contract June 1994 Q4

Answers

ANSWERS TO INTERROGRAMS

1. If the agent is to escape personal liability under a contract which he purports to make on behalf of his principal, he must act within the scope of his authority. There are a number of different kinds of authority:

   a) Express authority is the authority which has clearly been given to him by the principal. Where the authority given is capable of more than one interpretation, the principal may be bound even if the agent incorrectly interprets his authority (*Weigall* v *Runciman* (1916)), unless it is reasonable for the agent to seek clarification and he fails to do so: *European Asian Bank* v *Punjab & Sind Bank* (1983). If the agent exceeds his express authority, the principal may not be liable unless the other contracting party can show that the agent had some other kind of authority.
   b) Incidental authority is the authority to do all those things which are not specifically referred to in the appointment but which are incidental to carrying out the purpose for which the agent was appointed. For example, if P goes abroad and asks A to sell his car for him, A probably has incidental authority to advertise the car and show it to prospective buyers. If a solicitor is asked to form a company for a client, he has incidental authority to do all the things necessary to the formation of the company even though these may not be specifically mentioned. This type of authority is interpreted fairly strictly. For example, an agent employed to sell has no incidental authority to receive payment: *Mynn* v *Joliffe* (1834).
   c) Usual authority is the authority which an agent of a particular type usually has. For example in *Watteau* v *Fenwick* (1893) the manager of a public house contracted to buy cigars in his own name and the seller was permitted to sue the owner of the public house since this was within the usual authority of a public house manager. However this type of authority only applies where the agent belongs to a well known class of agents: *Jerome* v *Bentley & Co* (1952). Otherwise the plaintiff must rely on establishing customary or apparent authority (see below).
   d) Customary authority is authority to act in accordance with the custom of the market in which he is operating (*Graves* v *Legg* (1857)), but this only applies

where the custom is not inconsistent with the principal's express instructions: *Perry* v *Barnett* (1885).

e) Apparent authority (sometimes referred to as ostensible authority) is the authority which third parties are entitled to assume that the agent has because the principal has placed him in a particular position or otherwise made a representation to the third party that the agent is entitled to act in the transaction. It appears that there is some overlap with usual authority but, as stated above, usual authority only applies where the agent belongs to a clearly-defined class of agents who have clearly understood authority. Some examples of apparent authority include *Summers* v *Solomon* (1857) where the manager of a jewellery shop who bought jewellery from a supplier which was paid for by the owner of the shop continued to buy jewellery on this basis after he had left his employment. It was held that the owner was liable. In *Freeman & Lockyer* v *Buckhurst Park Properties Ltd,* K was permitted to act as managing director of the defendant company, even though he had not been appointed as such. He made contracts with the plaintiff architects which the company later sought to avoid on the ground that he had no authority to make them. The court held that he had apparent authority and the company was bound. A more recent case is *Panorama Developments (Guildford) Ltd* v *Fidelis Furnishing Fabrics Ltd* (1971) where the properly appointed secretary of a company entered into contracts which the company later sought to avoid on the ground that he had no authority. It was held that the modern company secretary has implied authority (usual or apparent) to enter into contracts concerning the administration of the company and the plaintiffs were entitled to assume from his position that he had the authority to make the relevant contracts.

The rules for determining apparent authority, which were set out in *Freeman & Lockyer,* are that:

a) there must have been a representation of authority;
b) the representation must have been made to the other contracting party;
c) the representation must have been made by the principal; and
d) the contracting party must have relied on that representation.

It is therefore not express authority alone which determines the principal's liability and regard will be had to the circumstances of the case to establish whether the agent did or did not have sufficient authority to make the contract.

2. The rule stems from the Latin phrase nemo dat quod non habet which means that a person who does not have good title to goods, eg a thief or a receiver of stolen property, cannot pass good title to a third party. There are a number of exceptions to that rule. The exceptions were determined under the case law but have been codified into statute law by the Sale of Goods Act (SOGA) 1979. These are as follows:

   a) The owner is estopped from denying the seller's authority to sell the goods, eg by holding out a person as his agent: s21(1).
   b) Where goods are sold by a factor to a person taking in good faith without notice of lack of authority: s21(2)(a).

c) Where goods are sold under a common law or statutory power of sale or a court order, eg by a bailiff or pawnbroker: s21(2)(b).
d) Where goods are held under a voidable contract (see identity mistake, Chapter 7), a person taking in good faith without notice of lack of title before the seller has avoided, may obtain good title: s23.
e) Where a buyer or seller is, with the other party's consent, in possession of the goods or documents to title, he or she may pass good title to a buyer who takes the goods in good faith without notice of the other's claim: s25.
f) Where the hirer of a motor vehicle sells it to a third party who takes in good faith without notice of the hire-purchase or conditional sale agreement, the third party will obtain good title: ss27–29 Hire Purchase Act 1965.

One common law exception which was abolished by statute was a sale in a market ouvert.

3. The unpaid seller has a wide range of remedies. These can be categorised into remedies against the goods and remedies against the buyer.

Remedies against goods

a) A lien on the goods, which is a limited equitable right to retain and to sell the goods if payment is not made. The seller must be in possession of the goods although property has passed to the buyer, but if he has extended credit, the lien does not arise until the credit period has ended: s41 SOGA 1979.
b) Stoppage in transit, which allows the seller to take possession of the goods while they are in the possession of a carrier if the buyer becomes insolvent. The goods are still in transit if the buyer rejects them but not if he takes delivery, if the carrier agrees to hold on behalf of the buyer, or if he wrongfully refuses to deliver the goods to the buyer. Sale or disposition by the buyer does not affect this right unless the seller has agreed or the document of title has been transferred to the buyer who passes it to a person taking in good faith and for value.
c) The right to withhold delivery if property has not passed to the buyer: s39(2) SOGA 1979.
d) The seller who has exercised any of the above rights only has a right to resell them if:

   i) the goods are perishable; or
   ii) he gives notice of his intention to resell and the buyer does not tender the price within a reasonable time;
   iii) a right of resale is expressly reserved in the contract.

Remedies against the buyer

a) Action for the price may be brought if property has passed or a date for payment has been agreed: s49 SOGA 1979.
b) Action for damages for non-acceptance. The measure of damages is estimated as the loss directly and naturally resulting in the ordinary course of events from the breach. Where there is an available market in the goods, this will usually be the difference between the contract price and the market price at the date of the

breach: s50 SOGA 1979. Otherwise the seller will be entitled to loss of bargain damages (see remedies in Chapter 12): *W L Thompson Ltd* v *Robinson (Gunmakers) Ltd* (1955); *Charter* v *Sullivan* (1957).

4. The doctrine of the undisclosed principal is applied in the situation where an agent apparently negotiates a contract for himself alone. There is a distinction between non-disclosure of the principal's name and non-disclosure of the existence of an agency. In the former case, whether or not the principal is bound by the contract is determined by the understanding between the parties. If the other contracting party accepts that there is an agency then the principal will be bound. If, however, the agent signs the contract without disclosing the existence of any agency at all, both he and the principal are bound by it and it may be enforced against either of them at the option of the other contracting party.

   Equally, the doctrine of the undisclosed principal states that, generally, either the agent or the principal may take the benefit of the contract. However, there are established situations where the principal will not be able to take the benefit. These are:

   a) it would be inconsistent with the terms of the contract to permit it: *Siu Yin Kwan* v *Eastern Insurance Co* (1994);
   b) the third party wished to deal only with the agent: *Collins* v *Associated Greyhound Racecourses Ltd* (1930); *Greer* v *Downs Supply Co* (1927).

   With regard to the first of these, the courts are often reluctant to allow the principal to be deprived of his rights: *Humble* v *Hunter* (1848); *F Drughorn Ltd* v *Rederiaktiebologat Transatlantic* (1919). Concerning the second, the other contracting party must demonstrate sufficient reason for not wishing to deal with the principal: *Nash* v *Dix* (1898); *Said* v *Butt* (1920). If he is unable to do so, in the last resort the other contracting party may be able to have the contract set aside for fraud or misrepresentation: *Archer* v *Stone* (1898).

SUGGESTED ANSWER TO QUESTION ONE

General Comment

The agency principle is a substantial exception to the doctrine of privity of contract, without which business would be unworkable. Stated simply, the principle is that one may enter into a contract for and on behalf of another and bind that other to the terms of the contract if the relationship of agent and principal exists between them. There are, however, many kinds of agency and the plethora of situations in which it can exist makes it a fertile topic for questions. The problem question here is fairly typical and requires the student to distinguish between different types of agency relationship within the same situation and analyse the transactions accordingly.

Key Points

- Where someone enters into a contract as agent for another, he is not bound by the contract but the other is

- There must be an express or implied appointment: *Heard* v *Pilley*
- The principal will only be bound if the contract was within the agent's authority
- Types of authority: express, incidental, usual, customary, apparent: *Weigall* v *Runciman* – *European Asian Bank* v *Punjab & Sind Bank* – *Mynn* v *Joliffe* – *Watteau* v *Fenwick* – *Jerome* v *Bentley & Co* – *Graves* v *Legg* – *Perry* v *Barnett*

The purchase at the auction

- Eric's actual authority was limited
- If the auctioneer did not know of the limitation Eric's apparent authority was unlimited
- Lovejoy is bound by the contract and must seek repayment from Eric

The painting bought from Gimbert

- If Eric failed to disclose the agency, both Lovejoy and Eric are bound
- The undisclosed principal (Lovejoy) cannot take the benefit if it would be inconsistent with the terms of the contract: *Siu Yin Kwan* v *Eastern Insurance Co* – *Humble* v *Hunter* – *F Drughorn Ltd* v *Rederiaktiebolagat Transatlantic*
- The undisclosed principal cannot take the benefit if the third party wanted to deal only with the agent: *Collins* v *Associated Greyhound Racecourses Ltd* – *Greer* v *Downs Supply Co*
- Misrepresentation could have vitiated the contract: *Archer* v *Stone*
- Gimbert may be able to avoid the contract if he had sufficient reason for not wanting to deal with Lovejoy: *Nash* v *Dix* – *Said* v *Butt* – *Dyster* v *Randall & Sons*

The items purchased from Tinker

- Where the principal holds out to a third party that another is representing him that other is his agent with ostensible authority
- Such a representation can be implied by putting the agent in a particular position: *Summers* v *Solomon*
- Merely leaving Eric in charge of the shop probably does not give him the necessary authority
- There may be sufficient authority in Lovejoy's express instructions to Eric
- Lovejoy is probably not bound to pay Tinker, who must claim against Eric

Suggested Answer

This question involves the topic of agency. Agency is an important exception to the doctrine of privity of contract which states that one who is not a party to a contract can neither enforce rights nor acquire liabilities under it. One who makes a contract on behalf of another (an agent) is not bound by the contract and acquires no rights under it, but the other (the principal) can claim the rights and incurs the liabilities. If Eric has acted as Lovejoy's agent in the relevant transactions, Lovejoy will be bound by them.

The first question is whether Eric has been appointed agent. Such appointment may be express or implied and may be made orally even though the contract which the agent is appointed to make must be in writing: *Heard* v *Pilley* (1869). Whether or not an agency has been created is a matter of interpreting the words used. An agent is one who acts on behalf of another, and Lovejoy's words to Eric: 'Mind the business for me and keep things ticking over', strongly suggest that Lovejoy intended to create a general agency with regard to his business. It also seems he expressly asked Eric to be his agent in regard to two specific transactions: bidding for him at the auction and purchasing the painting from Gimbert.

Having established that an agency has been created, it is then necessary to consider the extent of the agent's authority for, where an agent acts beyond the scope of his authority, his principal (the person on whose behalf he acts) is not bound. An agent may have different kinds of authority:

1. Express authority is the authority which has clearly been given to him by the principal. Where the authority given is capable of more than one interpretation, the principal may be bound even if the agent incorrectly interprets his authority (*Weigall* v *Runciman* (1916)), unless it is reasonable for the agent to seek clarification and he fails to do so: *European Asian Bank* v *Punjab & Sind Bank* (1983).
2. Incidental authority is the authority to do all those things which are not specifically referred to in the appointment but which are incidental to carrying out the purpose for which the agent was appointed. This type of authority is interpreted fairly strictly. For example, an agent employed to sell has no incidental authority to receive payment: *Mynn* v *Joliffe* (1834).
3. Usual authority is the authority which an agent of a particular type usually has (*Watteau* v *Fenwick* (1893)) and this only applies where the agent belongs to a well known class of agents: *Jerome* v *Bentley & Co* (1952).
4. Customary authority is authority to act in accordance with the custom of the market in which he is operating (*Graves* v *Legg* (1857)), but this only applies where the custom is not inconsistent with the principal's express instructions: *Perry* v *Barnett* (1885).
5. Apparent authority (sometimes referred to as ostensible authority) is the authority which third parties are entitled to assume that the agent has, because the principal has placed in him a particular position or otherwise made a representation to the third party that the agent is entitled to act in the transaction.

In the light of the above definitions, it is now necessary to consider each of the transactions in turn.

The purchase at the auction

As already stated above, Eric appeared to have express authority to bid on Lovejoy's behalf for the epergne. However, that authority was apparently limited by Lovejoy's express instruction: 'Go up to £3,000 if you have to.' While Eric was not expressly forbidden to bid higher, it is submitted that this was implicit in the instruction. It is, however, not necessary to decide this point if the auctioneer did not know of the limitation on Eric's authority. So far as he is concerned, Eric has been held out as Lovejoy's agent and he is entitled to assume that Eric had unlimited authority. Therefore, whatever Eric's express authority was, he had apparent authority to bid as high as he chose on Lovejoy's behalf. Lovejoy will therefore be bound by the contract and will have to seek repayment of the additional £2,000 from Eric.

The purchase bought from Gimbert

The situation here is a little different for, although Eric is clearly Lovejoy's agent with express authority to buy the painting on Lovejoy's behalf, Eric's statement to Gimbert that he is buying for a relative is rather ambiguous, in that it is not clear whether he has disclosed the agency but failed to reveal the name of his principal, or failed altogether to disclose the agency. An agent is not obliged to disclose the name of his principal and, where he does not do so, whether he acted as agent or principal in the transaction depends on the intention of the parties: *Southwell* v *Bowditch* (1876). Eric clearly intended to act as agent and it will therefore depend on how Gimbert interpreted his words. If both agreed that there was an agency, the usual rules will apply and Lovejoy will be both bound and entitled under the contract.

If, however, Eric failed to disclose the agency at all and led Gimbert to believe he was buying on his own behalf, the rule is slightly different. Both he and Lovejoy will be bound under the contract and either may enforce it or have it enforced against him.

The situation here is that Lovejoy wishes to enforce rights under the contract but Gimbert does not wish to sell to him. There are two situations where an undisclosed principal cannot take the benefit of a contract made on his behalf. Firstly, if it would be inconsistent with its terms (*Siu Yin Kwan* v *Eastern Insurance Co* (1994)), which would depend on an interpretation of the contract and how Eric had signed it. However, the courts generally show a marked reluctance to exclude the principal's rights in this situation (cf the contrasting cases of *Humble* v *Hunter* (1848) and *F Drughorn Ltd* v *Rederiaktiebolagat Transatlantic* (1919). Secondly, if the third party can show that he wanted to deal with the agent and no one else, eg because of the agent's reputation, (*Collins* v *Associated Greyhound Racecourses Ltd* (1930)), or because the agent owed money to the third party which was to be set off under the contract: *Greer* v *Downs Supply Co* (1927). This may be the case here but there is nothing in the question to indicate it.

Where the third party simply does not wish to deal with the principal there are a number of additional considerations. Firstly, if the agent expressly states that he is not acting for the principal, the contract can be avoided for fraud or misrepresentation, if this representation induced the contract: *Archer* v *Stone* (1898). However, it may be that Eric has not misrepresented the situation and he and Lovejoy are in fact related. The situation is then less clear. There are three relevant cases: *Nash* v *Dix* (1898). In the first, D, a vendor of land, disapproving of the proposed user, refused to sell to P. A then bought from D and sold to P but D repudiated his contract with A. It was held that A was not an agent but a reseller and P was entitled to take the benefit of the contract. It appears that, had A been an agent, P would not have been entitled to do so. The second case is *Said* v *Butt* (1920) where a theatre critic who was refused tickets by a theatre company had a friend purchase one on his behalf. It was held that the company were entitled to refuse him entry because the personality of the members of the audience was (in this case) a material consideration. In the third case, *Dyster* v *Randall & Sons* (1926), a somewhat different conclusion was reached. This too concerned the purchase of land by an agent where the vendor did not wish to sell to the principal. This time the principal was permitted to enforce the contract on the ground that refusal would be futile since the agent could assign his rights to the principal.

While this decision has been criticised by, inter alia, Trietel on legal grounds, it seems a sensible, pragmatic approach. However, even if one accepts that given the nature of land, the vendor has a right to be concerned about its ownership, it is submitted that this does not hold true for a painting, and the personality of the principal, in this case Lovejoy, is not a material consideration.

It is therefore submitted that Lovejoy can enforce the contract.

The items purchased from Tinker

In this situation, Eric has no express authority to buy the items in question and his own representation to Tinker that he is running the business for Lovejoy is irrelevant except insofar as it may give Tinker an action against Eric himself or enable him to avoid the contract for breach of warrant of authority or misrepresentation.

To enforce his claim against Lovejoy, Tinker would have to establish that Eric had apparent (ostensible) authority to buy the items on Lovejoy's behalf. If a principal represents to a third party that someone has authority then he is bound and the representation does not need to be express. It can be implied simply by placing the agent in a particular position. For example, in *Summers* v *Solomon* (1857) the owner of a jewellery shop employed a manager to run the shop and regularly paid suppliers for jewellery which the manager purchased for the shop. When the manager continued to make purchases from the suppliers after he had left the defendant's employment, the defendant was held liable to pay for them. Lovejoy's letter to Tinker merely states that Eric will be 'minding the shop' while he is away and it is submitted that, unless it is customary in the trade, or unless Lovejoy is accustomed to allow his shop assistants to make purchases for the shop, this does not represent that Eric has the necessary authority.

It is left only to consider the general terms of Eric's appointment and whether the transaction in question falls within those terms. Initially Lovejoy asked Eric to 'mind the business' and 'keep things ticking over'. It is submitted that there may be more authority implicit in these words than in the phrase used in correspondence with Tinker and that it could be interpreted to mean that Eric had authority to make purchases for the shop. However, the expressions used are very vague and it is submitted that Lovejoy's letter to Tinker may provide clarification of Eric's actual authority and may be interpreted as notifying Tinker of a restriction. While the expressions are vague and Eric may be taken to interpret them as he chooses, it would be up to him to seek clarification from Lovejoy before acting on them.

It is therefore submitted, in conclusion, that Lovejoy is not bound to pay Tinker and Tinker must seek payment from Eric himself.

SUGGESTED ANSWER TO QUESTION TWO

General Comment

The consequences of two contracts have to be discussed here. The contract between G and H was one for the sale of goods and requires discussion of the possible breach (or breaches) and the remedies available to G. The contract between J and G was a contract for services, again requiring discussion of the possible breach: in this latter contract the effect of the limitation clause will have to be examined.

Key Points

G's contract with H

- Defining the contract
- Sale of goods - application of s14 Sale of Goods Act 1979
- Nature of the breach
- Remedies - rejection of the boat?
- Damages, measure of and the question of remoteness of damage

G's contract with J

- Definition of the contract as one for the supply of services
- Application of s13 Supply of Goods and Services Act 1982
- Effect of the limitation clause

Suggested Answer

G's contract with H

The contract is one for the sale of goods. As H, the seller, sold the boat in the course of business the provisions of s14 Sale of Goods Act 1979 apply. Under s14(2) there is the implied condition that the goods were of satisfactory quality. As G explained the particular purpose for which he required the boat, s14(3) applies, under which there is the implied condition that it was reasonably fit for that purpose. There appear to be clear breaches of both these subsections, (It is assumed that these defects existed at the time of the sale, otherwise there would be little to discuss in this regard.)

The primary remedy for the buyer for breach of a condition under the Sale of Goods Act 1979 is rejection of the goods. However, in this instance G will be deemed to have accepted the boat under s35 of the Act by the delay and his use of the boat, and by virtue of s11(4) the breaches can only be treated as breaches of warranty. This limits G to a claim for damages.

In respect of the boat itself the measure of damages is provided for by s53(3) of the Act as being the difference between the value of the boat at the time of delivery and the value it would have had if it had fulfilled the terms of s14.

It also appears that G had spent a considerable sum stocking the boat with provisions. It is not made clear to what extent this sum has been lost but it is assumed that there has been some loss in this regard. This raises the question of remoteness of damage.

The rule stated in *Hadley* v *Baxendale* (1854) is that damages:

> ' ... should be such as may fairly and reasonably be considered either arising naturally, that is, according to the usual course of things, from such breach of contract itself, or such as may reasonably be supposed to have been in the contemplation of both parties, at the time they made the contract, as the probable result of the breach of it.'

For further discussion and application of this rule: see, inter alia, *Victoria Laundry (Windsor) Ltd* v *Newman Industries Ltd* (1949) and *The Heron II* (1969).

The expenditure incurred by G could not be regarded as arising naturally from the ordinary course of things, the first limb of the rule. But its loss could be said to have been in the reasonable contemplation of the parties as the probable result of the breach, the second limb of the rule. H was made aware that G intended to travel round the world and could have been reasonably expected to have contemplated that this type of expenditure would have been incurred, and would be wasted in the event of the boat being unserviceable. It should be noted that if damage can be contemplated recovery is not limited because the degree of damage could not have been anticipated: *H Parsons (Livestock) Ltd* v *Uttley Ingham & Co Ltd* (1978).

G's contract with J

This contract is one for the supply of services. It can be assumed that J, the supplier, was acting in the course of business, and under s13 Supply of Goods and Services Act 1982 there is an implied term that the supplier will carry out the service with reasonable care and skill. J was in breach of that term.

The breach of the implied term by J could only have resulted from his negligence and he will accordingly be liable for all the direct conequences of the breach, unless he can rely on the limitation clause which must now be considered.

This clause purports to limit J's liability to the contract fee of £300. However, under s2(2) Unfair Contract Terms Act 1977, the clause is subject to the requirement of reasonableness. (It is also subject to s3(2)(a) of the Act, which imposes the same requirement.) The reasonableness test is set out in s11(1) and, by s11(5), the onus of proving that the clause satisfies the test falls on J.

It is not possible on the present information to determine whether or not the clause would satisfy the test. Some guidance could be obtained from the speech of Lord Griffiths in *Smith* v *Eric S Bush* (1990), where his Lordship stated the matters that should always be considered. These were:

1. The respective bargaining strengths of the parties.
2. Whether there was an alternative source of the advice.
3. The difficulty of the task being undertaken.
4. The practical consequences of the decision: this would require consideration of the ability of the parties to bear the loss involved and the question of insurance.

The application of (4), the practical consequences criterion, would suggest that the clause would not satisfy the reasonableness test, but this must remain a tentative view.

SUGGESTED ANSWER TO QUESTION THREE

General Comment

This problem is relatively straightforward and concerns the application of the Sale of Goods Act 1979 to a 'consumer' contract and the effect of the Unfair Contract Terms Act 1977 on attempts by the seller to exclude or restrict liability under the 1979 Act.

Key Points

- There may be an implied condition as to satisfactory quality: s14(2) Sale of Goods Act (SOGA) 1979
- The meaning of 'satisfactory quality' in this context: s14(2A) and (2B) SOGA 1979 - *Jewson Ltd* v *Kelly* - *Bartlett* v *Sydney Marcus* - *Lee* v *York Coach and Marine*
- The statement as to restoration may be a misrepresentation, exclusion of liability for which under cl 44 is subject to the 'reasonableness' test: s3 Misrepresentation Act 1967, as amended by s8 Unfair Contract Terms Act (UCTA) 1977
- Clause 44 may also be void under s56(3) Consumer Credit Act 1974
- Clause 45 is totally void as H was dealing as a consumer: ss12 and 6(2) UCTA 1977
- Clause 46 is also subject to the 'reasonableness' test
- Liability of Lom's Garage: s75(1) Consumer Credit Act 1974 - *Shanklin Pier* v *Detel Products Ltd* - *Andrews* v *Hopkinson*
- Application of the Unfair Terms in Consumer Contracts Regulations 1999

Suggested Answer

It is firstly necessary to determine what, if any, is the breach of contract as between Fortin Finance and H.

The contract between H and Fortin Finance is one of sale of goods (it is, apparently, a credit sale, and not a hire-purchase agreement) and one must examine whether there has been a breach of the implied condition in s14(2) Sale of Goods Act 1979. Section 14(2) provides that:

> 'Where the seller sells goods in the course of business, there is an implied condition that the goods supplied under the contract are of satisfactory quality.'

However, under s14(2C) the term implied by s14(2) does not extend to any matter making the quality of goods unsatisfactory:

> '(a) which is specifically drawn to the buyer's attention before the contract is made; [or]
> (b) where the buyer examines the goods before the contract is made, which that examination ought to reveal ...'

Fortin Finance clearly sell in the course of a business. It does not appear that any defects were specifically drawn to H's attention, so that the proviso in s14(2C)(a) does not apply. H examined the car thoroughly before taking it out for a test drive, which suggests that the proviso in s14(2C)(b) may be relevant. However, one can assume that H's examination would not have revealed a defect in the brakes. Section 14(2) probably applies and the question is whether the car was of 'satisfactory quality'. Satisfactory quality is defined as being of a standard that a reasonable person would regard as satisfactory having regard to description, price and all other relevant circumstances: s14(2A) and (2B). In *Jewson Ltd* v *Kelly* (2002) the court reaffirmed the 'satisfactory quality' test under s14(2) generally.

The car in question is a second-hand 1936 model. A second-hand car 'is satisfactory if it is in usable condition, even if it is not perfect' (per Lord Denning MR in *Bartlett* v *Sidney Marcus* (1965)); but a car which is unsafe to drive is clearly unsatisfactory: *Lee* v

York Coach and Marine (1977). A car whose brakes fail is patently unsafe to drive. The definition of 'satisfactory' in s14(2A) and (2B) requires that regard be had to the price – £4,000 is a not an inconsiderable price. The definition also requires reference to 'all other relevant circumstances'. In this context one must examine the statement of the sales manager of Lom's Garage. He said that the car was not in concours (the word is misspelt in the question) condition. This means that the car was not in superb condition, fit for exhibition. He added that H would 'have to buy it as found'. But he also said that the car was 'restored'. This can only mean that it was restored so as to be able to function safely as a car. Fortin Finance are, it is submitted, liable for this statement. It is safe to assume that Lom's Garage was acting as agent for Fortin Finance. (There might be deemed to be this agency relationship by s56(2) Consumer Credit Act (CCA) 1974.)

In conclusion, therefore, Fortin Finance are liable for the breach of the implied condition as to satisfactory quality. What now falls for discussion is the effect of the exclusion clauses on this liability.

The clauses are stated to be incorporated in the contract. This does not have to be further discussed. Nor is it necessary to discuss whether, as a matter of construction, the clauses cover the breach and are otherwise effective at common law. This is clearly so. What requires examination is the validity of the clauses under the Unfair Contract Terms Act (UCTA) 1977.

Clause 44

This clause purports to exclude liability for the statement made by the sales manager of Lom's Garage that the car was restored. If this statement was a misrepresentation, then the provisions of s3 Misrepresentation Act 1967 (as amended by s8 UCTA 1977) would make this clause subject to the requirement of reasonableness. If the statement was a contractual term then, paradoxically s3 would not apply: see *Cheshire, Fifoot and Furmston's Law of Contract*, 12th edn, p195. But arguably Fortin Finance are in breach of the implied condition as to merchantibility even in the absence of this statement. In any event cl 44 of the agreement might be rendered void by s56(3) CCA 1974.

Clause 45

H was 'dealing as a consumer' within the provisions of s12 UCTA 1977. Accordingly s6(2) of UCTA 1977 applies. This renders the clause totally void.

Clause 46

This clause falls within s4 UCTA 1977 which makes such an indemnity clause subject to the requirement of reasonableness as set out in s11. In *Smith* v *Eric* S *Bush* (1990) Lord Griffiths refers to factors which should always be taken into account in determining whether a clause satisfies the requirement. Among the factors he mentions are the bargaining strength of the parties and their respective financial resources. It can be assumed that H was confronted with a standard form contract with little or no opportunity of negotiating its terms. The parties were, consequently, of unequal bargaining strength. It seems to me also that it is indisputable that Fortin Finance have the greater financial resources, including the greater facility to cover themselves by insurance.

It is therefore submitted that Fortin Finance are liable to H for the loss he has suffered and cannot rely on the indemnity clause in the event of J, the other driver, pursuing a claim against them.

Finally, as to whether Lom's Garage have incurred liability to H at common law. By statute, under s75(1) CCA 1974 Fortin Finance and Lom's Garage might have incurred joint and several liability. At common law it appears that Lom's Garage would be liable on a collateral contract for the statement of the sales manager that the car had been restored, on the principle in *Shanklin Pier Ltd* v *Detel Products Ltd* (1951). This principle was applied in *Andrews* v *Hopkinson* (1957), a case particularly relevant to the situation under discussion.

While the UCTA 1977 disposes of the problem in this instance, it is necessary for the sake of completeness to mention the Unfair Terms in Consumer Contracts Regulations 1999. The Regulations apply to contracts between 'consumers' and sellers of goods or suppliers of services. They apply only to terms which have not been individually negotiated, ie the seller/supplier's standard terms, but they apply to any kind of term, not just excluding and limiting terms. Such a term will be deemed 'unfair' if it does not satisfy the requirement of good faith and if it causes 'a significant imbalance in the parties' rights and obligations under the contract to the detriment of the consumer'. The concept of 'good faith' was recently examined by the House of Lords in *Director General of Fair Trading* v *First National Bank* (2002). It was held that the concept is a subjective one and that each case must be decided on its own facts. A consumer is defined as: 'a natural person who, in making a contract to which these Regulations apply is acting for purposes which are outside his business'. The guidelines are, however, much the same as those for determining 'reasonableness' under the Act. If the clause is adjudged unreasonable under the Act, it will probably also be unfair for the purposes of the Regulations.

Unannotated Cracknell's Statutes for use in Examinations

New Editions of Cracknell's Statutes

£11.95 due 2003

Cracknell's Statutes provide a comprehensive series of essential statutory provisions for each subject. Amendments are consolidated, avoiding the need to cross-refer to amending legislation. Unannotated, they are suitable for use in examinations, and provide the precise wording of vital Acts of Parliament for the diligent student.

Constitutional and Administrative Law
ISBN: 1 85836 511 2

Equity and Trusts
ISBN: 1 85836 508 2

Contract, Tort and Remedies
ISBN: 1 85836 507 4

Land: The Law of Real Property
ISBN: 1 85836 509 0

English Legal System
ISBN: 1 85836 510 4

Law of International Trade
ISBN: 1 85836 512 0

For further information on contents or to place an order, please contact:

Mail Order
Old Bailey Press
at Holborn College
Woolwich Road
Charlton
London
SE7 8LN

Telephone No: 020 8317 6039
Fax No: 020 8317 6004
Website: www.oldbaileypress.co.uk

Suggested Solutions to Past Examination Questions 2001–2002

The Suggested Solutions series provides examples of full answers to the questions regularly set by examiners. Each suggested solution has been broken down into three stages: general comment, skeleton solution and suggested solution. The examination questions included within the text are taken from past examination papers set by the London University. The full opinion answers will undoubtedly assist you with your research and further your understanding and appreciation of the subject in question.

Only £6.95 due November 2003

Company Law
ISBN: 1 85836 519 8

Employment Law
ISBN: 1 85836 520 1

European Union Law
ISBN: 1 85836 524 4

Evidence
ISBN: 1 85836 521 X

Family Law
ISBN: 1 85836 525 2

For further information on contents or to place an order, please contact:

Mail Order
Old Bailey Press
at Holborn College
Woolwich Road
Charlton
London
SE7 8LN

Telephone No: 020 8317 6039
Fax No: 020 8317 6004
Website: www.oldbaileypress.co.uk

Law
Update
2004

Old Bailey Press

The Old Bailey Press integrated student law library is tailor-made to help you at every stage of your studies from the preliminaries of each subject through to the final examination. The series of Textbooks, Revision WorkBooks, 150 Leading Cases and Cracknell's Statutes are interrelated to provide you with a comprehensive set of study materials.

You can buy Old Bailey Press books from your University Bookshop, your local Bookshop, direct using this form, or you can order a free catalogue of our titles from the address shown overleaf.

The following subjects each have a Textbook, 150 Leading Cases/Casebook, Revision WorkBook and Cracknell's Statutes unless otherwise stated.

Administrative Law
Commercial Law
Company Law
Conflict of Laws
Constitutional Law
Conveyancing (Textbook and 150 Leading Cases)
Criminal Law
Criminology (Textbook and Sourcebook)
Employment Law (Textbook and Cracknell's Statutes)
English and European Legal Systems
Equity and Trusts
Evidence
Family Law
Jurisprudence: The Philosophy of Law (Textbook, Sourcebook and Revision WorkBook)
Land: The Law of Real Property
Law of International Trade
Law of the European Union
Legal Skills and System (Textbook)
Obligations: Contract Law
Obligations: The Law of Tort
Public International Law
Revenue Law (Textbook, Revision WorkBook and Cracknell's Statutes)
Succession

Mail order prices:

Textbook	£15.95
150 Leading Cases	£11.95
Revision WorkBook	£9.95
Cracknell's Statutes	£11.95
Suggested Solutions 1999–2000	£6.95
Suggested Solutions 2000–2001	£6.95
Suggested Solutions 2001–2002	£6.95
Law Update 2003	£10.95
Law Update 2004	£10.95

Please note details and prices are subject to alteration.

To complete your order, please fill in the form below:

Module	Books required	Quantity	Price	Cost
		Postage		
		TOTAL		

For Europe, add 15% postage and packing (£20 maximum).
For the rest of the world, add 40% for airmail.

ORDERING

By telephone to Mail Order at 020 8317 6039, with your credit card to hand.

By fax to 020 8317 6004 (giving your credit card details).

Website: www.oldbaileypress.co.uk

By post to: Mail Order, Old Bailey Press at Holborn College, Woolwich Road, Charlton, London, SE7 8LN.

When ordering by post, please enclose full payment by cheque or banker's draft, or complete the credit card details below. You may also order a free catalogue of our complete range of titles from this address.

We aim to despatch your books within 3 working days of receiving your order.

Name
Address

Postcode Telephone

Total value of order, including postage: £

I enclose a cheque/banker's draft for the above sum, or

charge my ☐ Access/Mastercard ☐ Visa ☐ American Express
Card number

☐☐☐☐ ☐☐☐☐ ☐☐☐☐ ☐☐☐☐

Expiry date ☐☐☐☐

Signature: .... Date: ....